1996 Best Newspaper Writing

WINNERS: THE AMERICAN SOCIETY OF NEWSPAPER EDITORS COMPETITION

EDITED BY CHRISTOPHER SCANLAN

The Poynter Institute
and
Bonus Books, Inc.

00 99 98 97 96   5 4 3 2 1

International Standard Book Number: 1–56625–065–X
International Standard Serial Number: 0195–895X

The Poynter Institute for Media Studies
801 Third Street South
St. Petersburg, Florida 33701

Bonus Books, Inc.
160 East Illinois Street
Chicago, Illinois 60611

Book design and production by Billie M. Keirstead

Cover illustration by Phillip Gary Design, St. Petersburg, Fla.

Photos for cover illustration were provided by Chuck Zoeller
of the Associated Press and are used with permission. Photos
of Susan Smith, the Alfred Murrah Federal Building, and the
Unabomber sketch courtesy of the Associated Press.

Photo credits: AP photographers Eric Draper (O.J. Simpson),
Nati Harnik (salute to Rabin), Beth A. Keiser (Dennis
Rodman), David Longstreath (Oklahoma City bombing),
Toby Talbot (Jerry Garcia), and Eyal Warshavsky (Rabin
funeral). Photos of ASNE award winners and finalists were
provided by their newspapers.

Printed in the United States of America

This book is dedicated to Robert J. Haiman,
who created our home and guided its spirit
as president of The Poynter Institute from 1983–1996.
With gratitude to a caring leader, inspiring colleague,
and good friend to all who came to work and learn here.

About this series

The Poynter Institute for Media Studies proudly pub lishes the 18th volume of its series *Best Newspaper Writing,* valued since 1979 by students, teachers, and professionals as an indispensable text on clear, effective, and graceful newswriting.

As in past years, *Best Newspaper Writing* is a joint venture of the Institute and the American Society of Newspaper Editors. In 1978, ASNE made the improvement of newspaper writing one of its primary goals. The Society inaugurated a contest to select the best writing from newspapers in the United States and Canada, and to reward the winning writers with monetary prizes. The Institute volunteered to spread the gospel of good writing by publishing the winning entries along with notes, commentaries, and interviews. That first volume, *Best Newspaper Writing 1979,* sold out long ago and has become a collector's item.

Best Newspaper Writing 1996 is edited by Christopher Scanlan, an experienced newspaper reporter and writing coach, who is the director of Poynter's writing programs.

The ASNE Writing Awards Competition is augmented by the Jesse Laventhol Prizes for Deadline News Reporting for individual and team reporting. David Laventhol, editor-at-large for the Times-Mirror Co., endowed the prizes in 1995 in honor of his father, a longtime Philadelphia newspaperman. Laventhol said he wanted to encourage and recognize high quality in this key component of newspaper reporting: "While much of the journalistic world's prizes tend to focus on investigative reporting, special projects, and analysis and explanation, the fact is that more than half of what appears in most newspapers each day is based on events that occurred in the last news cycle before publication."

This year's award categories are deadline news reporting (individual and team categories), non-deadline writing, commentary, editorial writing, and sports writing. A committee of 18 judges, chaired by John

Carroll, editor of the *Baltimore Sun*, judged this year's entries:

Ken Brusic, *The Orange County Register*
Michael Fancher, *The Seattle Times*
Gregory Favre, *Sacramento Bee*
Jim Herman, *The Wausau* (Wis.) *Daily Herald*
William Hillard, retired from *The Oregonian*, Portland
Mike Jacobs, *Grand Forks* (N.D.) *Herald*
Pamela Johnson, *Arizona Republic*
Beverly Kees, Freedom Forum, Oakland, Calif.
Bill Ketter, *The Patriot Ledger*, Quincy, Mass.
Craig Klugman, *The Journal-Gazette*, Fort Wayne, Ind.
Wanda Lloyd, *USA Today*
Ron Martin, *Atlanta Journal and Constitution*
Diane McFarlin, *Sarasota* (Fla.) *Herald-Tribune*
Tim McGuire, *Star-Tribune*, Minneapolis
Mary Jo Meisner, *Milwaukee Journal Sentinel*
Matt Storin, *The Boston Globe*
Don Wycliff, *Chicago Tribune*

The Institute congratulates the winners and finalists of the ASNE Distinguished Writing Awards, and thanks the judges for their fine work and dedication to good writing.

* * *

Founded in 1975 by the late Nelson Poynter, chairman of the *St. Petersburg Times* and its Washington affiliate, *Congressional Quarterly,* the Institute was bequeathed Poynter's controlling stock in the Times Publishing Company in 1978. It invests its dividends in educational activities in four areas of print and broadcast journalism: writing, reporting, and editing; visual journalism; leadership and management; and media ethics. The faculty teaches beginning and midcareer professionals as well as news executives, publishes teaching tools such as this book, and conducts educational and research projects, all of which seek the same goal: to raise levels of excellence in newspapers and the communications media generally, so that journalists can fulfill their responsibility to empower citizens by informing them.

Robert J. Haiman, President
The Poynter Institute

Acknowledgments

Congratulations and thanks to the news organizations, editors, visual journalists, and reporters whose work makes this annual collection possible. Special thanks to the winners of this year's Distinguished Writing and Jesse Laventhol Awards for their willingness to explore the way they report and write, and to the finalists for their illuminating essays on the writing lessons they learned. As always, this is their book.

Publication, however, would have been impossible without support from my colleagues on the faculty and staff of The Poynter Institute for Media Studies, especially Roy Peter Clark, Bobbi Alsina, Joyce Olson, and Rita Estrada. Outside the Institute, Don Murray provided his usual eagle eye. Important contributions also came from our copy editor Vicki Krueger; Lee Stinnett, executive director of the American Society of Newspaper Editors, and his staff; and John Carroll, editor of the *Baltimore Sun* and chairman of the writing committee. Chuck Zoeller of the Associated Press again generously provided the news photos used on the cover. The guiding hand of Billie Keirstead, publications manager at The Poynter Institute, makes production of a book on a journalism deadline possible.

Contents

What the best writers learn; What they can teach us

"We like to pretend that it's easy, that stories write themselves, that you knock them out," says *Los Angeles Times* columnist Peter King. "It doesn't happen that way. At least the good ones don't happen that way. And I'm reminded of it twice a week, and I should have been reminded of it more when I was a city editor. It is a terrifying process, and it's hard work."

King learns that lesson about the terrors of the blank screen twice weekly when he writes the column that won the 1996 Distinguished Writing Award for commentary from the American Society of Newspaper Editors. His comments are echoed by the winners and finalists whose work fills this edition of *Best Newspaper Writing* with the powerful combination of civic clarity and literary grace that marks the finest in American journalism.

Selected from some 550 entries, the six winners and 12 finalists also share their reflections on writing that offer vivid illustrations that even, perhaps especially, the best writers continue to learn their craft every day. For reporters, writers, and editors interested in improving their skills, the journalists you will meet in these pages have valuable lessons to teach.

BARTON GELLMAN: NO EXCUSES

Before he went overseas as Jerusalem Bureau Chief for *The Washington Post,* Barton Gellman covered the Pentagon. Where others saw only a hostile gulf between the military and the media, Gellman perceived common ground. "We are both in the no-excuses profession. When you get a mission in the military, or you get a story assignment for a newspaper, nobody in the world wants to hear all the good reasons why you couldn't do it....You just have to do it."

On the night Israeli Prime Minister Yitzhak Rabin was assassinated, that lesson enabled Gellman to beat a remorseless deadline and in a few hours seize control of a fast-breaking, highly emotional story. For his graceful work under pressure, Gellman won the Jesse Laventhol Award for deadline reporting.

As his *Post* colleague, Glenn Frankel, told ASNE editors, Gellman followed the first lesson of the deadline writer: "Keep it simple. And that's what he did. Straight lead, then a couple of paragraphs of narrative about what happened, then a paragraph about the killer —who the shooter was, the alleged shooter was—then immediately into the question of the significance of the event, and he captures it in a couple of paragraphs and does an analysis of the meaning of this event, then back to the narrative. Straightforward, chronological, keep it simple, get it done." The result:

JERUSALEM, Nov. 4—A right-wing Jewish extremist shot and killed Prime Minister Yitzhak Rabin tonight as he departed a peace rally attended by more than 100,000 in Tel Aviv, throwing Israel's government and the Middle East peace process into turmoil.

The lone gunman met Rabin, 73, as he walked to his car in the Kings of Israel Square in front of Tel Aviv's city hall. The prime minister had just stepped off a massive sound stage where he had linked hands with fellow ministers to sing "The Song of Peace." Identified by police as Yigal Amir, a 27-year-old law student, the assassin fired three shots into Rabin's back at close range.

A cordon of security officers bundled the gunman away as Rabin was rushed by ambulance to Ichilov Hospital, just a few blocks away in the heart of Tel Aviv. He arrived there with no pulse and no blood pressure, according to Health Minister Ephraim Sneh, and died on the operating table at 11:10 p.m. (4:10 p.m. EST), an hour and a quarter after being shot. Seven minutes later, shouting over the sobs and gasps of policemen and journalists, Rabin's senior aide, Eitan Haber, announced his death.

MARTIN MERZER: SIGNALS TO THE READER

"You cannot produce a good newspaper story without vivid, excellent, aggressive reporting," says Martin Merzer of *The Miami Herald.* He recalls a favorite bit of advice from Gene Miller, two-time Pulitzer winner and *Herald* writing coach: "If you're having trouble writing a story, you probably need to do more reporting."

For their gripping deadline account of the hostage-taking of a school bus filled with disabled children, Merzer, Gail Epstein, Frances Robles, and more than a dozen of their *Herald* colleagues won the Jesse Laventhol Award for deadline reporting by a team.

Merzer, who wrote the story, credited the reporters, columnists, interns, and others who hit the streets the morning of the bus hijacking with feeding him the details that enabled the *Herald* to compete the next day with a story already given saturation broadcast coverage. Details produced by aggressive reporting are the way the newspaper, in a time of intense competition and instantaneous delivery, can send an important message to the reader. "You're not going to put an editor's note on top of it saying, 'Read this because we know more than you do.' But it's a signal to them that we do."

"Terror Rides a School Bus," which combines the digging of the investigative reporter with the compelling voice and style of the storyteller, opens this way:

> A waiter fond of poet Ralph Waldo Emerson attends morning prayers at his church, steps across the street and hijacks a school bus. Owing $15,639.39 in back taxes, wielding what he says is a bomb, Catalino Sang shields himself with disabled children.
>
> Follow my orders, he says, or I will kill the kids. "No problem, I will," says driver Alicia Chapman, crafty and calm. "But please, don't hurt the children."
>
> The saga of Dade County school bus number CX-17, bound for Blue Lakes Elementary, begins.

With that kind of detail, from "the hijacker's tax deficiency to the cent, to the number of the school bus, it's awfully hard to misfire," Merzer says.

RICK BRAGG: GETTING PERSONAL

Rick Bragg, national correspondent covering the South for *The New York Times,* lives by a rule that editors have been preaching for decades: "Show, don't tell."

But the lesson that underscores the special quality of his writing is another editor's never-forgotten comment: "You don't have to be ashamed to make stories personal."

"He didn't mean that my feelings necessarily had to show," says Bragg, "but that it was all right to make them seem as though the reader were kind of wading through. To give the images and the details and to care about 'em one way or the other."

One of the nicest compliments he can get, Bragg says, is when people come up and say, "I kind of felt like I was there."

Bragg's stories consistently evoke that feeling, whether he's writing about a black laundress who left her life savings to a Mississippi university or the county sheriff who drew a confession from Susan Smith, the mother who drowned her children in a South Carolina lake.

His storytelling skills earned him the Distinguished Writing Award for non-deadline writing, as well as a Pulitzer Prize for feature writing. They are obvious in this passage from his story about aging inmates in an Alabama prison:

All Jessie Hatcher's life, the devil in him would come swimming out every time a drink of whiskey trickled in.

"It was 1979 down in Pike County," he said, looking down some dusty road in his memory for the life he took. "Me and this boy was drinking. He thought I had some money, but I didn't have none. We took to fighting, and I killed him. Quinn. His name was Quinn. Killed him with a .32. I was bad to drink back then. I never drank another drop."

...he has a life history of violence. He shot a woman several times with a .22 rifle in 1978, but she lived and he served less than a year. He was drunk then. The murder of the man in Pike County sent him away for life.

He's 76 now and limps on a cane because of a broken leg that never healed right. He works all day in the flower garden, where he has raked the dirt so smooth you can roll marbles on it.

"My favorites are the saucer sunflowers," he said, "because they're so beautiful."

The young man, the one whose life was washed away on a river of whiskey, seems to have vanished inside this wizened little man on his knees in the mud, plucking weeds and humming spirituals.

"They could take the fences down and I wouldn't run," he said. "This is the right place for me."

PETER KING: HARD WORK

The difficult, "terrifying process" may be painful for Peter King, but it pays sizable benefits for Peter King's readers. Witness this stunning passage from a column about downsizing called "One More Styrofoam Parachute":

The first signs were subtle. The top executives quit bothering to flash pretend smiles when they wandered through his department. He began to notice how new office clerks no longer were brought around for introductions. Before too long, there were staff meetings and memos on a singular topic: "Belt-tightening."

Now the company was flush. In fact, its war chest of ready cash was a regular source of industry speculation. The best the worker bees could figure, the belt-tightening clamor was aimed at Wall Street. Investors like lean, and they adore mean. Corporate Darwinism, and all that. Or maybe the CEO simply didn't want to risk ridicule among his right-sizing buddies....

His supervisors went first, strapped to traditional golden parachutes. The new bosses promptly changed all locks. "Just for your security," he was assured. And then everyone in the department was summoned for an individual "chat" with an executive freshly arrived from New York. This one wore a gray suit, smiled wide with fine white teeth, and talked excitedly about how much fun it would be, bringing the department "into the 1990s."

Right away, our boy knew he was sunk. "Once he started talking about bringing us into the '90s, I quit listening and started to study his teeth. He lost all human form. All I could see was a big barracuda smiling at me. He had jaggedy, razor teeth, and they were worn down— like he'd been using them a lot. And his eyes were in a feeding mood. I said to myself, 'Start swimming for shore.' "

"You have to gather your concentration at some point, and that is one of the hardest parts, the beginning; the rewrite bank talks about cutting off the notes. Jim Hayes, who was a college professor of mine in California, referred to it as 'buckling a seat belt,' which basically meant, OK, the fun is over now; it's time to write. I have to remind myself of that every time."

DANIEL HENNINGER: STAND-UP ON THE EDITORIAL PAGE

When Daniel Henninger sits down to write or edit editorials for *The Wall Street Journal*, he often remembers a comment by comedian Joan Rivers: "I always figure when I go out on stage, or a stand-up comic goes out on stage, I've got about five minutes. And if I don't have that audience with me in five minutes, I might as well leave because they're never going to stay with me."

Newspaper readers are just as tough. "They'll turn the page at a drop," so timing is everything, Henninger says. "You have to sense when you're beginning to bore them. Or when you're over the top. When to shut it off. When to pump it up. You've got to be conscious of it, or you'll lose them."

There's little fear of that with editorials that blend word play, invective, and moral outrage as Henninger's do. His work won him the Distinguished Writing Award for editorial writing.

Here he goes for the funny bone with "The Nationalized Pastime," an editorial about the baseball strike:

The trouble with baseball is it ain't a railroad.

Back in the good old days—when men were men, the Oval Office had a spittoon and Babe Ruth thought the President was just a fella who made less money than he did—the person who sits where Bill

Clinton sits would have known how to deal with a bunch of oligopolists and their strikers.

He would've ordered those railroad magnates into his office, whomped them across their gold watch chains with a copy of the Railway Labor Act of 1926, locked them in a room with a referee from the National Mediation Board, and dadgummit if that didn't work, he'd order the Army out to get the railroads running again.

Golly, but the times have changed. Today the President calls the oligopolists of baseball into his office and "sets a deadline" for the two sides to settle their strike. That deadline passes—strike one! Then the President sets another deadline, and it passes—strike two! But Bill Clinton's not about to strike out completely with a third deadline, so he tells Congress to go in and bat for him.

It figures. We'll bet Bill Clinton managed to never actually strike out in a childhood baseball game. Oops, gettin' late; gotta get home for dinner; too dark; looks like rain; got something in my eye; I think that plane's gonna crash!

MITCH ALBOM: CHIPPING AWAY AT THE MARBLE

Besides consistently writing award-winning columns, Mitch Albom of the *Detroit Free Press* is also a gifted musician and songwriter. "I live by the credo of a musician, Dizzy Gillespie, the trumpet player, who said, 'It took me my whole life to learn what *not* to play.' That's been the hardest thing, but I'm learning it slowly."

What Albom tries to leave in his stories are physical descriptions, personality tics, and other details that create flesh-and-blood characters instead of stick-figure sources. His powerful stories, focusing on the lives of ordinary athletes on and off the playing field, won the Distinguished Writing Award for sports writing.

"If you just put 'said such and such, comma quote' and give his title, it doesn't say a lot," Albom says. "But if you talk about having a bullet hole in the leg or someone noticing someone's teeth or whatever—every time you do that, you chip away at the marble that keeps these people distant from your reader and you start to cut a figure of a real human being."

Here is the beginning of his unforgettable portrait of a young gunshot victim trying to find redemption in sports:

> The first gun in his life was a gift from a relative, a rifle that had been snapped in half. "Let the kid have it," his step-grandfather said. So Dewon Jones took it and fixed the trigger and the barrel, and soon he had a weapon instead of a toy. One day, he was playing with his best friend James. Dewon put the gun in his pocket and danced liked a cowboy. The gun went off.
> "I'm shot!" he yelled. "I'm shot!"
> At the hospital, doctors used tweezers to remove the bullet. Dewon and James made up a lie to police. They said they were on the porch when someone drove past and fired four random shots, and one hit Dewon's leg. The police wrote this down. It was not so unlikely, not where these kids live. No one was arrested. No one was charged.
> Dewon Jones went home the next day, wearing the unofficial tattoo of his city: a bullet hole.
> He was 10 years old.

In his new book, *News Values: Ideas for an Information Age,* Jack Fuller, the Pulitzer Prize-winning publisher of the *Chicago Tribune* and novelist, says that "people come to a newspaper craving a unifying human presence—the narrator in a piece of fiction, the guide who knows the way, or the colleague whose view one values. Readers don't just want random snatches of information flying at them from out of the ether. They want information that hangs together, makes sense, has some degree of order to it. They want knowledge rather than facts, perhaps even a little wisdom."

As long as readers can continue to find stories that make sense, have order and knowledge—and yes, wisdom—a blend that's in abundance in the work and work habits of these winners, the newspaper's chances for survival don't seem so bleak.

A NOTE ABOUT THIS EDITION

The discussions with most of the ASNE winners in this book are based on tape-recorded interviews, conducted by telephone, that lasted between two and four hours. For reasons of clarity or pacing, I reorganized some questions and answers, and in some cases, inserted additional questions. The edited transcripts were reviewed for accuracy and, in some instances, revised slightly by the subjects.

Christopher Scanlan
June 1996

1996 Best Newspaper Writing

Barton Gellman
Deadline Reporting

Barton Gellman covers the Middle East as *The Washington Post*'s correspondent based in Jerusalem. After graduating with highest honors from Princeton University in 1982, he earned a master's degree in politics from University College, Oxford, where he was a Rhodes scholar. Gellman was editor of his high school paper, had internships at *The Miami Herald* and *The Washington Post,* and worked for Gov. Bruce Babbitt of Arizona before coming to the *Post* full time in 1988. He served as Pentagon correspondent for the *Post* from 1990 to 1994 and covered D.C. Superior Court from 1988 to 1990, where he produced prize-winning coverage of the drug trial of Mayor Marion Barry. He has won two Front Page Awards from the Baltimore-Washington Newspaper Guild for local and national reporting. Author of *Contending with Kennan,* a study of George F. Kennan's foreign policy views, Gellman has written on politics and government for *The New Republic, National Journal, Washington Monthly,* and *American Oxonian.*

The night Israeli Prime Minister Yitzhak Rabin was assassinated, Barton Gellman had just a few hours to bring the news home to his readers. With the clock ticking, he wove an account rich with detail about what happened and insight into what it meant to prospects for peace. Then, after realizing he had interviewed the accused assassin months before, he mined his notes for another story, an evocative piece that shed light on the mindset of a political killer.

Israeli Prime Minister Yitzhak Rabin is killed

NOVEMBER 5, 1995

JERUSALEM, Nov. 4—A right-wing Jewish extremist shot and killed Prime Minister Yitzhak Rabin tonight as he departed a peace rally attended by more than 100,000 in Tel Aviv, throwing Israel's government and the Middle East peace process into turmoil.

The lone gunman met Rabin, 73, as he walked to his car in the Kings of Israel Square in front of Tel Aviv's city hall. The prime minister had just stepped off a massive sound stage where he had linked hands with fellow ministers to sing "The Song of Peace." Identified by police as Yigal Amir, a 27-year-old law student, the assassin fired three shots into Rabin's back at close range.

A cordon of security officers bundled the gunman away as Rabin was rushed by ambulance to Ichilov Hospital, just a few blocks away in the heart of Tel Aviv. He arrived there with no pulse and no blood pressure, according to Health Minister Ephraim Sneh, and died on the operating table at 11:10 p.m. (4:10 p.m. EST), an hour and a quarter after being shot. Seven minutes later, shouting over the sobs and gasps of policemen and journalists, Rabin's senior aide, Eitan Haber, announced his death.

Amir, who studied law and computer science at Bar Ilan University, was among the founders of an illegal Jewish settlement called Maale Yisrael that was built this summer in defiance of the then-impending deal to extend Palestinian self-rule to much of the West Bank. Israel Radio and Television reported that he spoke calmly to police tonight, telling them he acted alone, planned the assassination with a sound mind and had no regret.

Under Israeli law, Foreign Minister Shimon Peres becomes acting prime minister but the government is deemed to have fallen. That means it is up to President Ezer Weizman, a political maverick, to select a party leader to attempt to form a new governing coalition. The choice boils down to Peres or Binyamin Netanyahu, leader of the opposition Likud Party. At a 2 a.m. news conference, Weizman declined to discuss his next move. "The man has not yet been buried," he said. Rabin's funeral is scheduled for Monday.

Rabin's death is likely to advance elections that already were shaping up as a decisive test of the government's historic movement toward peace with its Arab neighbors, the Palestine Liberation Organization above all. The Israeli public is profoundly divided, and Rabin's Labor Party-led parliamentary coalition—dependent on opposition defectors and back-room deal-makers loyal only to Rabin—has hung on until now by a thread.

In no case can elections be later than scheduled, a year from now, and under many scenarios they will come sooner.

There had been no political assassination since Israel's founding in 1948. Tonight, the country reeled.

"This is a great, tragic moment in Israel's modern history," said Yaron Ezrahi, a political scientist at Hebrew University. "There's no question it will have profound effects on Israeli politics, the peace process and the government well beyond the next election. This is an event whose reverberations are so large that it is hard to assess it at this moment."

Many commentators, from right to left, have expressed alarm since summer at the increasingly violent cast of Israeli street politics. Jewish demonstrators have repeatedly blocked roads, set fires and clashed with police in protests against what they have called a "junta" and a government of "traitors" and "murderers."

Tonight's Tel Aviv demonstration was aimed at countering the past months' rallies of the right, in numbers and tone. Organizers, including the Labor and Meretz parties and the advocacy group Peace Now, brought the largest turnout in memory to the Kings of Israel Square—a traditional site for national political demonstrations—and deliberately chose a light-spirited tone.

The slogan of the night was "Yes to peace, no to violence." But an upbeat, carnival atmosphere prevailed, with popular singers such as Ahinoam Nini providing entertainment, and even Rabin and Peres joining in song.

Miri Aloni, a liberal activist, sang her signature number, "The Song of Peace," and passed the microphone to Rabin and Peres as they linked arms and swayed on the stage.

"Just sing a song of peace, don't whisper a prayer, sing a song of peace loudly," went the refrain.

Peres, alluding to the government's uncertain musical talents, drew a big laugh from the crowd by quipping: "We know how to make peace. We don't know how to sing. But in the making of peace we won't be off-key."

Later, his head bowed and voice breaking with emotion, Rabin's lifelong Labor Party rival said the prime minister had folded the song's lyrics and placed them in a breast pocket before descending from the stage.

"The bullets ripped them apart," Peres said.

Rabin's speech to the rally, his last, was confident and brief.

"I was a military man for 27 years," said the former army chief of staff, who was Israel's youngest brigade commander in the 1948 war of independence. "I fought as long as there was no chance for peace. I believe now that there is a chance for peace, a great chance, and we must take advantage of it."

Moments before descending from the stage, Rabin gave a final radio interview.

"I always believed that most of the people are against the violence that lately has taken a form that harms the basic system of Israeli democratic values," he said. "And they support peace. People have doubts about their personal security, but they do not have doubts that the path of peace should be pursued. I think this rally gave voice to many of the people."

A few minutes later, the program ended with the singing of "Hatikva," the Israeli national anthem. At 9:55 p.m., with many demonstrators still dancing in the square to a live concert by rock star Aviv Geffen, the three shots rang out.

Before tonight, there had been some recent disturbing signs of willingness to translate the anti-government rhetoric of Jewish protesters into anti-government violence.

Environment Minister Yossi Sarid, traveling in his government sedan, was run off the main Jersualem-Tel Aviv highway by a West Bank settler in an adjacent car who recognized the left-wing Cabinet official and swerved his car repeatedly into Sarid's.

Then, a month ago, right-wing demonstrators attacked the car of Housing Minister Binyamin Ben Eliezer as he arrived to cast his ballot on a vote of confidence in the government. They damaged the car and nearly upended it, according to Eliezer's account at the time. The government narrowly survived the parliamentary vote, 61 to 59.

That same night, a right-wing extremist leader was photographed holding a Cadillac emblem that had been torn from Rabin's official sedan in a similar attack. Although Rabin was not in his car at the time, some extremists said they had proved they could penetrate his security, and would do so again.

Also that night, tens of thousands of right-wing demonstrators massed in Jerusalem under the slogan that "the people did not sign" the Sept. 28 West Bank peace accord with PLO leader Yasser Arafat, an effort to remove legitimacy from Rabin's government. The rally featured speeches by Netanyahu and other Likud leaders.

A larger-than-life effigy of Rabin, dressed in the uniform of the Nazi SS, stood out that night from a sea of anti-government placards. Netanyahu, who later criticized the effigy, did not do so during the rally and delivered his speech as planned.

Environment Minister Sarid, who described Rabin tonight as "the most important statesman of this time, maybe in the whole world," blamed the mainstream Israeli right for creating the climate of his assassination.

"He fell victim to a lot of incitement and hatred and hostility," Sarid said. "For a long time we said that this is giving legitimacy to murder. But our admonitions went unheard, and there was encouragement, and the blood was spilled. One man did it, but there were many more inciters."

Until tonight, Netanyahu has walked a careful balance, distancing himself from violence but holding Rabin and his policies chiefly responsible for creating the public rift that made it possible.

Netanyahu declined to take questions tonight, but in a statement to Israel Radio expressed "deep mourning and severe shock."

"We must vomit from our society anyone who infringes the most basic rule of human society, 'Thou shalt not kill,' " he said. "I pray that we learn to maintain restraint and unity in the face of one of the most difficult tragedies that has befallen us since the beginning of the state."

Ori Orr, a fellow former general and key ally of Rabin in parliament, told Israel Television tonight that "None of us can digest this:

"He died in the most important battle he fought, at the hands of evil Jews. Today there is nothing we can do. We can only cry."

Writers' Workshop

Talking Points

1) Gellman's job here, he says, is to "forge a coherent narrative" from the stream of information that emerges from a breaking news story. Examine his deadline account of the Rabin assassination and evaluate how well he achieved that goal.

2) This story effectively weaves information, context, and poignant details so that the reader experiences the event as well as understands it. Pay close attention to each of these elements. Focus on the ways Gellman places the events in Jerusalem in a larger context and how well he answers questions raised by the assassination.

3) Before his posting abroad, Gellman covered courts and the Pentagon for *The Washington Post*. But, he says, "whether at the courthouse or Army unit or foreign country, you have to accumulate a body of knowledge that far exceeds what you can say in any one story. That knowledge helps the reporter frame the story and throw in that small explanatory line or paragraph that provides context for the reader. That's the voice my editors are looking for." Identify those lines in Gellman's story. Study how economically he can convey history and political impact in a phrase.

Assignment Desk

1) List the questions asked and answered in the first four paragraphs. Shift the order in a different arrangement and rewrite the lead. Do other approaches work?

2) Compare the stories of the Rabin assassination produced by at least three other news organizations with this version. How do they differ from the *Post*'s approach? Which is the most effective in your opinion?

3) One story form that Gellman says he favors is the "tick-tock," a strict chronological retelling account that uses the clock as its organizing device. Try to rewrite this story using that form.

In June, suspect talked of Israel's 'weak backbone'

NOVEMBER 5, 1995

JERUSALEM, Nov. 4—On a windswept hill in the upper West Bank, the man police accuse of gunning down Prime Minister Yitzhak Rabin gave a coldly furious interview in June.

Yigal Amir, an intense, dark-haired student of law and computer science, was standing in an illegal new Jewish settlement called Maale Yisrael, or "ascent of Israel." All around him were the placards of the apoplectic right. "The Land of Israel is in Danger!" screamed one black-on-yellow banner, stretched between the improvised structures of the week-old encampment.

A portable toilet stall invited settlers, by using it, to express their contempt for the government's peace policies with each call of nature. A hand-lettered sign dubbed the toilet the "Oslo Agreement"—a reference to the Norwegian-hosted accord that began the shift to Palestinian self-rule in September 1993.

Amir, who said he was 25, explained that he hitchhiked to Maale Yisrael each day from classes at Bar Ilan University in suburban Tel Aviv, a campus known for its affinity to religious nationalists. No matter what Rabin's government tried to do, he said, Jews would control the West Bank forever.

"This is the most holy land," he said. "Two thousand years ago, most of the population of Israel was here, in Samaria and Jerusalem."

The government's "backbone is very weak, and maybe that is the reason they are willing to give up everything for peace," he said.

Amir said the government would not survive to complete its program. He did not elaborate, and there was no indication at the time that he meant anything more than the usual opposition vow to bring down Rabin's coalition at the polls.

He did not shout or curse, the way some demonstrators do. Slender and self-controlled, he gave the impression of holding more detailed views he did not care to share with an American reporter.

Asked, for example, about the Arab villages in view and their orchards of almond and apple trees, Amir said that just because Arabs worked the land "doesn't mean it belongs to the Arabs."

Would settlers move to those places next, his visitor asked.

"Maybe," Amir replied.

Police officials here, speaking to Israeli reporters after disarming Amir and pinning him to a wall as Rabin fell bleeding, said the alleged assassin spoke with almost surreal calm. Informed that Rabin had succumbed to his wounds, the officials said, Amir expressed satisfaction.

Amir confessed, according to Israeli broadcast reports, that he had intended to kill Rabin for most of a year and at least twice had traveled to the sites of Rabin's scheduled appearances—in January at the Yad Vashem Holocaust memorial, a visit Rabin did not make because of a terrorist bombing in Beit Lid that day, and in September at the dedication of a new highway interchange.

Israel Television aired file footage tonight of Amir at the September event, some distance from Rabin. He was screaming about the abandonment of 140,000 Jews, a reference to the West Bank settlers, and police removed him forcibly from the scene.

Amir hails from Herzliya, an affluent beach-front suburb north of Tel Aviv, where his mother is a kindergarten teacher and his father a biblical calligrapher. Israel Radio reported he did his army service in the elite Golani combat brigade and served as an immigration emissary of the Jewish Agency in the former Soviet Union. Both of those are sterling credentials, obtained by stiff competition in Israel.

Avishai Raviv, the chief of a right-wing extremist group called Eyal, which has been linked to violence against Arabs, said that "we knew him through our activity" but denied that Amir was a member.

"He was always nice and moderate," Raviv said.

A classmate from Kolel, a community seminary where Amir studied, told Israel Radio that Amir did have "a connection with the Raviv gang."

"I think he was brainwashed and did not act alone, as he claims," said the acquaintance, identified only as

Arik. "The truth is there were signs. After every attack
and during demonstrations on the lawn at Bar Ilan, he
said things like, 'Rabin should be taken care of' and
'the government should be taken care of.'"

Asked whether he had ever reported such remarks,
Arik replied: "Listen, you live with people and you
cannot believe that a person who is close to you is ca-
pable of carrying out such an insane act. It is true that
he is right-wing. So am I. But this is frightening.... It
is exactly like people who knew about violence in the
family and were silent for years."

Others who knew Amir said he worked for a security company and, like many Israeli men with army
service, was licensed to carry a weapon.

Amir's case serves to illustrate the ability of violent
extremists, including also members of banned groups
such as Kach and Kahane Lives, to mingle seamlessly
with mainstream members of the political opposition.
Kach activists, violent followers of the late rabbi Meir
Kahane, often manage to infiltrate Likud party rallies
and attract television cameras with chants such as
"Death to Rabin!"

At one spontaneous demonstration, which coa-
lesced at the scene of an August terror bomb in Jerusalem's Ramat Eshkol neighborhood, the extremists
whipped up a large enough crowd to physically
threaten President Ezer Weizman and prevent him
from speaking.

At Maale Yisrael, where Amir was interviewed in
June, he lived and worked openly amid senior repre-
sentatives of the Yesha Council, the umbrella organization for Jewish settlers, and of Likud Youth.

Likud leaders supported the illegal settlement, and
Likud banners were raised at the site. One of them, a
turnabout on Rabin's 1990 election slogan ("Israel is
Waiting for Rabin") read, "Israel is Disappointed in
Rabin" and was signed, "The Likud."

"Sadly, many nonviolent politicians on the right
were encouraging extremists to adopt violent means
because they themselves were using extremist rhetoric," said Yossi Alpher, an Israeli strategist who is
Jerusalem representative of the American Jewish
Committee.

Menachen Friedman, an expert on Israel's religious right from Bar Ilan University, said extremists routinely demonized left-wing leaders and believed that their elimination could change the course of events.

"I think...in that act he thought he would stop the peace process," Friedman said.

Rabin's own stubbornness gave his assassin his final opportunity. Members of the prime minister's inner circle said tonight they had urged him for months to wear body armor under his clothes.

They said he waved them off, saying he was not afraid.

Writers' Workshop

Talking Points

1) In this story, Gellman puts the killer of the Israeli prime minister in his physical and socio-political environment. Study and describe the elements he uses to achieve this effect.

2) Sometimes it's the absence of things—not a quote, but silence; not what a person is wearing, but what's absent (a soldier in civilian clothes, for instance). Notice what Gellman said is missing in the suspect's behavior.

3) Working feverishly into the early hours of the morning, Gellman wrote this story based on the notes from his earlier interview with the assassin, his recollections, and a variety of sources. Identify as many of the sources of information in this story as possible. Pay close attention to how Gellman tells you where he gets his information. Consider whether he could have made more of the fact that he had interviewed Rabin's killer months before. Would you have? Why?

4) Deep in the story, Gellman writes a classic "nut graph" paragraph, one that seeks to place the event in a larger context. "Amir's case serves to illustrate the ability of violent extremists, including also members of banned groups such as Kach and Kahane Lives, to mingle seamlessly with mainstream members of the political opposition." In some newspapers, such as *The Wall Street Journal,* that passage would probably have appeared higher in the story. Discuss whether you agree or disagree with its placement and why.

Assignment Desk

1) Gellman chose to end this story with a description of how Rabin's stubborn refusal to wear body armor under his clothes "gave his assassin his final opportunity." Rewrite the story with a different ending.

2) For this story, Gellman had to reconstruct an interview that was five months old. Could you do it? Go back to the notes and your memories of an event or interview from the past and write a story based on them.

A conversation with
Barton Gellman

CHRISTOPHER SCANLAN: Tell me the story behind "Israeli Prime Minister Yitzhak Rabin is Killed." Can you do a tick-tock for me with this story?

BARTON GELLMAN: As the world knows now, Rabin was assassinated at a peace rally in Tel Aviv. I decided not to go to the peace rally. I thought a pro-government rally, organized by the government, isn't such a big story unless, of course, something happens. It was a Saturday night and I had a friend who was having a baby shower. I decided not to go, and sent a stringer, just in case.

The baby shower was full of journalists. I had two or three beers, which is a lot for me, and one of the journalists gets a phone call right around 10 at night. The first report is, "There have been heard what sounded like shots at the rally; no one knows quite what it means, but the prime minister has been sped away in his car." This sounds like news. We all jump on our cellular phones, and the next 15 minutes develop the story that there were definitely shots fired in the direction of the prime minister. At first there's no knowledge about whether he's hurt or not, and then there is a very tentative report that he may have been injured.

At this point, it's past 10:30. I am an hour's drive from Tel Aviv, in Jerusalem, and I called my desk. I had a dilemma. Every instinct tells me to go as fast as I can to the scene of the news, but it's an hour drive each way. I didn't think I was going to be able to breeze right into Rabin's hospital room if he was at the hospital. I wasn't sure I should go. I talked to Gene Robinson, our foreign editor, who was on duty that day. We agreed that if, in fact, the prime minister of Israel had been shot, whether or not he was badly wounded, this was a story of such significance that they wanted me to be able to write the story and not have it done essentially by rewrite in Washington with me dictating whatever notes I could get from the scene.

Why did you want to write the story?

I wanted my voice to be the one to tell readers what happened here and what it was going to mean. On my way back to my bureau, I was on my cellular phone calling everyone I could think of. I was able to reach two government ministers and the United States ambassador in their cars on their way to the hospital, and all of them sounded grave but none of them, except maybe Ambassador Martin Indyk, actually knew what had happened at the time I talked with them. In any case, none of them told me. They said that they'd been told that Rabin had been hit, he was injured, but they didn't know more than that.

It was 11:10 at night when Rabin died, and some minutes after that when one of his closest aides came out and announced that the prime minister was gone. This was done on live radio, and I heard it live. My Hebrew isn't great, but it was good enough to understand that. There was just an enormous, surreal sense of shock over my whole household. My stringer was back from Tel Aviv, having rushed back assuming I would want help. Another translator who works for me had come in for the same reason. My wife and babysitter were there, and we're all just looking at one another in disbelief.

What was going through your head?

I am, as I said, half-drunk, although rapidly sobering up, and desperately telling myself, "I have to figure out a way to convey the enormity of this story and I better start thinking fast because it's nearly 4:30." To tell you the truth, I came into my office and I shut my door and I was actually screaming at myself, sort of slapping myself in the face and saying, "Snap out of it. This is a really big story. You've got to rise to this."

It was about as much stress as I can ever remember experiencing. I knew that history was happening here. There's only a few times in your career in journalism when you're sure that what you're seeing is something for the history books and not just some footnote.

Almost every first draft I write is full of clichés and mixed metaphors and too many adjectives. This was a huge, sort of desperate challenge to me at the time. I really didn't know what I was going to do. You almost feel as though if this is the biggest story you've ever covered, then it's got to be the best story you've ever written. But it doesn't really follow that way, and you don't always have the material right there at hand. But that was more or less the standard I was subconsciously setting for myself.

What did you do?

First of all I said that the facts themselves were so dramatic that they didn't need a lot of dramatic language. That simply stating the bald fact that someone walked up to the prime minister of Israel and shot him to death at a peace rally, right after he sang the "Song of Peace," was so powerful and so dramatic that I should just tell it simply, without a lot of elaboration.

And then I thought, "I've got to simultaneously tell people the facts and I've got to raise all the rather large questions that get raised very quickly when a country is in the middle of a huge history-making decision already, which is how to transform a bitter 100-year-old conflict; indeed, whether to transform this conflict into some new relationship with its neighbors, and right at that moment lose the man who was guiding the ship." So I just sat there and I wrote a lead.

What kind of reporting were you doing?

I was trying to find out as much as I could about what had happened. I'm still making phone calls to the housing minister, the health minister, everybody I can think of who's on their way to the scene, because everyone in the government is rushing there. I've got my translators listening to the live radio and watching the live television broadcasts, and coming in and feeding me new details as they emerge. I'm starting to hear, for the first time, the name of the assassin and a tiny bit about him. I figure that I need at least some kind of a context quote, I need someone to say, not in my language but in someone else's language, some first cut at what is going to be the meaning of this, and so I called one of the smartest people I've ever met, a political scientist at Hebrew University. I'm always in danger of overusing him because every time I call him he says something smart.

I get that out of the way and then I decide, "I'm not going to have a lot of talking heads in this story; there's too much plain fact that's going to need telling," but I had to have at least one.

What are the various sources of information that were streaming in?

I had two translators. Eetta Prince-Gibson was listening to the radio and Talya Ezrahi was watching the television. They were coming and telling me stuff, and keeping a running log in writing of other details. I kept telling them, "I want small details, fine details, the little stuff that will help me make this as concrete as possible." The most important thing I learned in my early days of journalism was to show, not to tell. Don't say something was dramatic; show the readers enough little details that they will experience a sense of adrenaline. I tried to cut back on my first draft tendency to use a lot of adjectives and, instead, to come back with a lot of concrete details that help you build a mental picture of the sights and the sounds and the smells or whatever it is that I know.

How did you come to write the story about the suspect?

Three or four or five paragraphs into writing the main story, I'm trying to assemble all the news as it's breaking around me. There are conflicting early reports about exactly who did this and what we know about him. And suddenly, it dawns on me that I think I might just have talked to this assassin five months earlier.

The name itself, Yigal Amir, meant nothing to me. It sounded just like any other Israeli name. But then, as I was trying to write this main bar, every few minutes something else comes in. "He's 25 years old, he went to Bar Ilan University, he seemed to have been studying computer science; no, he was studying law; no, he was studying Talmud—wait, he was studying all three of them," and all of a sudden that rings a bell. I'm thinking,

"Why does that ring a bell?" and the next piece comes in and the radio says, "He seems to have been involved in illegal settlement activity on the West Bank."

All of a sudden, I have a very clear picture in my head of talking to this very intense young guy on a hilltop in the West Bank at a place called Maale Yisrael. I remember, in great detail, this conversation because I remembered thinking at the time, "That's an interesting triple major; you're studying Talmud, computers, and law," and I remembered his style, I remembered some of what he'd said, and I was pretty sure that I had interviewed Yigal Amir.

Once you realized that, what did you do?

It was getting very late, and I called my wife, Tracy, into the office and I said, "Here is a big pile of notebooks. I'm pretty sure I interviewed Yigal Amir. Can you see if you can find his name?" I had no idea when. I do save my old notebooks, and they're more or less in chronological order, and pretty quickly we found it. I had this very strange sensation of seeing the name of the prime minister's assassin in my own handwriting in one of my old notebooks. Now, to the world, Yigal Amir is a very familiar name. At that time, it was still new.

As calmly as I could, because it's part of the culture of being a foreign correspondent that nothing ever rattles you, I picked up the phone and called Washington and said, "I'm going to do a profile of Yigal Amir because it turns out I've interviewed him." And the editor said, "What!?" And I said, "Yeah, I mean, just pure dumb luck, I talked with the guy five months ago."

A lot of people have asked me whether anything about the interview at the time suggested that he could be an assassin. The answer is no. I thought at the time that he and what he said were so *unexceptional* that he didn't even make my story, which I had on the front page the next day. He was one of those little footnotes that stays in the back of your notebook.

Is there something that's transferable about the experience that would make it possible to replicate it back in the United States?

Getting away from your desk and getting out as much as possible. It's actually one of the things I love about being a foreign correspondent, that you get so much good stuff by being out there, reporting with your own eyes and ears.

And that's something I did try to do when I covered the courthouse. The cases are about something. They're about people and places and things that happened, and so I tried not to just do them from the courtroom. I tried to do what I observed that good reporters, much more senior than I was covering more important beats like the Supreme Court, would always do, which is not to write the cases just from the briefs and the arguments. But if a case is about free speech in a school out in Minnesota, just get out there and see things and talk to people. It invariably pays off.

How do you focus your story? How do you decide what you're going to write, how you're going to write it, the kind of thinking and planning that precedes the writing?

Our readers are relying on us to tell them the information that they most want to know, as they most want to know it, or we're going to lose their attention. I thought, what's the first most important thing? The prime minister is dead. And this has thrown not only this country but the larger historical process of reconciliation with the Arabs into turmoil.

And then I thought I'd better say a little bit more about what actually happened, as spare and clean an account as I could: who had done what and when. I wanted to give a sense of scene, because if I didn't do that, then I thought it was going to look like, "Old news, we know that already." I wanted people to feel immediately as though they were thrust into this scene.

So you say, "The lone gunman met Rabin, 73, as he walked to his car..." and you say, "Kings of Israel Square." And then you use the detail, "...a massive sound stage where he had linked hands with fellow ministers to sing the 'Song of Peace'...fired the shots into Rabin's back at close range." Those are the details you're looking for?

I couldn't stop to explain any of it at any length. I wanted to have every phrase convey at least some mental picture. It helped people who were not right here in the middle of it and surrounded by it experience some of the power of this event.

Did you have any concern that by the time the *Post* hit the streets, most Americans will already know?

I thought, "What are they going to want to know?" I knew from the Gulf War and other events I've covered that also have had live television saturation coverage that after awhile this sort of data stream is so thick and so long and so contradictory. When you're watching live television, you're learning many of the things that I'm learning in about the order I'm learning it, full of contradictions, false starts, pieces separated by an hour or two, and you have to put them together. I thought my job was to somehow forge a coherent narrative out of all this by putting together all the best details that I knew to be true.

Did you write down any of these questions, or is this your thought process?

I had no time to be systematic. I was really struggling, honestly, to remain calm. I was in something like the initial state of shock that I think the whole country was in for weeks afterward, months in fact. This was a huge, huge thing that had happened, and virtually no one had expected it and no one knew where it was going to lead, and so I was, frankly, struggling to keep my composure about this.

I knew all the questions that were flashing into my mind were going to flash into a reader's mind. "Well, who did this? Now what happens?" I'd never thought about it. I didn't know anything about the law of succession in Israel. It never occurred to me I would have to worry about that. So I started reporting that, to find out, and I figured I'd have to say very high in the story who was running the country now and how long that was going to last and what was going to happen next.

I admired this paragraph: "Later, his head bowed and voice breaking with emotion, Rabin's lifelong Labor Party rival said the prime minister had folded the song's lyrics and placed them in a breast pocket before descending from the stage... 'The bullets ripped them apart.'"

Peres has a sense of theater—he knew he was good copy at that moment and he was, I think, in some sense trying to say something appropriate to the emotions of the occasion. It actually was not true—because eventually I was able to look at the lyrics and, in fact, the bullets had not ripped them full of holes, but they were full of Rabin's blood.

What's the lesson from that?

What I wrote was accurate. I sourced it. Peres said it. But the lesson always is to keep looking and check and go back and get as close as you can to the source. I don't know whether that's such a hugely important detail, but I do find that first reports of dramatic events are often wrong and need to be reassembled later.

How did you gain the knowledge that enabled you to write, "Under Israeli law, Foreign Minister Shimon Peres becomes acting prime minister but the government is deemed to have fallen."

Some of it came on the radio, and some of it came when I was talking to government ministers. I have had to do a couple of legal stories here and I have learned from covering the courthouse that it's very important to get legal details right. I know some lawyers here, and I thought I understood how to write the sentence, but I called one who knew the basic law of Israel on the formation of government and bounced it off him.

Every time I have to write something but I'm not sure enough about it and I decide I can't skip it, I make another quick phone call to nail it down.

I often discover what I'm missing while I'm writing. I rarely get to do my reporting in one phase and then my writing in a second; I almost always think of questions or problems as I'm writing that require another phone call or another looking up something in a book.

So a good Rolodex is really vital to you at that moment?

I'm an obsessive collector of phone numbers. In the courthouse I made sure I sort of snuck a look at the phone number in each courtroom because there were phones in the courtrooms in D.C. In the Pentagon, I passed through Andrews Air Force Base and I would go take a look at what the phone number is in the VIP waiting lounge. Here I ask people for their home numbers, their car phones. Israel is completely wired.

Many people have more than one cellular phone, and a beeper, and if there were such a thing as a wrist watch radio, they would have that, too. It's a place where you could have 10 phone numbers for one person, and I'll take all 10.

Where'd you learn that?

I don't remember but, I'll tell you, the first time I really, really needed to talk to someone and I had no idea how to reach them, I figured out that it's good to just store these things up for a rainy day.

Where do you keep them?

On my computer. I believe in using a computer to store stuff that I would lose on scraps of paper, and I print out the Rolodex every so often and carry around the printout, but I usually just tell the computer, "Go find me so-and-so's number."

I had to call Cabinet members. And so I thought to myself, "Where are they going to be? They're probably going to be in their cars," so I was glad I had some car phone numbers.

Did you write an outline? Do you write outlines for stories?

I write outlines for some big magazine stories or long features sometimes, but I certainly don't on deadline; I simply don't have the discipline or it's just not my way. I write stuff, I rewrite it, I move it around. Sometimes, as I think a stray thought, I jot down a phrase in the B-matter of the story, and just leave it there, knowing that I'll come across it after I scroll down through the screen and say, "Oh, yeah, I've got to write a paragraph on this." And as often as not, I'll move that up somewhere.

Do you know how long you had to do this story?

He was dead at 17 minutes past 11:00 at night, and by around 3:00 or 3:15 I had filed two stories, the main bar and the Yigal Amir profile. I don't think that's particularly fast, frankly, from the point of view of a wire service. I know that the wires had long, impressive stories faster than that, but I knew exactly how much time I had and I used every second of it. I made my deadline, but I didn't make it by much.

And are you writing with your eye on the clock?

Very much so. And that's part of the pressure because, as I said, I'm really not that experienced at writing under extreme deadline pressure, and I don't think I'm particularly fast or particularly slow among my colleagues. I think I'm sort of right there in the middle.

Turning to the story of the suspect, how much time did you have for that one?

A little less than for the main bar, but it was a much simpler story. Because there was so much going on in the main bar that I kept on thinking I just don't know what to do next. I kept experiencing this conflict between carrying a narrative, telling a chronological tale—"Rabin went to a peace rally"—but I had to keep interspersing that the government was changing, that Israel is in the middle of an enormous social debate about exactly the subject that seems to have led to the assassination, and so on. But for the Amir profile, all I had to do was set a scene to tell what I knew about this guy and then to weave into the story what sparse biographical details we knew in a couple of hours after the event.

When you had finished these stories, how did you feel?

I was wiped out emotionally, physically, and at the same time, I knew that I was at the beginning of a very long roller-coaster ride. That day I filed two stories, the next day I filed two stories, the next day I filed two stories, the next day I filed just one story, and on that day, my editor said, "For the weekend we need a giant profile of Yigal Amir." I didn't know exactly how all that would go, but I knew that I was about to start a very, very intensive period of reporting on the fallout of this huge event. So the last thing I did before I went to bed was to make arrangements for somebody to listen to the 6 and 7 a.m. radio news and wake me if there were important developments, because there would still be time to correct the story or add to the story for the same newspaper. And I talked a little bit to Jackson Diehl, the assistant managing editor for foreign news and a former correspondent here, about what we should do next.

How much sleep did you get that night?

Three hours.

Do you like your job?

It's the best job I've ever had. Because the scope of it is a whole country, a whole region. Because the story line is very rich. Because of the independence from my bosses, the fact that I am very far away in time and space and, therefore, have an unusual degree of autonomy, the ability to set the agenda. Because the culture of the foreign staff at *The Washington Post* is to trust the correspondent to tell them what's important and what needs doing most of the time. And because so much of the reporting is direct reporting and not sitting on the phone talking to an official and getting spun by people who talk for a living.

What is the most challenging or difficult aspect of the job?

Feeling like you're doing justice to a whole country, a whole culture, feeling like you really "get it," you understand what's happening, that you're able, with some confidence, to look to the second and third levels of meaning to get beneath the obvious.

What do you think enabled you to rise to the occasion? What in your past experience or training enabled you to do this?

I just knew I had to do it. When I used to cover the Pentagon, there were a lot of hostile audiences and a lot of people think there's virtually nothing in common between the military and the media, and there's endless discussions about the conflict between the military and the media. When I talked to a military audience at one of these media and the military days, I would talk about some points in common that we had, and one of them was that we are both in a no-excuses profession. When you get a mission in the military, or you get a story assignment for a newspaper, nobody in the world wants to hear all the good reasons why you couldn't do it. You know, the computer crashed and my tire was flat and the sun was in my eyes and I had a couple of beers and whatever else may have happened; it's simply not relevant. You just have to do it. And I guess I'd absorbed enough of that ethic over the years that I didn't consider any other possibility.

What were you doing before this job?

I started covering the Department of Defense and the U.S. military just a few weeks before the Gulf War broke out, and I stayed on that assignment for almost four years. It was a little bit like preparation for a foreign posting because it has its own kind of arcane language, its own cultures and subcultures. I spent a month in Somalia when the Marines first landed, and would go more or less wherever U.S. troops were around the world from time to time.

How long have you been at the *Post*?

I came to the *Post* in August 1988 as a reporter on the metropolitan staff. I was covering the D.C. Superior Court, so it was your basic courthouse reporting with a little bit of everything, from a guy who was being prosecuted for stealing a snake from a pet shop to the Marion Barry trial for drug use and perjury and various other charges.

Did you always want to be a reporter?

I did always want to be a reporter. I guess I can date it from when I joined the junior varsity gymnastics team in high school and found out that I wasn't ever going to be any good at it, so I went down the hall and tried out at the student newspaper. And since then I more or less knew that was what I was going to do.

What about that experience persuaded you?

I got hooked early by a confrontation with my high school principal. I had written a couple of articles one year; the next year they decided to make me the editor. I wanted to have a splashy first issue, so I commissioned three related articles on the problems of teen-age pregnancy. My principal thought that was a really bad idea, and when the issue came out—we had in fact prepared it in some secrecy because we thought she would think it was a bad idea—she confiscated the whole press run and fired me as editor and actually shut down the newspaper.

We sued her in Federal Court, myself and my two collaborators on the project. It went all the way through my whole senior year of high school and well into my first year of college before we got an out-of-court settlement that said we had the right to publish the articles. By that time I was long since graduated, but I had also long since gotten the bug for journalism and wanted to keep doing it.

Why did you choose to study in the Woodrow Wilson School?

I was interested in the subject matter, especially in international relations and the way that societies relate, and I guess I rationalized later that I had made the right choice because there are two main schools of thought on how you prepare for journalism. One is that you study journalism formally as a profession with a body of professional knowledge that needs to be acquired, and the other is that you study something else, you learn something about the world, and you approach journalism more as a craft, something to which you apprentice yourself and learn it by doing it. For better or worse, that's the way I did it. The high school paper, the college paper, summer internships, and then, eventually, the *Post.*

Having taken that road, do you have an opinion on whether one of them is preferable?

I guess I like the one I took. It's valuable for us in journalism to know something about something. It would be good if there were more people with real mastery of other subjects. There's a shortage of scientists in journalism, a shortage of people with other kinds of direct experience in another world besides our own.

I think I learned something about the world. I was able to study something deeply besides my own profession, and I think that I learned a good deal about how you become a reporter by doing it. I learned as much from my own student editors at the college newspaper, the *Daily Princetonian,* as I learned anywhere else. That brought me from zero to some working understanding of how you do this job. I spent a summer at *The Miami Herald,* where I watched some real telephone artists at work and got assignments all over South Florida.

What's a telephone artist?

There were people there who just opened my eyes to the idea that there's a hundred different ways to get someone to open up to you, to tell you something that they weren't sure they wanted to tell you, or even just to hang on the line and not hang up on you. There was a guy named Ron Ishoy in the Broward County bureau at that time, and they sat me next to him because he was a veteran reporter and I just used to listen to him and I was only hearing one side of the conversation, but it almost always would start off with, "Now, wait a minute, ma'am, please don't hang up, just hear me out for a second." Before I knew it, two hours had gone by and he's still on the phone with her and he would write just some wonderful, vivid picture of what had happened, never having left his chair. Now, I've come to be a big believer in getting out of the chair and driving off and seeing things and hearing things with your own senses, but it's an absolutely basic skill to get people to talk to you and to get people to want to talk you.

Are there specific things that you've found most helpful in terms of getting people to talk to you?

There aren't really any tricks, or if there are any I haven't come across them. I've seen people much better than I am at drawing people out. In fact, I'm a little bit shy, and so I have to work at this. But what I think about a lot is human behavior and human motivation. I try to empathize, not in a clichéd sense of, "I feel your pain," but "What is going on for this person right now, what is this person's relationship to the story, how is he or she experiencing what's happening, and what does he or she really want?"

How does this process work?

At the beginning of a story, I try to think about in what order I should speak with people. At the Pentagon beat one time, I had the problem of trying to reconstruct one of the friendly-fire deaths in the Persian Gulf War. This had been one of the major controversies of the war, and it was something that nobody in the military likes to talk about. I decided I would like to do a ticktock, from beginning to end, on one case of a friendly-fire death. I had to start with the fact that the Pentagon would not identify any occasion of friendly fire. But eventually there were a lot of records about the Gulf War, and assembling all the data that was known with the names of all of the dead and which units they were in and where those units had been on which days, I was able to come up with half a dozen cases that I was pretty sure were friendly fire.

I zeroed in on one of them, and I'm trying to figure out how do I get these people to talk about a subject that is so hard for them to talk about, so emotional. After a while, I made the fairly obvious deduction that it would be easier to get the people who were shot *at* to talk than the people who had done the shooting. And so I started cold calling them, hoping that their own need to talk about the trauma, probably untinged by a sense of their own personal guilt, would get me started. I figured once I had the picture fairly clear from that side, then I might be able to bring that picture to people on the other side who would naturally want to show what it looked like from their point of view, and that's more or less how I approached it.

Did it work?

It ended up being a fairly compelling account. Not so much because it was friendly fire, but because it really was a story from both points of view of a combat engagement, and that is something you rarely get.

How do you define a tick-tock?

The oldest storytelling device: a chronological account. Start with the beginning, go through the middle, then finish at the end. I think that is the natural way people tell stories, it's the natural way that people want to hear stories, and although we have to work with the inverted pyramid and nut graphs and all sorts of other devices that we've grown up with in journalism, sooner or later I find most of my good stories and most of my long stories move into a chronological telling, because that's the way people expect to hear things.

How have you managed, despite a natural shyness, to do work that requires a fair amount of assertiveness?

Just by doing it. By choosing the career I chose, I was trying to force myself out of it. I picked this career that's constantly pushing me into people I haven't met before and changing the circumstances on me.

The main thing I do is I think about what interests me about the subject at hand, what's going on, what do I find intriguing about it, and just start asking people questions about what they're doing or what's happened or what's going on. People often like to talk about themselves, like to talk about the world in which they live, if they sense that your agenda is simply to find out and understand it and spend the time.

My style is to do longer interviews than some of my colleagues do. Certainly, I do longer interviews than most of my subjects expect. I have a somewhat disorganized interviewing style. Part of it's on purpose and part of it's just because I don't really know what I'm after until I start to hear it. And I tend to want to go into much more detail than I'm ever allowed to use in the paper because I really feel like the great bulk of what's going on in a story has to be going on off the page, especially when you're a beat reporter.

If you're covering something that's at all technical or complicated, whether at the courthouse or Army unit or foreign country, in my experience you have to accumulate a body of knowledge that far exceeds what you can say in any one story, and that helps you frame the stories and throw in that small, explanatory line or paragraph here or there that provides context for the reader. That's the voice that my editors are looking for, and the reason that they're spending the enormous sums of money to keep a foreign correspondent overseas. It's not that there isn't excellent coverage by wire services and other news sources. It's that they want to have the voice of their own correspondent who has accumulated a sense of the place and can put things in context.

Where did you learn to write? And how?

I learned to write fundamentally in college from two experiences. One was my freshman composition class, which I vividly remember. I got a B+/C− on my first essay. It was a two-page essay and my section leader probably wrote as many words of commentary as I'd written in the essay. I mean, she basically told me that I was a blowhard; that I was using long, multi-syllable words because I liked the sound of them and not because they were the best words; that I was making elementary mistakes like splitting infinitives and so on and so forth. I had actually come to college thinking I was a pretty good writer. I mean in my high school I was a pretty good writer, and I realized I had a lot to learn.

The second experience was joining, sometime in my first semester at Princeton, the *Daily Princetonian,* and going in and writing three or four stories a week like a beginning college journalist, and just writing so many words and getting edited so many times that I was bound to learn something.

Are there writers who have influenced you or people that you've read who have shaped you as a journalist, as a writer?

I have some colleagues at *The Washington Post* I admire enormously for their ability to find just the detail that makes you feel like you were there.

I was lucky enough to take a course in my senior year with John McPhee, the great *New Yorker* writer. He teaches a small seminar, called "The Literature of Fact." He doesn't actually like to have too many student journalists. He thinks that we end up overly formulaic or more interested in the fact than in the execution of the writing. There's an essay competition to get into his seminar. He gave enormously close attention to what I did and was one of the most empathetic readers I've ever had. He didn't assign his own writing, but all of us were moved to read a lot of him and I think he's extraordinary.

What made McPhee such an empathetic reader?

I'd always heard that people who are great writers aren't such great editors. They're two very different skills. He had the ability to look at what I was doing and put himself inside it and go to just the right weak point and say, "Is this really what you mean here? Is this really the right image? Might it not be something a little bit more like that?" And all of a sudden, changing four or five words transforms the whole structure of the piece and gives it a coherent theme that you didn't even quite know was there.

I've read William Howarth's introduction to McPhee's reader about his planning process. Did he teach that as well?

It's idiosyncratic. A lot of us have idiosyncrasies, and in fact I've learned not to fight them. I mean, I think writing is so hard that if you only feel comfortable doing it on a lined yellow pad with three sharp No. 2 pencils, then that's the way you should do it. And, you know, he only wants to use a certain size notebook. He has these tiny little notebooks, and he makes bezillions of cards and he starts taping them to the walls and surfaces and it's a very elaborate process. He told us all about it, and he said that at the end of this very long and elaborate process, the step he always took was he went outside and lay down on his back on his picnic table, looked at the sky, and said to himself, "I absolutely cannot do this thing. I just can't do it. I cannot do this piece." And I found this enormously reassuring because that's essentially the sort of panic I always have when I'm doing something I think is important, and I guess it was nice to know that even John McPhee has the same experience.

What are your idiosyncrasies?

Me, I have no idiosyncrasies. It's just a question of arranging things physically in a way that I find comfortable, and I like certain computer software and I like to have my screens organized in a certain way and I also have a preference for a particular size of notebook.

Are there other writers in your family?

My father wrote for his newspaper in college and he did some sports writing for the *Evening Bulletin* while he was stringing in college in Philadelphia. He moved out of journalism fairly young, but he always encouraged it in me.

How about your mom?

She's a schoolteacher in Philadelphia. And she's always been my most faithful reader. She'd read any crap I wrote and think it was great. This is probably a cliché too, but I do think about her as a reader when I'm writing, because she is smart and interested in the world around her but usually not knowledgeable about the subject I'm writing about. So if I'm writing a story from a courtroom or from kind of a complicated religious or nationalist conflict or from the deck of an aircraft carrier, I'm thinking how I need to tell the story so that she is going to find it understandable and interesting.

What's the best reflection or piece of advice you ever got about writing on deadline?

Show, don't tell. Find the details that will tell the story for you, and in some ways the story writes itself.

I'll give you a small example: I heard that Rabin died soon after he had been on the stage, linking hands and singing. And if you ever knew anything about Rabin you would realize what an extraordinary fact that is because he was one of the least likely people in the world to stand on a stage and sing a song. And so I asked, "What song?" And then, when I found out it was the "Song of Peace," I said to Eetta, "I've got to get the lyrics. I want to know exactly what the words were." And I picked one of them and put it in the story.

If a friend called and said that they were faced with the same kind of high-pressure breaking story, what advice would you give them?

"Take a deep breath and try to imagine sitting down and telling this story almost as in a letter to a friend." Sometimes we do get caught up in either the mechanics or in the conventions of daily journalism, and forget how to tell a story. All of us are natural storytellers in our own daily lives. We need to remember how we do that when we're searching for inspiration.

I would just add one last thing: I guess I would ask him, "What do you know that your readers don't know, and why does it matter?"

THE ARIZONA REPUBLIC

David Cannella
Finalist, Deadline Reporting

David Cannella has been a reporter for *The Arizona Republic* since 1980, covering a variety of beats, including community news, crime and courts, health and medicine, and general assignments. Among his stories was the 1993 outbreak of hantavirus in the Southwest that killed more than a dozen people, mostly Native Americans. He has won numerous awards from the Arizona Press Club, the Arizona Newspaper Association, and the Arizona Associated Press. He was also selected Child Advocate of the Year by the state chapter of the American Academy of Pediatrics for his reporting on children's health issues. He is a graduate of the Walter Cronkite School of Journalism and Telecommunications at Arizona State University and is completing a master's degree in media ethics at the university's School of Justice Studies.

Cannella's deadline account of the assisted suicide of a 27-year-old man crippled by Lou Gehrig's disease provides a detailed and poignant look at the right-to-die movement through the prism of one patient and his family.

27-year-old Lou Gehrig's sufferer helped with suicide

MAY 13, 1995

SOUTHFIELD, Mich.—After two canceled appointments with death, Nicholas Loving died smiling Friday.

The 27-year-old Phoenix man, wasted by Lou Gehrig's disease, is the 23rd, and youngest, person assisted in suicide by Dr. Jack Kevorkian. It was the second suicide this week at which Kevorkian was present.

Death came, finally, for Nick at 9:45 a.m. in an unremarkable home in this suburb 20 miles north of Detroit, said his mother, Carol, who was at his side when he died.

Lying on the living-room couch, Nick made a slight movement of his left hand to release carbon monoxide from a small tank, then breathed deeply through a plastic mask over his mouth. The deadly gas went deep into his lungs, and in minutes, he was dead.

It is what he wanted; there were no second thoughts, not a moment's hesitation when Kevorkian told him he could trigger the device "whenever he felt comfortable."

"He let out a beautiful sigh," his mother said. "I turned to Dr. Kevorkian and said, 'He's gone to heaven. He's finally happy.'"

He did not gasp or choke.

"It was," she said, "a good way to go."

Nick called his final appointment his "deliverance." And he died with a smile on his face, with Pink Floyd's *Dark Side of the Moon* playing through his earphones.

His last words: "I love you, Mom. Aren't you going to hold my hand?"

She did.

Once Nick was dead, his mother, Kevorkian and an assistant left. Fearful that a neighbor was spying on them and would call the police, they spent an hour at a restaurant.

"I didn't like the idea of leaving Nick there all alone," Carol Loving said. "But he was peaceful. We put an afghan on him, a blue and white one, just up to his chin, not covering his head."

When they came back, they pulled the old sedan that Kevorkian was driving into the double garage, closed the door and went in to retrieve the body. They loaded Nick into Kevorkian's infamous primer-gray Volkswagen—the van in which Janet Adkins, the first patient Kevorkian assisted with his suicide machine in 1990, died.

With Nick's body stretched out on the floor, a pillow under his head and a blanket covering him, they drove to the Oakland County Sheriff's Office, parked in the back, then crossed the street to a Big Boy's. Kevorkian anonymously called the Sheriff's Office, "There's a van in your parking lot with a body in it."

That set in motion a scenario all too familiar to Sheriff John Nichols.

"It's nothing different," he said Friday afternoon. "What the hell."

Carol retreated to a hotel in Southfield, checking in under an assumed name. Kevorkian vanished, and his lawyer, Geoffery Fieger, spoke to the media, saying stoically that Kevorkian is committed to his mission and that the medical community should begin to listen.

It was a long journey for Nick, a young man whose vitality had been drained by Lou Gehrig's disease, leaving him unable to walk, unable to feed himself, unable to speak clearly.

"I was never the kind of person to chew my cabbage twice," Nick said last month, while awaiting his date with Kevorkian. "Now, I'm repeating myself all the time. I was the guy who always was the life of the party, always laughing, always joking. Now, people can't even understand me when I call their name."

During the midnight flight from Phoenix to Detroit, he said he had no second thoughts.

"I've said my good-byes," he said. "I'm ready. I know I'm going to a better place. Anyplace is better than this."

What he sought deliverance from were the ravages of the rare and incurable neurological disease, which Nick had suffered from for nearly two years. He understood what was ahead: slow and sure muscular deterioration until all he could do was blink his eyes.

Death, he knew, was coming in one of two ways. He'd either choke on his own saliva because he couldn't swallow or slowly stop breathing when his lung muscles failed.

"It's no life," he told Kevorkian in a videotape made shortly before his death.

He reiterated that it was his choice to die. When Kevorkian asked him on tape if he had any last words, Nick quoted the Rev. Martin Luther King Jr.: "Free at last, free at last, God Almighty, I'm free at last."

"I was beginning to think it would never happen," he said on the airplane. Kevorkian had canceled two previous appointments with him. "Each time I would get excited, only to get disappointed."

Kevorkian was his last resort, he said in April. He regretted letting the disease progress beyond the point where he could kill himself.

"I've thought about suicide since the day I was diagnosed," he said then. "I put it off until I had no control, no strength to do it. I told myself I wouldn't let myself get this far, but I guess you hang on to life all you can."

He hung on, but as the disease progressed, he slowly retreated to his room in the two-bedroom apartment he shared with his mother in Sunnyslope.

"It's hard on him, it's hard on all of us," said Drew Loving, Nick's fraternal twin. "We have to support his decision because we know that's what he wants, but it's hard."

Luke, the youngest of Carol's four children, visited often over the past several weeks, but no day was harder than Thursday, when the two brothers had to say good-bye, had to let go.

"He's more than a brother to me," said Luke, 25. "He always looked out for me. I always looked up to him.

"Our dad walked out on us all when we were little, and Nick stepped in. He was always taking care of us."

On Thursday, the brothers spent most of the day and evening at the Sunnyslope apartment. A sister, Hannah, 29, is no longer close to the family. Nick hadn't seen her for months. But his brothers, mother and an uncle, whom he was particularly fond of, took turns entering his bedroom, trying to make conversation with the man a day away from death.

"What can you say?" Drew said. "I just told him I love him, and we'll all remember him, always."

Nick's last meal was his favorite: pizza with sausage and extra cheese. He cheered for the last time for the Phoenix Suns, his favorite team. And after the Suns won, Nick was the one who had to remind his mother that he'd better get dressed, because he didn't want to miss his flight.

Drew left first, after a tearful farewell. Moments after he left the bedroom, Nick called out, wanting to see him one last time, but Drew was gone. Nick had his mother phone his brother's apartment, knowing he'd get an answering machine.

"Remember I love you," he told the machine. "I want you to take care of Mom."

He had left his fishing pole to Luke and his stereo and expensive compact disc collection to Drew.

Listening to music, loud rock and roll, and watching television was about all Nick could do to pass the time over the past few months. It was on late-night TV, which he often watched on those sleepless nights, that he saw an interview with Kevorkian. It inspired his plea for help in ending his life.

"I thought he was a good guy," Nick said. "I think he's doing the right thing. I felt very positive about him, so I asked my Mom to write him. I thought it was a shot in the dark, but I couldn't continue like this. I had no idea if he'd answer me, but it was worth a try."

Carol drafted a one-page letter and sent it, along with her son's medical records, to Kevorkian on March 20. To their surprise, he answered with a telephone call on March 23; he agreed to help.

"It was like winning the lottery, that's how I felt," Nick said.

A second call came two days later. This time, Kevorkian asked whether Nick wanted to be an organ donor. He declined.

Kevorkian reached them again two days later, telling them to make arrangements to arrive in Detroit on May 8. Kevorkian said he would help Nick die the next day.

"It can't come a day too soon," Nick said. And he got his wish.

Kevorkian called again, this time pushing the appointment up by one day, in order to accommodate two other people. It would be Kevorkian's first triple assisted suicide.

But on May 1, Kevorkian called to postpone. Nick again was in limbo, and he didn't like it.

His mood worsened on Monday, when he learned that Kevorkian had been present at the suicide of a 78-year-old retired minister with lung disease. That was once to have been the day of Nick's death.

"I felt cheated," he said. "I didn't know what was going on."

The third person apparently died of natural causes.

Still, Kevorkian assured Nick that he would help.

"He really played with our emotions," Carol said.

But Kevorkian did call on Wednesday, telling Carol he'd help her son on Friday.

And so they booked a flight, leaving Sky Harbor International Airport just before midnight on Thursday, arriving in Detroit just after 6 a.m. Friday.

The plan was to meet in a hotel parking lot in Bloomfield Hills, another Detroit suburb. Nick, dressed in a black Van Halen T-shirt that he bought at a 1988 concert, turquoise pants and a black Nike baseball cap, was uneasy during the limousine ride from airport to hotel, his mother said. But after a 10-minute wait, Kevorkian arrived in his beat-up sedan. Nick smiled broadly, and tears began to trickle from behind his mirrored sunglasses.

He was one hour away from the unremarkable home where he died.

"Anyone who tells you they're not afraid of dying is probably lying," he said earlier. I've never been truly happy since this happened to me. There are times I laugh, but they are few and far between.

"I've always had this feeling that I'm just doing time, and that's no way to live."

Lessons Learned

BY DAVID CANNELLA

It had taken several months to get to this point—a motel room at the Holiday Inn in Southfield, Michigan. I had two yellow pads filled with notes, several file folders of supplemental material, everything from medical journal articles to magazine pieces on Dr. Jack Kevorkian.

On a table sat my laptop computer, an ancient Radio Shack model.

It was about 11 a.m., and the telephone rang. It was my city editor, Steve Knickmeyer.

"You've been through a lot," he told me. "You've got a lot of emotions built up. Dig deep down into your gut, and use them. Let it flow."

Earlier that morning, a 27-year-old Phoenix man I had come to know and interview killed himself with his mother and Kevorkian at his side.

Nicholas Loving and his mother, Carol, had agreed ahead of time to let *The Arizona Republic* tell his story. I made two promises to Nicholas—we would not publish until he was dead, and we would not run photographs of him in his wheelchair. He hated that wheelchair.

Loving suffered from Lou Gehrig's disease. He was frustrated that he couldn't find relief, and saw no hope. A bright and articulate man, he said upon our first visit that he wanted to tell his story because it wasn't fair that he could find no one to help him die.

I tried to stay objective with this story. Many people—coworkers, family, friends—have asked me what I thought about his decision.

After several interviews with him, including a red-eye flight from Phoenix to Detroit, I came to understand his rationale. That's what I wanted readers to see. That's what I hope came through the several articles in the two-day package on the life and death of Nicholas Loving.

And I wanted details. Kevorkian, through his loud-mouth attorney, wouldn't speak with me. Nor was I allowed to be present when Nicholas died. I had hoped to, and the family said it was fine with them, but when it became clear it would jeopardize Nicholas's standing with Kevorkian, I agreed to stay in the motel room.

I organized my notes by time and subject. When the interviews took place was important to the story, since I had talked with him several times and would have those quotes in a story that noted in the lead that he was dead, I wanted readers to be clear. I also had notes on such subjects as assisted suicide, the right-to-die issue, Lou Gehrig's disease, and the legal and ethical troubles of Kevorkian.

I went over all those notes, and waited to hear whether Nicholas went through with his plan.

Carol Loving called once her son was dead and dropped off in a van at the morgue. Over the phone, I grilled her about the details—where did it happen, what did the house look like, what color was the couch, what did Nicholas, she, Kevorkian say?

I had plenty of detail leading up to his death, including his final meal—pizza with sausage and extra cheese. Now I wanted to know how he died. Did he flinch? Was he sure? Did he seem in any discomfort?

I attended subsequent news conferences called by Kevorkian's attorneys and made calls to the governor's office, the medical examiner, and the sheriff's office.

But I kept my focus on Nicholas. That was my story, not Kevorkian and all his baggage.

Nicholas was the 23rd person to die with the help of Kevorkian. He knew his death would make a blurb in papers across the country. Every time Kevorkian acts, there's some kind of story.

What Nicholas wanted, what I wanted, was for his story to stand out.

And so I dug deep down, took a deep breath, and let what I had come to learn and feel flow out onto the computer screen. It was Nicholas's story. I just promised him I'd tell it.

KNIGHT RIDDER

Michael E. Ruane

Finalist, Deadline Reporting

Michael E. Ruane is the Pentagon correspondent in the Washington bureau of Knight-Ridder. He joined the bureau in August 1994 after 12 years with *The Philadelphia Inquirer* where he covered police, urban disaster, and wrote features about rural Pennsylvania. He started in the newspaper business in 1969 as a copyboy at the old *Philadelphia Evening Bulletin,* and later worked there as a police reporter, general assignment reporter, and rewrite man until the paper folded in 1982. He has bachelor's and master's degrees in American history from Villanova University and was a Nieman Fellow at Harvard in 1991–1992.

At the Pentagon he's covered, among other things, the U.S. Army's deployments to Haiti and Bosnia. His touching Christmas Eve dispatch from an American Army outpost in Croatia conveys the loneliness of a holiday away from home and the weary resolve of soldiers who must look into themselves to find a way to celebrate it.

U.S. troops spend
tough Christmas

DECEMBER 25, 1995

ZUPANJA, Croatia—Staff Sgt. Alan Hartman would spend the holy night curled on the floor of his Bradley Fighting Vehicle, "Angel"—his head resting against the ready box of 25mm armor-piercing ammunition, the starry sky visible through the open hatches above.

Lt. Bridget Murphy, an Army nurse, would be staffing the admitting desk of the 212th MASH tent, on the 8 p.m. to 7 a.m. shift. And "Top" Sergeant David Brown, a Texas sharecropper's son whose eyes fill when he speaks of his duty to his men, would be up all night, prowling and checking, like a weary father on his sleeping children.

Christmas Eve for the men and women of the American Army waiting to cross the Sava River into Bosnia was a day of unshaven faces and calloused hands, of tired eyes and dusty boots, sprained knees and cut fingers.

It was a day of Christmas trees decorated with empty soda cans, steel tie-down shackles, chemlights and tiny vials of Tabasco sauce; of a candlelight service held in a warehouse; and of Christmas carols sung in musty tents under a sliver of orange moon.

It was a day when a 23-year-old medic from Shreveport, La., got an engagement ring mailed by her fiance; when a young lieutenant from Delta, Ohio, was handed a commemorative coin by a four-star general; and when a bunch of guys from a Bradley vehicle filled a PX box with a treasure trove of toilet paper, Pringles, Chips Ahoy and Coke.

And it was a day when Chief Warrant Officer Rena Johnson, 37, a bridge maintenance technician from Abilene, Texas, stood amid the roar of bulldozers at the river bank, loaded down with gas mask, flak vest and night-vision goggles, and said of her duty in the Balkans:

"This is my gift to the world. If I pray for peace on earth, this is my small contribution. I'm finally in a position to contribute something important to peace in the world. So this is my gift, my small drop in the bucket toward world peace."

Christmas Eve at this small lumber and sugar mill village—whose Catholic church, St. Ivan Krstitelj, still bears shrapnel holes from the war—was an unusually balmy day, and a hazy, breezy night.

Down by the river, Army engineers continued to swarm in bulldozers and graders over the sites where a pontoon bridge is expected to be placed across the river, perhaps sometime this week.

The bridge will carry the scores of tanks and armored vehicles and about 15,000 soldiers of the 1st Armored Division, the heart of America's contribution to NATO's Bosnia peace force.

There was some excitement about midday when a four-star general, William Crouch, the commander of the U.S. Army in Europe, arrived at the river bank with a large entourage to visit the troops.

As top generals often do, he handed out some colorful commemorative coins and said of the men and women:

"These soldiers do a tremendous job. All you have to do is look at them...I'd say to their parents, their families, that they ought to be darn proud of what these troopers are doing, the way they're going about it. They're great Americans and they're doing a great job."

One of those who got a coin from the general was Lt. Jay Shininger, of Delta. "It's a little attaboy generals often give out," he said afterward. "It's better than a handshake, less than a ribbon to put on your chest. Somewhere in between...I don't know if I'll show my grandchildren but I'm going to start a collection."

Another gift had been received earlier by Pfc. Heather Beauregard, 23, of Shreveport. It had come sewn inside a teddy bear and shipped via the mail and some friends from back home. It was a small box containing a diamond engagement ring.

She cried when she opened it and then stuck it under her flak vest, near her heart: "He said it was going to be itty bitty...it isn't itty bitty."

A few miles away, 1st Sgt. David Brown, 39, of Whitehouse, Texas, was also thinking about gifts—to his men and to this tortured region.

"One of the things that I do feel deeply about this Christmas season is that I have an opportunity to do something for other people, and give them the right to just live and see another Christmas.

"We as Americans a lot of times take for granted a lot of the things that we have...If we could slow down a little bit and take a look at this place, as primitive as it may seem, these people, they only want the basics in life, and that's to live."

He must give his men the same, he said: "You can find a lot of people here that are here for ego, to make themselves a name. My major concern for these soldiers here," he said, pausing with emotion, "is to get every last one of them back alive...That's all I want."

Lessons Learned

BY MIKE RUANE

Don't forget now, my boss was telling me over the phone from Washington, you gotta give me a Christmas story.

I was sitting in a hotel room in Zagreb, Croatia. For the past week I'd been covering the American military deployment to Bosnia: bouncing between the U.N. headquarters in Zagreb, a big American staging base in Hungary, and a handful of little towns along the Sava River in eastern Croatia.

I'd been trying to get a handle on when, where, and how the U.S. 1st Armored Division was going to roll its bulk across the river, which marks Bosnia's northern border with Croatia, and into the American zone of operations around Tuzla.

It had been fascinating, like something out of World War II, with tanks being hauled across Europe on trains and Army engineers humping bulldozers and pontoons to ready a bridge across the Sava River.

But now came Christmas.

Beforehand, we figured the GIs' Christmas in Bosnia would be a potentially rich story. Not one of great geopolitical sweep, which I don't care for anyhow, but a good old-fashioned yarn.

The trouble was the Americans weren't all the way in Bosnia yet. A few had been airlifted into Tuzla. But most of the U.S. force was still strung out over hundreds of miles between Germany and the little Croatian river town of Zupanja, where they were assembling the bridge.

Plus, now that it was time to do the story, it didn't look so rich. Zupanja was a flat, bleak place that the Army was fast churning to mud. Few tents had been set up. Many grunts were living out of their tanks—which is worse than living out of your car. And they all badly wanted a shower. Things were screwed up. People were tired and sour. It was not a heart-warming scene.

Still, as my editor, Larry Williams, said, that's where the Army was. So on Christmas Eve I repaired to Zupanja.

Now, everybody's been called on to do Christmas stories. It may be fun the first time. After that it's a pain. Christmas happens every year. It isn't new. It has no motion. And it happens the same way over and over. People like it that way.

My experience has been that there are two basic ways to try for a good Christmas story, or a story about any subject that has no locomotion and too much familiarity:

A) If you're lucky, you stumble upon an eloquent person you use as a metaphor for all mankind. But this is rare. More often you fall back on B) Frantically trying to create a mosaic out of the odd collection of images, quotes, color, and impressions you might gather.

As a newspaper reporter on such a story, you are also hampered by timing. Readers are going to be reading your piece Christmas morning. But, unlike television, you can't tell them what happened that morning. You have to present them with information from the day before—which TV also may already have told them. So you have to figure out a way to tell it better.

I think a good way to do that is an old standby: details. Most TV has trouble with detail. TV needs motion and color. It wages a primitive assault on the eye. Print aims for the brain. And, there, details have explosive impact: a calloused hand, a discarded cigarette butt, an unshaven face, a muddy combat boot. The effect on the imagination can be terrific.

Quotes are, in a way, another kind of detail. But I think quotes are overrated. Especially in Washington, where I work, big shots are adept at making their mouths move while ensuring that what comes out is utterly worthless. One lesson I have learned is, with some exceptions: The more important the personage, the more vapid the quote.

But there is another side to the lesson: With some exceptions, many of the most beautiful things I have ever heard humans say have come from the mouths of the plainest folk.

This held true in Zupanja, where one worried, nail-bitten reporter found himself saved by the details and by plain, human eloquence.

Like that of Rena Johnson, for example, a 37-year-old Army warrant officer with a shy smile and crushing handshake, who stood in ankle-deep mud and said her participation in the deployment was her Christmas gift, "my small drop in the bucket toward world peace."

And David Brown, 39, a tired-looking first sergeant, who grew teary as he watched his men, many of them teenagers, line up outside a PX truck. "You can find a lot of people here that are here for ego, to make themselves a name," he said. "My major concern for these soldiers here is to get every last one of them back alive...That's all I want."

These were average people who paused in the midst of a busy day and out of the blue uttered pretty sublime statements.

They and mundane things I'd barely noticed—like the ragged outdoor Christmas tree hung with tiny vials of Tabasco sauce—turned out to be gems in the desperate act of writing the story later.

In fact, they made the writing much less desperate. Having chosen, or been forced to choose, option B—the mosaic approach—the task required only time and a careful sifting and ordering of the jewelry into categories. (The sifting and ordering actually starts as soon as the reporting does.) I tried to add movement via some chronology, and a strong understructure of beginning, middle, and end.

Basic chronology is always available, and so is simple beginning-middle-end structure. Afterward, I realized that jewels are almost always there, too, strewn in the mud and grime of an assignment. I just have to remind myself always to look hard enough to find them.

The Miami Herald
Team Deadline Reporting

When a busload of disabled school kids is taken hostage by a man who may have a bomb, more than a dozen *Miami Herald* reporters with an eye for the telling detail and the dramatic moment hit the streets. Back in the newsroom, Martin Merzer, in the time-honored role of "rewrite," stitches his colleagues' reports into a riveting narrative that displays the digging of an investigative reporter and the pacing and style of a storyteller. Their story demonstrates how, even in an age of images, the power of the word endures.

Martin Merzer was born in New York City, served in the Army from 1966 to 1968, and graduated from Hunter College, City University of New York, in 1973 with a bachelor's degree in English. After six years as a general assignment reporter and business news writer for the Associated Press in Miami and New York, Merzer joined *The Miami Herald* in 1979 as a business writer. He became the *Herald*'s Jerusalem bureau chief in late 1983 and now is senior writer on the enterprise team in Miami.

Gail Epstein is the *Herald*'s senior police reporter. A native of New York, she graduated from the University of Florida in 1978 with a bachelor's degree in journalism. Before joining the *Herald* in 1991, she was a reporter and editor for the *Atlanta Journal and Constitution.*

Frances Robles joined the *Herald* in 1993 after a three-year stint at *The Plain Dealer* in Cleveland, Ohio, where she covered schools and neighborhood issues. Robles covered higher education and school crime for the *Herald,* and is the most recent addition to its crime team.

Contributing to the story were *Herald* staff writers Elinor Brecher, Maria Camacho, Ina Paiva Cordle, Tom Dubocq, Joan Fleischman, Manny Garcia, Rick Jervis, John Lantigua, Grace Lim, David Lyons, Jodi Mailander, Arnold Markowitz, Patrick May, and researcher Elisabeth Donavan. Terry Jackson edited the story.

The Miami Herald

Some of the journalists who worked on the *Herald*'s coverage of the school bus hijacking (starting at front center and moving clockwise): assistant city editor Terry Jackson, reporters Frances Robles, Jodi Mailander, Gail Epstein, Arnold Markowitz, John Lantigua, Patrick May, Tom Dubocq, Manny Garcia, Joan Fleischman, editorial researcher Elisabeth Donovan, and reporter Elinor Brecher.

Terror rides a school bus

NOVEMBER 3, 1995

By Gail Epstein, Frances Robles, and Martin Merzer

A waiter fond of poet Ralph Waldo Emerson attends morning prayers at his church, steps across the street and hijacks a school bus. Owing $15,639.39 in back taxes, wielding what he says is a bomb, Catalino Sang shields himself with disabled children.

Follow my orders, he says, or I will kill the kids. "No problem, I will," says driver Alicia Chapman, crafty and calm. "But please don't hurt the children."

The saga of Dade County school bus No. CX-17, bound for Blue Lakes Elementary, begins.

Soon, a phalanx of squad cars trails and flanks a bus load of innocents. Two desperate parents jump into their own cars and join the pursuit. Also in the caravan is Dade Schools Superintendent Octavio Visiedo in his black Buick Park Avenue. Someone has abducted 13 of his students.

Now, traveling at 20 mph, a trooper pulls within six inches of the bus, tossing in his personal cellular phone. "I was scared to death," says officer John Koch. "But I had to do what I had to do. I've got a little girl. She's 3. She's my life."

Word spreads. The workday is halted, a region temporarily frozen with dread. Motorists gaze in astonishment; office workers gather at windows to watch the 15-mile, slow-speed chase. Somehow, the odyssey of O.J. Simpson has blended into the movie *Speed,* and it is unfolding—live and real—here in South Florida and on national television.

Finally, after 95 minutes, it ends Thursday outside Joe's Stone Crab, a landmark known around the world. It ends with gunfire from a police marksman named Derringer and with shattered glass and with officers diving into danger to rescue young hostages.

It ends with a deranged man dead and one student injured, a sliver of glass in his eye.

It ends with cops wearing bulletproof vests hugging kids carrying Lion King schoolbags.

It ends about as well as it can. The kids are alive.

Most are in Joe's, drinking Coke and ginger ale, eating french fries and vanilla ice cream. They can have a balanced meal some other time. Now, they need comfort. Some already are reliving the experience.

"A bad man on a bus made us drive a long way," says Brian Morales, 7, subjected to an unexpected lesson about life in the 1990s. "He was a very bad man and he was keeping us on the bus."

As Brian says this, Sang's body is sprawled under a yellow tarpaulin, surrounded by officers still tingling with adrenaline. Sang was 42, an immigrant from the Dominican Republic. Married. Two children, one of them an honors student at Killian High.

He owned two Chinese restaurants, but they were consuming his resources. So he waited tables at Joe's and was known to recite Emerson's verse as he dished up the stone crabs and mustard sauce. His favorite poem was "Success": "The profoundest thought or passion sleeps as in a mine, until it is discovered by an equal mind and heart."

Sang, who was known as Nick, quit in a huff Wednesday night. Co-workers said he was talking to himself, seemed weighted with stress.

But that is only part of the story.

SHE FOLLOWED RULE NO. 1

Another part belongs to Chapman, the bus driver, 46 years old, on the job only 17 months. Largely because of her, 13 children are alive today.

"She followed the most important rule: You protect the lives of the children," said Henry Fraind, spokesman for the Dade school system. "We are taught to protect the children at all costs. We would classify the driver as a modern-day hero."

And another part belongs to the police—men and women who train for these situations hoping never to employ that training, men and women suddenly confronted by the most intense challenge imaginable, men and women who stormed that bus and saved those kids.

"Had we known he was not armed, we would not have shot him," said Metro-Dade police director Fred

Taylor. "But we did believe that he was armed. He [the police marksman] did exactly what he was trained to do."

Based on accounts from participants and witnesses, this is the story of school bus No. CX-17, an ordinary bus on an ordinary run that turned into an extraordinary experience.

* * *

Eight-fifteen a.m., Thursday, Nov. 2, 1995. Another school day. The kids—all with learning disabilities—were being picked up for the trip to Blue Lakes, a school with 618 students, about one-third of them in special education programs.

Chapman was on her usual run. She was widely regarded as an excellent driver, one with real concern for the children.

She stopped the bus at 7821 SW 56th St., just across the street from the Alpha & Omega Church, which serves an Evangelical congregation. Two children normally were picked up here.

'HE WAS NOT RATIONAL'

Chapman had no way of knowing that Sang was distraught and had just left the church. "He was yelling," Taylor said. "He was not rational at the time. When he left his home this morning, he told one of his daughters to pray for him."

Sang was under considerable pressure. The income from his job at Joe's was being used to subsidize his two restaurants. But no one knows precisely what set him off Thursday morning as bus CX-17 followed its route.

One of the children waiting at the bus stop was Daniel Castellanos. His mother, Nubia, was with him.

A few minutes later, a neighbor pounded on the Castellanoses' front door. It was opened by Maurice Castellanos, Daniel's father.

"She said, 'Don't panic, but some man pushed Nubia onto the bus,'" Castellanos said. "I reacted in a way that was more like puzzled. A bus?"

Later, his wife filled him in.

"This guy crosses Miller [Road] and motions to her that he has something on his side. He told her, 'Get inside!'

"My wife sat down and he told the bus driver to close the door and proceed. He told them it was a kidnapping and he was in trouble with the IRS. He went to the back of the bus and he was placing things under the seats.

"She thought it was a bomb. She was hysterical [within] but managed to stay collected."

As the bus worked its way toward the Palmetto Expressway, the hijacker ordered the driver to call authorities over her two-way radio. She did, but it proved unreliable. He demanded a cell phone from police, then ripped the radio from the console.

Sang told Nubia Castellanos and Dorothy Williams, an adult aide aboard the bus, to open the windows. He soon released Williams, who has diabetes, and the bus rolled on.

TWO KIDS, A MOM LET OUT

Castellanos began to engage Sang in conversation.

"She pleaded with him not to hurt anybody," said Maurice Castellanos, who hurried to the bus stop. "He said he had children, too, and wouldn't hurt anyone.

"He told her to get off the bus with my son and another child who was crying a lot. I feel like she was able to save that child."

That child was Brian Morales, the 7-year-old who spoke about the "bad man" on the bus.

As this was happening, Castellanos returned home. He thought he was calm. He thought he was confident. After all, how far could a hijacker get on a school bus?

Then, he realized he was collecting photos of his wife and son. In case the police needed them.

"That's when it hit me," Castellanos said. "I might never see them again."

* * *

State trooper John Koch, a nine-year veteran, was on patrol nearby when his radio crackled with the news. With the bus now on the Palmetto, Koch joined the chase.

This is his account:

"The bus came by very slow, 20 mph. The driver opened the door and yelled at me, 'He's on the floor!'

The bus curved onto State Road 836, heading east toward downtown Miami and Miami Beach.

THE MIAMI HERALD 55

"I heard on the scanner that he needed a cellular phone and that if he didn't get it, he was going to start hurting the children. At that point, I said the hell with it.

"I knew they said he had a bomb and a gun, but I also knew if I didn't do something quickly, he would do something to the children.

"I pull up next to the bus, on the right side, where the door is. I look in and see the bus driver looking back behind her. I thought he was going to pop out and shoot me. I couldn't shoot because I didn't know where the kids were.

"I was six inches from the bus. I said, 'I got the phone. I got the phone.' I know the guy is right there. She says, 'Throw it!' I tossed the phone; it was my personal phone. Threw it right in her lap and then I backed off.

"That was very scary for me. I knew if he wanted to take a shot, he wouldn't have missed at that distance, but I couldn't leave the children there."

* * *

Using the cell phone, Sang told police he wanted to exit at around 82nd Avenue and stop at an Internal Revenue Service office. They told him he already was beyond that exit. OK, he said, we'll go to Joe's Stone Crab instead.

Nevertheless, remembering the disaster at the federal building in Oklahoma City, believing that Sang had a bomb, authorities blockaded the federal building in downtown Miami.

Sang directed the bus across the MacArthur Causeway. Still trailed by police, it approached the restaurant.

Now, the bus had turned the corner of Biscayne and Washington, coasting toward Joe's new front entrance. One of the students jumped out. The Metro-Dade Special Response Team, a SWAT unit, stood ready, armed with SR-15s, a police version of the AR-15 assault rifle.

According to police commanders and others, officer Joe Derringer—crouched about 30 feet from the bus— saw a movement from Sang that suggested he was about to detonate a bomb. So Derringer, his name hauntingly evocative of a 19th-century gunsmith and the weapon he created, fired a single shot through a window, apparently striking Sang.

The bus lurched ahead. Not knowing if Sang was wounded, other officers assaulted the bus—some smashed side windows as a distraction, others crashed through the front door.

One of those officers was Jose Fernandez.

"He's ordered to storm the bus," said C. Michael Cornely, a police union attorney. "The kids are yelling like crazy. The guy was reaching for something under the coat. Fernandez shot him twice on the bus."

Fernandez and others dragged Sang to an adjacent alley, where the hijacker died.

Trooper Koch again, who ended up at the climactic scene:

"After the shooting, they pulled him along the ground, away from the bus. Someone yelled 'Bomb!' and they just scattered.

'GET OUT OF THE BUS!'

"But the problem was that the kids were still in the bus. I ran inside and started handing kids out. Two or three other people ran in also.

"The kids were all strapped in. The bus driver was still trying to get one kid out who was still stuck in his straps. I'm trying to get his legs to bend to get him out of the straps. I'm looking for the escape route. Where is it?

"I got him out and handed the kid down. I was the last person out the back of the bus, but that bus driver was tough, tough as nails.

"I had to yell at her to get her out of there. 'Get out of the bus, lady!'"

Finally, she did—and he did. The saga of school bus CX-17 was over.

Herald staff writers Elinor Brecher, Maria Camacho, Ina Paiva Cordle, Tom Dubocq, Joan Fleischman, Manny Garcia, Rick Jervis, John Lantigua, Grace Lim, David Lyons, Jodi Mailander, Arnold Markowitz, and Patrick May contributed to this report, as did Herald researcher Elisabeth Donovan.

Writers' Workshop

Talking Points

1) For powerful writers, details are the gold standard of reporting. "Terror Rides a School Bus" is packed with the kind of specifics that give the readers the sense that they know these people, are there on the scene, coming as close to experiencing the event as may be possible. The lead contains the first two of many specific details: "A waiter fond of poet Ralph Waldo Emerson..." and "Owing $15,639.39 in back taxes...." Study this story and isolate as many details as you can. Discuss their impact on the reader. Consider how the reporters on the story obtained them.

2) If scenes are the "2-by-4s" of stories, as Mitch Albom says, then transitions are the nails that hold them together. Martin Merzer skillfully uses transitions to pace the story, lead the reader along, and provide commentary to accompany the drama. Some, like "But that is only part of the story," mark obvious shifts. Others are more subtle. Identify other transitions in this story and describe what purpose they serve.

3) Newspaper storytellers bring their own lives to the keyboard every time they write. When they choose to draw on their own personal observations, invariably they contribute one of the most engaging elements of narrative: the writer's voice. In paragraph 11, Merzer describes a scene in which the rescued children are drinking sodas and eating vanilla ice cream. "They can have a balanced meal some other time. Now they need comfort." Notice the lack of attribution. "It just came from me," says Merzer. Is there any doubt that this is the writer's conclusion? Debate the rewards and risks of such writing.

Assignment Desk

1) Merzer chose to tell the first half of this story in present tense, a decision ASNE judges called "risky" but worthwhile. Shift to past tense in the first five paragraphs and consider the effect of the revision. Which do you prefer? Why?

2) "The saga of school bus No. CX-17" is a phrase that reappears in the narrative, once as a beginning and again as the ending. Write alternative endings to this story and explain your reasons for choosing them.

A conversation with
Martin Merzer

CHRISTOPHER SCANLAN: What was your job on the story of the hijacked school bus?

MARTIN MERZER: I was the writer. The new-fangled term is "anchor." Being a little older than a lot of people in this room, I prefer the term "rewrite man," although I'm not sure either one is completely appropriate.

How did you get the assignment?

I was working at home on another story. It began with a phone call from my editor, John Pancake, the state editor, who said, "I think we're going to need you down here today." I had no idea what he was talking about. I had apparently turned the TV off nanoseconds before this story broke. I flipped on the TV and saw that all the local stations were already going completely live on it, so I hopped in my car and drove on down.

A lot of times in these situations, I'll go to the scene, even though I know I'm going to be the writer. I try to go to the scene to get a mind's eye view of what's happening, pick up a little bit of color, maybe a quote or two. It helps to have an eyeball picture. But this time the story was essentially over, so I just went straight to the office.

We had a problem here that newspapers have more and more these days. This thing happened at 8:30, 9 o'clock in the morning. We couldn't get it in the paper for another 24 hours. All the local TV stations were already on it full time, obliterating their other programming. Local news was on it, it was on CNN live, and we still had 24 hours to go. Anybody who didn't know about this during the day was going to know about it at night. So one of the choices that's open to you is to try to tell it better, in more detail, so that people who think they know a lot about this story figure out real soon that there's more to know and that we're going to tell it to them.

I figured our best contribution would be to tell the story in a different fashion with compelling detail.

Is that why you decided to tell the first half of the story in present tense?

I remember somewhere along the line that day noticing that my fingers had written it in present tense and then, later on, had switched into past, but never thinking a whole lot about it until the next day when I got a message from some editor saying, "You know, that was pretty gutsy, using the present tense and then switching into past," and I remember thinking, "What in the hell is he talking about?" and then going back to look at it and saying, "Yeah, well, I guess so."

We needed to really tell a story, and when you tell a story, you usually do it in present tense. We needed to recreate a sense of immediacy and that also calls for present tense. When the material started coming in, that just seemed right.

What's a story to you?

A good yarn, a good tale.

Why did you think this is one that's got to be a yarn?

Our options are somewhat limited. If we go in with a hard news lead, you know, "A man hijacked a bus Tuesday morning, holding 13 children hostage, and was ultimately shot to death outside Joe's Stone Crab," I mean, no one's going to read into the third paragraph because they figure they know that.

But there are signals in here that we're going to tell them stuff that they don't know. It was intentional. I knew that we needed to write a top that signaled to readers, "You think you know everything about this, but you don't, and we're going to tell you some more." And that's what Ralph Waldo Emerson is doing up there and that's what the 39 cents is doing up there. That's saying, "We've got detail. Maybe you know everything you need to know about it, but if you're interested in this incident, we've got a little more to tell you. Stick with us."

And that's what the CX-17 is doing up there, the number of the bus, and that's why we've got the superintendent in his black Buick Park Avenue, not just his car. You can overdo that, but I think in a case like this, careful use of very precise detail sends a signal to the reader. It says, "We're going to tell you some stuff in here that you thought you knew, but you didn't."

You're pretty swamped with material? How do you keep track of it all?

The next day, I look back and I can't for the life of me imagine how. You've got wires and feeds coming in very frequently. And it seems like an unwritten law of journalism, the closer you are to deadline, the faster the feeds start to come in. You have people who are coming over to you to talk, reporters, editors. Electronic messages are coming hot and heavy. You've got TVs to keep an eye on, ideas that are coming from various people. Some are good, some aren't so good, some false reports, some false leads.

How do you organize it?

I usually try to create a file and swap into it material from the feeds that I'm sure is going to get used, sort of like skimming the cream right there. I try real hard to read all the feeds so that later on, if there's a crucial detail or a fact or a sequence, I know it's there someplace. As the day goes on, there are times when you just can't read everything. I create a master file with that material in it and sometimes try to organize it in a sequential fashion that often becomes the foundation for the story. In our computer system, we have two screens that we can keep live all the time.

I try to take the early feeds myself. That gives me a chance to talk with the reporters and find out what they're hoping will come up later. If I see a hole developing, I can ask somebody to try to help me close it. But there does come a time when you have to cut that off. Every good reporter who has a great fact or detail wants to tell the writer about it. I do the same thing when I'm out in the field. But there comes a time when you have to cut it off, or else you just can't get the story written. That time tends to vary, but two or three hours before deadline, I usually find myself saying, "That's great, but I've got to give you over to somebody who'll take the dictation."

Are you asking for things like $15,639.39?

That was a pre-Christmas gift from David Lyons.

And CX-17?

I saw that on TV. I knew that was the kind of detail I wanted. I saw the kids carrying their Lion King lunch boxes on TV—and I knew that was the kind of thing I wanted. I drove a couple of reporters nearly crazy. I try to keep things kind of light and loose, but I did ask a couple of them what kind of ice cream the kids ate at Joe's. I could feel them hanging up saying, "Geez, what is this guy doing?" Finally one of the reporters found out it was vanilla, and I could call the other reporters off that and let them get back to work.

Why did you want to know the flavor of the ice cream?

That's the Gene Miller rule. Gene is associate editor of the *Herald* and a writing coach. In fact, I told some of the reporters that, "If we don't tell the readers what kind of ice cream they were eating, I'm not going to hear the end of it tomorrow from Gene. So you've got to help me out here, you've got to find out what flavor they were serving these kids." It's one of those details that just makes a story hit home.

What is the Gene Miller rule?

"Get as much detail as you can possibly get in your notebook. You may not want it, but get it in your notebook. And don't just tell them it's ice cream; tell them what flavor of ice cream." I did a post-*Challenger* story and got to the guy who uttered the famous phrase, "Obviously a major malfunction," Steve Nesbitt from NASA. I had him reconstruct what happened later on in his day and he told me he went home, went to the mall, couldn't find anything to do with himself, went home, opened up the freezer, ate ice cream for dinner, went to sleep. And I remember thinking, "Man, that's great stuff." And then, you know, my heart skipped a beat when I realized I hadn't asked him what kind of ice cream. And then I had to call this guy back a week later and remind him who I was and say, "Listen, this is going to sound really odd, but I need to ask you what kind of ice cream you ate." And it was chocolate chip. To this day, when *Challenger* comes up in the newsroom, somebody invariably says, "Yeah, and the guy was eating chocolate chip ice cream that night." It's just the kind of detail that sticks in people's minds. It would be a signal that we've done our work. But you can get carried away in the writing of it: "Joe Blow put his hands behind his neck and leaned back in his green Barcalounger and tied the shoe with his brown shoe lace..." You've got people so bored, they're looking forward to the editorials.

"Most are in Joe's, drinking Coke and ginger ale, after eating french fries and vanilla ice cream. They can have a balanced meal some other time. Now, they need comfort." To me, that's voice. Why don't you talk a bit about why you inserted a sentence like that in the story?

That just came from me. It's part of telling a story. If you're a parent—and I am—and you're reading that these kids came off the bus and for lunch they had Coke and ginger ale and french fries and vanilla ice cream, my brain just made a connection. I thought, "Boy, that's a pretty unbalanced meal," and right behind it came the thought, "So what? They can eat a balanced meal some other time. These kids had a rough morning." And given the nature of this story, it wasn't a hard news story where every other paragraph had to be attributed to police, it just felt right.

It's the voice of the storyteller.

I'm sure I broke three or four rules in there, but sometimes you take a chance.

Did you always do that?

No, no, no. I began at the AP back in 1973. I was really green. On any given day, you'd be writing a hard news story, sort of like this one, but on the spot. You'd take a traffic fatal from a radio reporter and turn it into a radio feed. It was just great training. And I was terrible. Every single thing I did for the first two months would get rewritten. I would pick up my ego and print out what I had written and print out how it turned out after an editor got his hands on it and I'd take it home and that's how I learned my trade.

Where did your storytelling voice come from?

I think that developed before I was a writer. It developed when I was a reader. I grew up in New York City and Jimmy Breslin and Pete Hamill and people like that were major influences on me. Those are the kind of touches that you would find in their work. A lot of it would be in columns, but sometimes they would write a daily news story. I guess they called it "new journalism" back then. That voice would be in it and it just stayed with me. And I guess there are times when it comes out.

Is the *Herald* hospitable to that?

It's always been known as a writer's newspaper. It still is. There are limits, though. If this story had happened at 6 o'clock at night, I wouldn't think of writing it this way. And it would be wrong if I did, and it would have been changed.

What does "a writer's newspaper" mean to you?

A place where you can take some chances, where you can be "risky," again within limits. We've got lots of levels of editors who are going to keep an eye on this sort of thing. But it is a place that encourages and rewards good writing, sometimes on the edge. They realize we're trying to do something different and they give you the freedom to try something a little different.

What role did editors play with this story?

Very little, to tell you the truth. They told me what my role was and then they pretty much left me alone to do it. This story was being read over my shoulder electronically. You know that's going to happen these days because everybody's got the capability to do that, but this story really was. I was getting messages from people in other departments about it. I assume that our highest-ranking editors were reading it, too, and, you know, I never heard from them. No news is good news.

Are you aware that people are reading over your shoulder, even though it's electronically?

You have to block out a lot when you're doing this. At a certain point you just focus on writing the story, yet having somehow to stay aware of the messages and the continuing feeds and the changes in the actual facts that might be coming at you and so on. I tend to forget that people are reading it as I'm writing it.

How do you focus?

I try to emulate some of the things I saw at the AP. It's just the ability to be able to focus on the story. It sort of carries you along. An important thing is to know when you have to just focus on writing the story. It is a common mistake to keep talking to people, to keep walking around the newsroom and talking to every reporter who wants to talk to you. At a certain point, you just have to say, "I'm sorry, I can't do that now. Let me get this done on this deadline and I'll come on over and talk to you after." And again, trying to keep cool, trying to keep everybody loose, that's fairly important, too.

You mean the people who are out there doing the reporting?

When a deadline comes close, there probably isn't time for it, but earlier in the day, in the middle of the reporting, just maybe send a message to somebody who's on line out in the field, or joke with somebody who's on the phone and just kind of keep everybody, including yourself, reminded of the fact that we're supposed to be having fun while we do this. This is hard work, man. If you can't have a little bit of fun at it, what's the point?

I was struck by the organization of the story. You've got those opening three paragraphs that billboard the story. And then you switch to the bus driver and say, in effect, "Based on accounts, this is the story." It's almost like a second lead or turn.

Right, and it's probably too far down. I wanted that top section to be shorter—and I still do, to tell you the truth. This is sort of a hybrid. We wanted to share detail and like any good story, it usually begins at the beginning and ends at the end. But at the same time, it's a newspaper story, the lead newspaper story of the day. I had it front loaded with some of the hard news, just in case somebody had just flown into town that night and picked up the paper the next morning and didn't know how it ended and that only one kid was injured and the guy was shot dead. It was a compromise, trying to tell it in story form, but front loading the introduction of the story with a sketch of how it ended— because you're not going to put an editor's note on top of it saying, "Read this because we know more than you do." But it's a signal to them that we do.

Are you conscious of what the length of the story must be when you're writing it?

I'm always struggling with length, and I'm frequently negotiating for more length, sometimes directly with the news desk, which in our operation are the people who draw the lines and decide how much copy's going to fit on the page. And if I see that I really need another five inches, I'll sometimes send a message right over there and say, "Hey, I could really use another five inches. Do you think we have a shot here?" And we've got a great desk and more times than not, they say, "Yes, sure." But there are limits.

What makes it a great desk?

Flexibility. Their ability to do on deadline what the reporters and writers are doing on deadline.

"Sang was 42, an immigrant from the Dominican Republic. Married. Two children, one of them an honors student at Killian High." Staccato. Sentence fragments. Why do you do this?

For emphasis. For pacing. Because it seems right to my ear.

Are you trying to anticipate the reader's experience?

We're trying to tell a story largely the way people might tell it to each other, but also observing some newspaper conventions. There was a rather long sentence just before it or two sentences before. The reader's eye or ear needed a breath, needed a chance to slow down.

You then say, "He owned two Chinese restaurants, but they were consuming his resources. So he waited tables at Joe's and was known to recite Emerson's verse as he dished up the stone crabs and mustard sauce. His favorite poem was 'Success.'" How do you know these things?

Reporters had spoken to his fellow waiters at Joe's, and one of them had told him that he often walked around the dining room reciting poetry.

As soon as I heard about the poetry and we found out who his favorite poet was, I knew that had to be in the lead or near the top. I went diving into the library to come up with the poem itself. And that was the line in it that seemed the most applicable to the story and the event.

It's often better to let people just talk in their words, rather than in yours, even if they don't necessarily scan into perfectly orderly newspaper sentences—what we try to do here is let the people do it in their words to the extent that they can, get out of their way to the extent that we can.

The long section from State Trooper John Koch is a monologue.

Gail Epstein got to him. This is a feed that came late in the process.

I would have hated myself if I didn't use virtually everything he told her and she would have hated me, too. I mean, just look at what he's saying. I hated to interrupt it there with that one sentence.

I thought I had to break him up after his first quote. But he's got a terrific story to tell within the larger story and we're blessed with some space in the newspaper to let him do it. I mean our job is to get out of his way. We can't say it better than he just said it.

I wish I was good enough to improve on that, but I'm not. The only thing I am is smart enough not to get in his way.

Did you have a plan for the story?

I did not have a plan to use present tense and switch into past tense or to let the trooper speak where he did. The plan was to do a re-creation with as much detail as we could, and just let the story flow. To begin the story at the beginning and to try to end it at the end, but to observe some of the conventions of newspapering at least near the top of the story. I wish I could say I had this really terrific plan to do this, but I didn't. It just sort of happened.

How long did you spend writing this story?

I probably started writing it around 2:00, based on what we knew at the time, maybe a little earlier than that. The deadline was around 6:00 or 6:30. I try to start writing as soon as I can because as you get closer and closer to deadline, the material is going to come in in ever larger batches. So it's a mistake to wait until all the material is in. I always feel better getting something down and then going back and adding, making it better and better or at least richer and richer, or adding material to it and making it longer and longer.

Between editions, Gail Epstein had come back and she sat down next to me and read it through and fixed up a couple of points, sharpened a few points, added a few things. Frenchie [Frances] Robles came back an hour or two later and read it in the system and made a suggestion or two.

What's the best advice you could give somebody who's in the same position?

Get there early, talk to the reporters yourself as best you can, and start writing as soon as you have any significant material at all. It's always easier to update it, to make it better, than it is to start from scratch. I have seen people with a 6 o'clock deadline schmooze around the office, read some of the wires, and look at some of the notes, but never start to write until 4:30 or 5 o'clock, and they've been real unhappy when 6 o'clock came along.

Start writing as early as you can, even if you end up writing it almost entirely over. At least you have the foundation. I'm always striving to get the thing done from top to bottom real early so I can just keep improving it.

What kind of advice would you give somebody who wants to do this kind of deadline storytelling?

Develop a calm demeanor or at least put on a good act.

Stay focused. At the end of the day, you're going to have to present a written story, so remember that's the goal. The goal isn't to chat with a lot of folks and talk about what a terrific story is developing; the goal is to sit there and start writing it. I see the anchor role as being more than a writer. It's sort of analogous to the quarterback on a football team. Editor Terry Jackson is sort of the coach. He's calling the plays, but on the field, it's up to me to tell the guy that if he's covered left, to go right, and that on that last play, I thought I saw a hole over there and maybe he could fill it. A lot of times that means just talking with the reporters: "What do you think the story should be?" I'll ask them, "What do you think the lead should be?" "Where do you think this is going?" "What do you think you'll have for the story by the end of the day?" "Is this word OK with you? Is that word OK with you?" You can't do too much of that because it'll consume a lot of time.

If the reporter is still in the field, I will take the time to read back the top to make sure it is consistent with what they're feeling out there, with what they're seeing, to make sure that the tone and some of the detail and where the story is going is accurate, and that they're comfortable with it because their name's going to be on it.

Not in this case, but from time to time, there could be resentment. "I'm out here reporting and somebody back there is doing the writing." It helps smooth that out if you're consulting with the reporter, if you're saying, "Does this sound OK to you?"

Did you learn or relearn anything doing this story?

The value of a lot of reporters doing some really good reporting. We wouldn't be talking now if someone didn't get that interview with the cop and do other things. I remember Gene Miller again. I've heard him say that if you have trouble writing a story, it's probably because you don't have the material you thought you had when you opened up your notebook. Get it all, whether you're going to need it or not. We're not writing fiction here. I could not write a good story if I or other people didn't report a good story.

Recalling deadline with Frances Robles

I was just pulling into the *Herald* and listening to a disco station when the DJ broke in and said, "Stay away from such and such a street because a school bus had been hijacked." As part of my higher education duties, I was also the school crime reporter. A bus being hijacked? That sounds like something I should be worried about.

So I went upstairs and checked in with the editors, and then I left to go follow the bus. I had a beeper, and the *Herald* sent me messages, like "Go to highway 836," and "He's past the toll plaza. Go toward the beach."

I got on the bridge that leads to the beach, and there was a police car blocking the entrance. I watch the bus go by, and police car, after police car, after police car. Once everybody passed, the police cars left and I was allowed to cross the bridge. I went to Joe's Stone Crab.

There's the school bus. And policemen running around, and the bus starts jerking back and forth, and whamming into the police car in front of it.

I was across the street and slightly down the block. I'm standing there on the phone with my editor, and I was saying, "Oh, my God. They shot him." She says, "How do you know?" "Well, because I recognize the sound of gunfire." They were watching it on TV in the newsroom. Most of those camera shots were taken from helicopters. They couldn't hear the gunfire.

I said, "He's dead." She said, "How do you know?" And I said, "Because I can hear the construction workers all clapping." And then they dragged the body out of the bus.

I went around trying to find people who saw it. The rest of the day, I was a captive of the police. I knew I couldn't leave; somebody needed to be there.

They had a second news conference, at the police station. And I was the annoying one, because I knew the *Herald* wanted detail. They wanted the time that this happened. And did the guy have his hand in his right pocket or his left pocket?

And the police were looking at me like, "Who is this lunatic? And why is she asking so many stupid questions?"

Earlier on in the day, they had been talking a lot about a canister that this guy had. I asked, "Well, whatever happened to the canister?" "Oh, it wasn't a bomb."

"OK. Well, what was it?" "Well, it was a kid's breathing device."

"So, was there a bomb on the bus?" "No."

"Did you ever say he had a bomb on the bus?" "You know, no."

"I'm sorry. Was that a yes?" "Uh, you know, we believe that he said..."

"No, no, no. Did he ever say..." So that one question of mine took five questions. And I had 25 questions.

When these major things happen, the *Herald* responds, and everybody is part of it. Joan Fleischman is the gossip columnist at *The Miami Herald*. She has a tag line on that story. Joe's Stone Crab is a very high-falutin' restaurant, and she's always writing items in her column about things that happen at that restaurant. So when we needed to find the manager of the restaurant, there was no question of who we needed to turn to.

One thing the *Herald* does really well is, when there's a huge story, you don't have to worry about every angle being covered, because there's going to be every single person in that office covering it—they're going to be interviewing the cockroaches at Joe's Stone Crab.

Deadline Tip:

Can I look at this story and say there was some big, exclusive thing I was able to provide? No. But there were things I was able to make happen. I saw things. I was there. When the police were running down the street saying there's a bomb on the bus. Or the way they stormed the bus and got the kids out. I was able to describe that the way it happened. Byline, tagline, no line. That didn't matter. What mattered was getting everything in the paper.

Frances Robles covers crime for The Miami Herald.

Recalling deadline with Gail Epstein

My colleague, Frenchie Robles, had gotten to the scene already. We agreed that I would handle the police version and she would try to get some of the real people kind of witnesses.

My role was basically to try to get as much as I could about the official police version. Other people were doing the victims and the family stuff. As the police reporter, I'm the one with the most established relationships to the formal and the informal structure of the police department.

I went to the police spokesmen who were there and listened as they answered questions, and also gave them a list of specific questions we wanted answered.

I had my tape recorder with me, which helped because when they came out finally to give us the most complete version of events they had up until that point, I just taped it. Then I came back to the office and I typed up what became the skeleton of the story.

I provided the first official account from A to Z of where they had picked this guy up, what had happened along the way, and then what ultimately happened at the end. That enabled us to do spin-off reporting.

That's when we learned that, in fact, it was a state trooper who had driven his car right up next to the bus and gotten a cell phone to Mr. Sang.

After I transcribed this tape, I called the Florida Highway Patrol and got them to get me in touch with this trooper who, fortunately, was still available for comment. He was great. Sometimes they'll fall into police lingo or they'll be official with you, but the guy was very straight up, very human. It was obvious that he had been affected by this. When I first started, he was just talking real fast. I said, "Wait, wait, wait, hold on, hold on, slow down for me because I want to get all of this."

He tells me about driving up next to the bus and how he's thinking of his own kid, and these kids are on the bus and what if this was his kid, and throwing the phone in there.

I typed that up and gave that to Marty [Merzer]. Marty is a phenomenal anchor. The guy can just take 20 million different pieces of information thrown at him and weave them together into this amazing tale.

I think that you need to be smart about what bases you're going to cover and how you delegate, and it really doesn't make sense to have too many people in one spot. I left the scene when we had three people there because we were all doing the same thing. I called my office and said, "I'm heading back," because I knew I could do something more productive somewhere else. And as it turned out, I could; I got the interview with the trooper.

I felt good about the interview because when I looked back at the story, it really is the closest we came in that story to someone who personally participated in a major way. His descriptions were powerful, and they were firsthand. For this kind of story, there's nothing that replaces that firsthand, immediate account.

Deadline Tip:

When I head out to a scene like this and I do my initial assessment, I talk to the people, do my first sweep, I pretty quickly can fashion in my mind what's the best I can get out of this and what's the worst I can get out of this. That way I can mine the gold and if I don't have as broad a sweep as perhaps someone else, I will have a much richer, narrower story. You have to get there and do all of your basic stuff first. But then you have to figure out where that nugget's going to be to use as the lead or the opening anecdote. Then I can go back and report this more, get the extra detail. "Well, what was he saying?" "What were you saying?" "What were you thinking?" "What were you hearing?" "What did it smell like?" "What did it taste like?"

That's what's going to make the difference between just telling what happened and telling a great story.

Gail Epstein is senior police reporter for The Miami Herald.

Recalling deadline with Terry Jackson

It was 10:30 in the morning, so what do you do for tomorrow's editions when television has basically cherry-picked the story? It's an interesting story, but it's going to be old by the time your readers come around. That's where teamwork comes in.

My first order of business was to get enough people into the street, blanket the area, and find out as much about everybody involved as you can. Move as many people quickly to the public records situation; get home addresses for as many people as you can find; run license plate numbers. Some parents of the children on the bus went to Joe's (where the hijacker brought the bus), and so we picked up some there. We were able to get to the victims' side of this fairly quickly. We did good, solid shoe-leather reporting. We knocked on a lot of doors, opened public record files, ran computer searches, and tried to gather as much information as possible, and we were pretty successful at it.

The one thing we can do better than anybody, meaning we as an industry, is tell a readable story. If you look at the stories that continually win awards for writing, they have beginnings and middles and ends, and they have anecdotes and allusions—all the things our high school English teachers taught us about. They have them in a journalistic style, but they are there.

For that, you've got to have an anchor person, which is one of the things newspapers are sometimes reluctant to do when you have a big story like this. You have every reporter, if they're worth their salt, wanting to get involved. And that's good. But when it comes time to sit down and write, many of those reporters want their words in the paper. If you try to be Solomon-like: "Well, you write paragraphs 3 through 7 and you write paragraphs 9 through 12," the story doesn't come out as a story, it comes out as a compilation of notes.

We brought in the person on our staff who is, I think, the best at this kind of work, Marty Merzer, and anchored him here in the office. He wrote the main-bar story. You have to demonstrate an ability to tell a story. But first and foremost, you have to be a solid reporter. You may be there pulling in stuff from everybody else, but in essence, the rewrite person or the anchor is a reporter unto himself. His sources are all the other reporters.

As an editor, I want to know I can go to someone who is going to deliver to me clean copy on time. And by clean I don't mean just noun/verb agreement; I mean a complete story. You can't turn in a story of this magnitude on deadline and have it be a mess. So I'm never going to go to a person who is a continual deadline pusher.

Marty is great at being able to put his head down, focus on the objective, and keep moving toward it. You won't find him scrambling like mad and throwing scraps of paper around, looking for this quote or that quote. He's methodical.

There's a two-fold benefit to that. He gets the job done on time. But, two, and I think this is probably almost equally important, he imparts to the editors around him a sense that everything is under control.

By using an anchor, the story speaks with one voice all the way through. That means the people who basically contribute don't get a chance to do what they got into this business to do, which is to write, but they do get a chance to report. The reporters came back and, really, all of them came back with nuggets that would have stood alone as stories.

Ultimately, we've got to worry about what we're trying to present to our readers: a tale, a story with a beginning, a middle, and an end. That, by and large, takes a single writer. I've tried it many different ways and, with rare exception, it's a mistake to try to put three people in a room together and say, "OK, write the story."

When they took the kids off the bus and took them into Joe's, I remember Marty saying he wanted to know what they fed them. Joe's is known for stone crab, but they fed the kids ice cream. Those kinds of details sometimes get overlooked or trampled in a story this big. When you have a good anchor, he looks for those sorts of things. You began to get questions from Marty as to what he needed. That became my job. I really became Marty's servant, making sure that we got the information he wanted and needed.

One of the things we didn't do on this story, to our credit, is we didn't overedit it. We have the ability to tell stories in depth, in detail, and to tell them in a literary fashion. And that's what we did in this story— telling a crime story in a fashion that went beyond the sensationalistic or the blotter.

I think there's a tendency as an editor to want to overedit these stories or hold them close to you. As an editor, I had very little to do with this story in the sense of why it came out the way it did. I mean, I can't stress enough that the smart thing I did was basically point people in the right direction and then get out of their way.

Deadline Tip:

A big story like this comes along and the reporter juices in an editor start flowing. You want to be a part of the big story. It's only natural. But the problem is your hat's changed; you have reporters to go out and do the reporting and to do the writing and that's what they do best. Your job is to be a leader. And being a leader doesn't mean getting out there and basically telling everybody, "Here, watch me while I do it."

I've learned that I can be more proud of the story if I'm able to accurately assess how the story's going, whether we're getting right information, whether the right people are in the right spots. And if I can answer yes to all those questions, then I don't need to stand over peoples' shoulders and say, "What about this?" "What about that?" Because it just communicates to reporters a sense of disarray or panic. On stories like this, the one thing you don't want to do is create a situation in your newsroom where people are panicked about the coverage of the story. They should be excited, motivated, but they shouldn't be panicked.

Terry Jackson is an assistant city editor for The Miami Herald.

The Washington Post

The Washington Post

Finalist, Team Deadline Reporting

When an assassin's bullet killed Prime Minister Yitzhak Rabin on Nov. 4, 1995, *The Washington Post* assembled a team of reporters whose extensive experience covering the Middle East brought a level of sophistication and understanding rare in the hectic pace of deadline writing. In addition to Barton Gellman, whose dispatches from Jerusalem were awarded this year's Jesse Laventhol Award for deadline writing by an individual, Glenn Frankel and Thomas W. Lippman in Washington and Daniel Williams in Rome produced a package of stories that gave readers a timely, accurate, and powerfully written account of a terrible deed, the climate that triggered it, and what the assassination meant to the fragile flower of a Middle East peace.

 Reprinted here is the obituary of Rabin, written in a few furious hours by Frankel. Now a special projects writer, he served as Jerusalem bureau chief from 1986–1989 and was awarded the 1989 Pulitzer Prize for International Reporting for his coverage of the Palestinian *intifada.* Author of *Beyond the Promised Land: Jews and Arabs on the Hard Road to a New Israel,* Frankel's command of history, language, and the life and times of Yitzhak Rabin resonate in every paragraph of his deadline profile of the slain prime minister.

The ultimate Israeli: A soldier who yearned for peace

NOVEMBER 5, 1995

By Glenn Frankel

No man—Israeli, Palestinian or American—was more essential to the Middle East peace process than Yitzhak Rabin, who was gunned down by an assassin in Tel Aviv last night.

Without his acquiescence, there would have been no secret talks between Israeli and Palestinian negotiators in Oslo. Without his support, the two sides would not have reached the 1993 agreement that granted Palestinians political autonomy, triggered Israeli military withdrawal from the Gaza Strip and Jericho and set the timetable for further withdrawal from much of the West Bank.

And without his blessing, delivered in the form of his historic handshake with Palestinian leader Yasser Arafat on the White House lawn in September of that year, the divided and wary Israeli people would never have accepted an arrangement that held great promise for peace but also contained great risks.

Rabin was constantly aware of those risks, and he spoke of them again just last month during his final visit to Washington to sign the latest agreement with Arafat. Contrasting the mood of hard-headed realism that day in the East Room of the White House with the euphoria of the famous handshake two years earlier, Rabin told the crowd: "Today, we are more sober. We are gladdened by the potential for reconciliation, but we are also wary of the dangers that lurk on every side."

That Rabin was killed by an Israeli Jew, rather than by one of the Arabs he had fought as a soldier and defense minister for decades, suggests the depth of emotion and hatred among the Jewish people over the peace process. Yet it belies the fact that of all Israel's leaders, Yitzhak Rabin was the most mainstream, the one whose hopes and fears and ideology most consistently reflected those of Israelis.

He was the first prime minister born in the territory that is now the state of Israel and the first to have served in the Israeli army. As military chief of staff in 1967, he was a hero of the Six-Day War, when in response to an Arab military build-up Israel launched a surprise airstrike and went on swiftly to defeat three Arab armies.

He served as ambassador to the United States and twice as prime minister. And he was defense minister in 1988 during the taut early days of the Palestinian uprising against Israeli rule, the *intifada,* when his "break their bones" policy won him international opprobrium yet domestic popularity.

Rabin was in many ways the quintessential Israeli —socially liberal yet fervently hawkish on defense matters. Because of his military background and his ruthless pragmatism, he touched the core of his countrymen's concerns—their obsession with security and their fear of destruction, yet also their yearning for peace. His front-line experience, his highly analytical approach to problems, his unflagging honesty, even his verbal crudeness—all of these impressed and somehow comforted Israelis. With him in charge, they felt in safe hands.

He was a hard man—he smoked four packs of cigarettes a day, drank heavily at times and often expressed great contempt for political allies as well as rivals. His staff feared him perhaps as much as his enemies. He had a warrior's disdain for sentiment. Yet it was these very qualities that allowed Rabin to do what his predecessors had not—to write a final chapter to the past, to shake hands with the Palestinians he had fought for decades and to take the existential leap into an uncertain future.

He was the ultimate product of Israel's military establishment. He and the Israeli military came of age together in the 1940s and '50s and, like the army, his personality was molded in the early years of combat and Israeli statehood.

His keen intellect, his skill at improvisation, his taciturnity—even his sometimes icy disdain for other people—all mirrored the values and lessons taught in the training schools and on the battlefields of the young Jewish state. But while he benefited politically from Israel's four decades of war with its Arab neighbors, he never worshiped combat. And when the time came, the old soldier was prepared, indeed eager, to become a force for change.

He was born in Jerusalem in 1922, the son of recent Russian immigrants. His father was a tailor, a humble and austere man, but his mother, Rosa Cohen, was a natural politician who became an important figure in the small Jewish community of Palestine, then administered by Britain under a League of Nations mandate. She had an iron will and intellect but a frail heart, and Rabin recalled in his memoirs running to fetch a doctor after each of her many bouts of heart disease, always fearing she would be dead when he returned. "Rachel [his younger sister] and I lived under the shadow of this dread throughout our childhood," he wrote. His mother died in 1937.

Rabin was serious, intense and disciplined, much like his mother, but painfully shy. Even as a child he was dour; at the agricultural school he attended as a teenager he was the only student without a nickname. Although he graduated at the top of his class, his acquired Hebrew was coarse, his humor often vulgar. He had hoped to continue his education, but the army intervened.

He received his first military training at age 13, and at 19 he became a full-time soldier in the fledgling Jewish army that quietly took shape under British rule. At 26, he was a brigade commander during Israel's war for independence, charged with defending the perilous, ambush-prone road through Arab-held territory from Tel Aviv to Jerusalem.

Prickly and tightly wound, he was no inspired leader of men. But he impressed his superiors with his keen mind, his love of detail and his willingness to obey orders. He did not hesitate to open fire in 1948 on fellow Jews aboard the Altalena, an arms ship docked off the Tel Aviv shore that was set to provide weapons to future prime minister Menachem Begin's rebellious paramilitary movement.

Likewise, as he recalled in his memoirs, he felt no compunction about using force to drive thousands of Arab civilians out of central Israel because their villages straddled the key supply line between Jerusalem and Tel Aviv.

He was in those days something of a primitive. When ordered to the island of Rhodes in 1949 to represent the military at armistice talks with the Arabs, he had never worn a necktie. As Robert Slater recalled in his book, *Rabin of Israel,* a colleague knotted a tie for Rabin before he left for Rhodes, and the young commander put it on each morning by pulling it over his head and pulling it tight.

Rabin rose quickly through the ranks of the young Israeli army. By age 32 he was a major general; 10 years later he was chief of staff. But while his strong intellect was undeniable, the human factor still seemed to be missing. Time and again throughout his career, he made decisions based on his reading of the strategic situation and overlooked or miscalculated the effect on people.

Critics said his mobilization of Israeli troops and other provocative moves during the weeks before the 1967 war prodded Egyptian President Gamal Abdel Nasser to escalate his own bombastic rhetoric and troop deployments and helped draw both countries toward a war neither really wanted.

The one time he tried to confide in a friend, he was betrayed. It happened just before the 1967 war, when, after weeks of late night strategy sessions, and unremitting pressure, he unburdened himself to Ezer Weizman, his top deputy, telling Weizman he feared he was leading Israel to military disaster. He asked Weizman if he should step down as chief of staff. Weizman sought to reassure him, persuading him that he was exhausted and merely needed rest. After a day off, Rabin returned to work and two weeks later led the army to its resounding triumph.

Seven years later, however, Weizman made the incident public in a blatant attempt to undermine Rabin's candidacy for the premiership. Rabin survived the attack politically, but he never forgot the harsh lesson.

After retiring from the army, Rabin asked for and received Israel's most important diplomatic post, ambassador to the United States, despite the fact that he had no prior such experience. In Washington, he studied the *Realpolitik* and global strategy of Richard Nixon and Henry Kissinger, whom he often described as the two leaders he most respected.

But he learned other lessons as well. He arrived in Washington in 1968 in time to attend the Democratic Party convention in Chicago, and in his memoirs he marveled over how even the strongest country in the world could tear itself apart, in this instance over the Vietnam War.

In 1974, the ruling Labor Party chose Rabin over arch-rival Shimon Peres to succeed Golda Meir as prime minister. Under his guidance, Israel pulled off the famed Entebbe rescue mission in Uganda in July 1976, but on the whole his first term, by his own admission, was a troubled and ultimately unsuccessful one.

Rabin wanted to negotiate accommodations with the Arab states, but he was a political neophyte. He felt constantly undermined and hemmed in by rivals, such as Peres, who was defense minister, and Meir. Still, as he later conceded, he made unnecessary enemies and alienated potential allies.

He was forced to resign in disgrace in 1977 in the face of a minor scandal involving a checking account that he and his wife Leah maintained in Washington in violation of Israeli law. Other men might have quit politics, but Rabin was haunted by his errors and by his enemies; he craved redemption and revenge.

For seven years he sat on the back benches of the Israeli parliament, the Knesset. He kept up a tempestuous feud with Peres that damaged both men and had more to do with ambition and pride than with ideology. Finally, they put their differences aside for the sake of the party and ran as a united ticket in the 1984 election.

Rabin was the Labor Party's most powerful vote-getter in the stalemated election of that year, and he was named defense minister in a new unity government —an office in which he always said he felt most at home.

He quickly became the center of gravity in the deeply divided Cabinet, frequently mediating between its warring components. No one dared challenge his authority or question his judgment on security issues. He was tough, demanding and uncompromising.

He and his father had been detained without trial under the British mandate in 1946, but Rabin himself

now employed similar weapons against Palestinian activists in the Israeli-occupied West Bank and Gaza
Strip—administrative detention, expulsion and house
demolition. "I've kicked out more Arabs than anyone
you can name," he shouted at a right-wing heckler
during the 1988 election campaign.

He was equally contemptuous of Jewish settlers in
the occupied territories. He called the Gush Emunim
settler movement "a cancer in the body of democratic
Israel." He detested Jewish fanatics and—in an eerie
harbinger of his own death—he expressed the fear that
their Messianic obsessions would destroy the state.

When the intifada broke out in December 1987, the
human dimension failed him once again. After several
harrowing weeks in which Israeli soldiers opened fire
all too frequently against unarmed Palestinians, he is-
sued his "break their bones" command. He said later
that the idea was to save lives by substituting clubs for
bullets in putting down the uprising.

But Rabin failed to realize how such beatings
would look on international television, nor did he con-
ceive of the searing, demoralizing impact such personal, hand-to-hand combat would have on his own
men. Their discomfort and disaffection with their role
was one of the factors that led Rabin to conclude that
the occupation came at too high a price for Israeli society, and he pressed Israel's right-wing prime minister, Yitzhak Shamir, to launch a peace initiative that
called for Palestinian autonomy in the territories.
When Shamir undermined his own peace plan in 1990
under pressure from his party's right wing, Rabin
joined Peres in an abortive attempt to bring down the
government.

Shamir won that parliamentary battle, forcing
Rabin and Peres to the back benches. But two years
later, the old soldier rose again. He first defeated Peres
in the Labor Party's leadership contest, then led the
party to victory over Shamir's Likud. Soon after Rabin
assumed the premiership, he patched up Israel's tat-
tered relations with the White House, then struggled to
come to terms with the Palestinians in negotiations in
Washington.

On his opening speech to the Knesset, Rabin said
Israelis had voted to change more than just their gov-

ernment; they had changed their entire way of looking at the world: "In the last decade of the 20th century... walls of enmity have fallen, borders have disappeared ...and it is our duty, to ourselves and to our children, to see the new world as it is now—to discern its dangers, explore its prospects and do everything possible so that the state of Israel will fit into this new world."

Rabin had promised to reach an agreement with the Palestinians within nine months, but the negotiations stalled. At a crucial point, he allowed his old rival Peres, now Israel's foreign minister, to authorize back-channel contacts with the outlawed Palestine Liberation Organization in Oslo. The result was the historic agreement reached in August 1993 and the Nobel Peace Prize for Rabin, Peres and Arafat.

Rabin's dour performance that day was memorable. His face etched in pain and self-doubt; he seemed to radiate all the misgivings, anguish and grim determination of the Israeli people. He stared at his shoes, at his fingernails, at an abstract speck on the horizon—anywhere but to his left where Yasser Arafat stood beaming. His speech took no more than six minutes, and the words were not especially profound. But the delivery was powerful.

In a weary yet emphatic voice, Rabin confessed that it was not easy for him to share a platform with the leader of the PLO. Nonetheless, he spoke clearly and without contempt or condescension to the Palestinian people: "Let me say to you, the Palestinians, we are destined to live together on the same soil, in the same land. We, the soldiers who have returned from battle stained with blood, we who have seen our relatives and friends killed before our eyes, we who have attended their funerals and cannot look into the eyes of their parents...we say to you today in a loud and clear voice: Enough of blood and tears. Enough."

The last two years were not easy for Rabin. He had pledged to Israelis that the agreement with the Palestinians would lead to greater prosperity and personal security. The former had come to pass, but the latter was sorely missing, and after each new suicide attack against Israelis by Palestinian extremists Rabin was denounced by the Israeli right as a traitor to the Jewish people.

Even while he guided Israel to its future, Rabin remained firmly rooted in the old mind-set that saw security issues as paramount and everything else as a distant second. He regularly denounced Israelis who expressed concern over human rights abuses in Gaza and the West Bank and fought to maintain the power of his security forces to use violent interrogation methods on suspected terrorists.

He expressed sweeping disdain for anyone who disagreed with his policies. Although he had been elected prime minister largely on economic issues, Rabin saw these as a distraction. He bemoaned the fact that young Israelis seemed as interested in acquiring nice houses and foreign cars and other symbols of bourgeois affluence as in defending their country. Yet he himself presided over perhaps Israel's greatest wave of economic prosperity—a prosperity that helped complete its transformation from a small, beleaguered garrison state to a modern, self-confident member of the community of nations.

"No longer are we necessarily a people that dwells alone, and no longer is it true that the whole world is against us," he told Israelis on his first day in office in 1992. "We must overcome the sense of isolation that has held us in its thrall for almost half a century. We must join the international movement toward peace, reconciliation and cooperation that is spreading over the entire globe these days—lest we be the last to remain, all alone, in the station."

Glenn Frankel is a former Jerusalem bureau chief of The Washington Post and author of Beyond the Promised Land: Jews and Arabs on the Hard Road to a New Israel.

Lessons Learned

BY GLENN FRANKEL

The phone rang that Saturday at around four in the afternoon. It was the Foreign Desk with the news that Yitzhak Rabin had been shot. No one knew how seriously. And we had a problem. Someone had searched the musty shelves for a Rabin obituary and found none. Maybe we wouldn't need it, but maybe we would. Could I come in?

On the way downtown, I thought about what I would want to say. Rabin was a towering historical figure, Israel's last Zionist patriarch. He had led his hesitant, wary countrymen to a date with destiny: the signing of a historic agreement with their arch enemy, Yasser Arafat and the Palestine Liberation Organization. He too had been wary. You could see it etched in his face on the day he shook Arafat's hand on the White House lawn. Later he described the butterflies he had felt that day. Israelis had felt them as well. He and they shared the same visceral emotions: intense fear and suspicion coupled by acute longing for peace. This was the source of his strength and the reason why they trusted him. Where he led they followed.

Then there was Rabin the person. He was a crude man, known for his fondness for cigarettes, scotch, and raunchy humor. He didn't tolerate fools and enjoyed terrorizing his subordinates. Israelis like their politicians rough around the edges; they even like their leader to have a bit of blood on his hands. It's not just machismo: there's a feeling that a man who has been there, who has himself squeezed the trigger, knows the price of violence, will be mature enough to weigh all the doubts and check all the alternatives before plunging in. Rabin, who had led an army and had ordered deportations, house demolitions, even assassinations, had the requisite qualifications.

A leader had been shot, but also a man. My piece had to be about them both.

Within minutes after my arrival, CNN and the wires had the word: Rabin was dead. It was after 4 p.m. and on Saturday everything closes early. I had three hours.

This was strictly a writing exercise. There was no time to make phone calls or check facts. Fortunately, I had written frequently about Rabin before, both in the pages of *The Washington Post* and in a brief portrait in my book about

Israel, *Beyond the Promised Land.* I knew the details of
what I wanted to say, even had ready phrases to fall back on.

Deadline makes its own rules, supplies its own adrenaline and sense of urgency. If you're lucky, that urgency
somehow finds its way into the prose and powers it forward.
But there are ways of helping it along. For starters, keep
everything simple. On deadline, there's no time for the
elegant, anecdotal lead. What was the most important fact I
wanted to convey about this person? That he was the essential man at a historic moment. So that became the lead.

I'm a big fan of triads. It's a vice of the incurably longwinded, but it's also a useful tool for a writer in a hurry. So
I jammed a trio into the lead paragraph ("Israeli, Palestinian
or American"), then played it back in the next two paragraphs with three sentences leading with "Without..." It
gave the piece a certain rhythm; when I read it out loud,
which I often do while I'm writing a piece, it seemed to
flow.

By the end of the third paragraph, I'd completed my lead
thought, stated my thesis, and hammered it home. Now was
a good time to come back in some way to the assassination.
I focused on the sense of risk and danger, elements that
have always been present when Middle Eastern leaders take
a chance for peace. I took a quote from Rabin's speech during his last visit to Washington. He had spoken then in general terms of risks, but now with his death, the quote took
on personal significance. And it gave me a chance to introduce Rabin's own voice, speaking in a chillingly foreboding
way about the dangers of the enterprise he had undertaken.

This will sound crass, but it's easy to write about someone who has been killed. The drama is already there; the
writer needs only to provide context. Take William
Manchester's *Death of a President.* The prose is solid,
workmanlike, probably no better than several dozen other
nonfiction, quasi-journalistic books. Yet it endures. It has a
majestic weight, a tragic overlay, even when Manchester begins with a long description of the petty rivalries of Texas
politics. That's because everyone knows what's coming.
Every reader knows the hero is about to die.

And so the awesome fact of Rabin's death became the
context for my sentences. I mixed the biographical and the
judgmental for the rest of the top 11 paragraphs, completing
the basic framework, then launched into a standard profile
structure: "He was born in Jerusalem...etc." Chronology is
the nonfiction writer's best friend. It is a rational, accessible
and relentless navigator, and it guided me through the rest
of the piece.

As I moved through the details of Rabin's life, I kept trying to return to his emotional makeup. So it seemed important to dwell on that moment when Rabin felt betrayed by a supposedly close friend who disclosed his nervous collapse two weeks before the Six-Day War in 1967. And on Rabin's determination to stay in the Israeli parliament after he was forced to resign in disgrace during his first term as prime minister. And finally on the key moment when he and Arafat signed their fateful accord. I also searched for the telling detail. The fact that he couldn't tie his own necktie at the 1949 armistice talks helped explain something about the man and the new country he represented as both made their first appearance on the world stage.

I have some regrets. I should have used Rabin's own voice more, more quotes, especially from his crusty 1979 memoirs. And I should have written longer. This was our last opportunity to put the man in the pages of our newspaper. The editors gave me 3,000 words; I should have insisted on 4,000. I was afraid I wouldn't have time. In fact, I was done early. It wasn't the most factually complete obituary; nothing on deadline will have every necessary detail. But it had the awful power of immediacy: it was fresh off the shelf, a portrait of a man suddenly and mercilessly swept away by the very forces he sought to vanquish.

The next day at the funeral service, President Clinton in his speech recalled the tie anecdote and embellished it with his own account of helping straighten the prime minister's bow-tie at a black-tie dinner. In capturing a man's life and a leader's death, it's the human details that count.

The Dallas Morning News

Finalist, Team Deadline Reporting

On the morning of April 19, 1995, when a bomb tore away the north face of the Alfred P. Murrah Federal Building in Oklahoma City, the blast rattled windows 12 miles away in the home of Arnold Hamilton, the Oklahoma bureau chief for *The Dallas Morning News.* As Ralph Langer, the paper's executive editor tells it, within moments Hamilton was on the phone to the Texas & Southwest Desk to report, "We've got a big one up here."

The paper's coverage of the Oklahoma City bombing reflected its determination to "become the leading news source on the tragedy" and also its sense that the *News* considers Oklahoma its back yard, Langer says. Its first goal, after placing a team of reporters and a command post in Oklahoma City, was to provide a compelling, comprehensive account for the early edition—the one circulated in Oklahoma City. Despite a tornado scare that emptied the newsroom in Dallas the night of the blast, the paper made its deadline with a report that "triumphed in content and timeliness," according to the Knight-Ridder Tribune News Service, which distributed the stories around the globe.

The *News* mobilized more than 125 reporters, editors, copy editors, photographers, and graphic artists to cover the story as it unfolded over the first several weeks. It provided readers with an obituary memorializing every person killed in the blast and led coverage of the multi-state investigation and search for suspects. The first day's report, represented here by Hamilton's main story and a heartbreaking account of the survivors' futile search for hope by J. Lynn Lunsford, delivers on the newspaper's promise to readers to be out front continuously on the coverage of this tragedy.

Arnold Hamilton has served as Oklahoma bureau chief for *The Dallas Morning News* since July 1, 1988. He formerly worked as a state Capitol correspondent based in Sacramento, Calif., for the *San Jose Mercury News* and spent five years with the *Dallas Times Herald,* including two as its chief political correspondent in Dallas and 2½ years as a state Capitol correspondent in Austin. Hamilton began his journalism career in Oklahoma, working five years for *The Oklahoma Journal* and two years for the *Tulsa Tribune.* A native of St. Louis, Mo., he is a graduate of the University of San Francisco and has a master's degree in political science from Oklahoma State University.

J. Lynn Lunsford is a staff writer for *The Dallas Morning News.* The son of a *Fort Worth Star-Telegram* printer, he knew he wanted to be a journalist from the time he was four years old, after visiting the newsroom with his father. After graduating from the University of Texas at Austin in 1986, he followed in his dad's footsteps, spending the next six years as an aviation and transportation writer for the *Star-Telegram.* Since he joined the *News* in 1992, he has covered a number of breaking disaster stories, including five major plane crashes, a van accident that killed 14 children, and the Oklahoma City bombing. He has won several awards for spot news reporting.

Scores missing in rubble of office building

APRIL 20, 1995

By Arnold Hamilton

OKLAHOMA CITY—A thundering explosion apparently caused by a car bomb blew away almost half a federal office building here Wednesday, killing at least 31 people in one of the worst terrorist attacks in U.S. history.

Officials said the death toll, which includes at least 12 children, undoubtedly would climb as rescue workers dig through more parts of the nine-story rubble that had been the Alfred P. Murrah Federal Building.

Twelve hours after the 9:04 a.m. explosion, authorities reported pulling at least two more victims from the rubble, including a 15-year-old girl.

Near midnight, more than 400 people had been treated at local hospitals and 200 more building employees were unaccounted for.

Federal investigators said they do not know who is responsible and do not know why Oklahoma City was targeted.

"Obviously, no amateur did this," Oklahoma Gov. Frank Keating said. "Whoever did this was an animal."

About 40 rescue workers continued their increasingly dangerous work by lights early Thursday. Hopes of finding more survivors grew dimmer with each hour as storms pelted the area, making the building more unstable.

"The rain and the wind are making it very tough. There's debris falling. The guys are staying in there wearing hard hats, though, because they're still finding people alive," a federal official said.

Names of the dead were not expected to be released until Thursday. Members of Oklahoma's congressional delegation, meeting late Wednesday with state officials, said they expect more than 200 dead, according to local radio reports.

"This is a place of unspeakable horror, that building," said Gov. Keating. "To the extent that we can find two or three more people and save their lives, that's fabulous."

Shattered in the explosion were not only walls and lives but the assumption that middle-sized, middle-America cities like this one were free from the unpredictable terrors of terrorist bombings.

There were no calls warning of the explosion, which was felt more than 70 miles away and plunged downtown Oklahoma City into chaos. Windows throughout the area were blown out. About 60 other buildings were damaged.

In Washington, President Clinton ordered tighter security at federal buildings throughout the nation. He described the fatal blast as "an act of cowardice and it was evil. The United States will not tolerate it, and I will not allow the people of this country to be intimidated by evil cowards."

Throughout the country, bomb threats caused government buildings to be evacuated and government workers to look over their shoulders.

More than 900 people were believed to be in the building when the bomb went off, including about 30 in the America's Kids day-care center.

By midafternoon, about 20 children were still unaccounted for.

Oklahoma City Police Chief Sam Gonzales said the blast was believed to be the result of a half-ton bomb placed in a vehicle parked on the north side of the federal office building. He said it left a crater about 8 feet deep and 20 feet wide.

ATF officials estimated that the bomb's power was greater than that which devastated the World Trade Center in February 1993.

"I was in Korea, and I never heard anything that loud," said Jerry Henry, a 61-year-old retired boat builder who was reading a novel at his apartment building about five blocks away. "I thought it was kind of like a sonic boom."

The destruction was incredible. Black smoke streamed across the skyline. Nine floors worth of brick, glass and other materials rained onto Northwest Fifth Street, killing several people outside the building and injuring scores of others. Cars burned on the street.

Assistant Fire Chief Jon Hansen described the first 30 minutes after the bombing as "pure mayhem." Streets were choked with walking wounded, some bloodied and their clothes in tatters, as emergency crews and passers-by swelled the downtown area.

Late Wednesday morning, six small bodies were taken to a nearby Methodist church that had been transformed into an makeshift morgue.

By noon, the only sounds rescuers in the building could hear were the ones made by other rescue workers, said Officer Adrian Neal of the Edmond Police Department. By 1:30 p.m., many of the medical personnel were being sent home.

"People from all the floors were just thrown down the middle like a rag doll," said Dr. D.S. Ahmad of Presbyterian Hospital. "We don't need doctors and nurses. What we need are body bags."

Gloria Titsworth, her husband and two daughters were in the local recruiting headquarters for the U.S. Army and U.S. Marine Corps when the blast occurred.

Ms. Titsworth was knocked unconscious by the blast, and awoke to find desks piled on top of her. Her husband had a gash in his throat and one daughter was missing. In the confusion of the rescue, Ms. Titsworth lost track of her husband.

Later on, in the basement of St. Anthony Hospital, the young woman begged a nurse not to take her upstairs to her room.

"No, no, I don't want to go up in any more buildings anymore," Ms. Titsworth sobbed. "I want to stay right here."

For hours after the blast, the horns and sirens of ambulances and fire engines dominated the air in the state capital's downtown area.

At one point, when they thought another bomb had been found, dozens of police and rescue workers sprinted up the street away from the Murrah Building, screaming at bystanders to run.

No other devices were located that were believed to be connected to the bombing, the FBI said.

At one point, rescue workers formed a human chain 30 yards long from part of the building, apparently to remove victims.

"We're systematically going through the building, one floor at a time," said Assistant Fire Chief Jon Hansen. "The building is very unstable. Our rescue crews are at tremendous risk right now....We're getting to people we know we can get to now. We're talking to people through floors.

"We have to crawl on our stomachs and feel our way and we're talking to victims who are in there and reassuring them that we're doing everything within the good Lord's power to reach them and get to them," Chief Hansen said.

JIHAD LINK ALLEGED

An FBI communiqué that was circulated Wednesday suggested that the attack was carried out by the Islamic Jihad, an Iranian-backed Islamic militant group, said a security professional in California who declined to be named. A spokesman for the Islamic Jihad later denied any responsibility.

The communiqué suggested the attack was made in retaliation for the prosecution of Muslim fundamentalists in the bombing of the World Trade Center in February 1993, said the source, a nongovernment security professional.

"We are currently inclined to suspect the Islamic Jihad as the likely group," the FBI notice said.

Authorities said they have no evidence that remnants of the Branch Davidian religious sect may have been involved. The bombing occurred on the second anniversary of a fire near Waco that destroyed the Branch Davidian compound.

Bob Ricks, special agent in charge of the Oklahoma FBI, said hundreds of calls had been received from people claiming responsibility for the bombing.

Agent Ricks, who was a key spokesman for the FBI during the Branch Davidian siege near Waco, said it was an "obvious coincidence" that the bombing occurred on the fire anniversary.

"But to say that it was one particular group or one individual, we're not anywhere near making a statement with regard to that. We have no indication with regard to group or with regard to reason," he said.

The Bureau of Alcohol, Tobacco and Firearms, which played a leading role in the Davidian siege, had offices in the Murrah Building along with the Drug Enforcement Administration, the Veterans Administration and the Secret Service. The FBI offices in Oklahoma City are in another building.

Lester D. Martz, special agent in charge of ATF's division office in Dallas, said ATF and FBI bomb experts began sifting through the building's wreckage around 8 p.m. Wednesday.

"They'll be working through the night, doing shift work," said Mr. Martz, ATF's senior agent at the scene. "It's gonna be a long night. You've got a lot of tired people."

The FBI announced Wednesday that it was searching for three men seen driving north from the scene in a brown Chevrolet pickup truck with tinted windows and a bug shield on the front hood.

FBI officials had no description of the driver but said two passengers appeared to be men of Middle Eastern descent, with dark hair and beards, wearing blue pants, black shirts and coats. One man was believed to be between 20 and 25, the other between 35 and 38.

YOUNG VICTIMS

In Oklahoma City, the day's horror was multiplied by the fact that so many of the victims were small children whose parents had just dropped them off at the America's Kids day-care center for federal workers.

Some news accounts said that of the approximately 30 children in the day-care center, only two were known to have survived, one in surgery and one in intensive care. The dead from the day-care center ranged from 1 to 7 years old. Some were burned beyond recognition.

Other children who attended a day-care center at a nearby YMCA also were injured by broken glass and flying debris.

People frantically searched for loved ones. Some children from the day-care center were taken away on stretchers. Others were scooped up by parents who ran to the scene. Some victims wandered around the streets in shock.

Carole Lawton, 62, was sitting at her desk on the seventh floor when the explosion hit.

"I was sitting there and all of a sudden the windows blew in. It got real dark and the ceiling just started coming down," said Ms. Lawton, an employee in the Housing and Urban Development office.

She said she then heard "the roar of the whole building crumbling."

The floor around her fell onto the floor below, forcing her to crawl through a window into a hall and down some stairways. She was not injured.

Todd Linder, who works two blocks away, said the last thing he remembers is "sitting in my chair and I remember the ceiling falling in. I heard a loud boom and after that it was just chaos."

Emergency crews set up a first aid center near the ruined building. The injured, with bloodied heads and arms, sat on the sidewalks awaiting aid. St. Anthony Hospital put out a call for more medical help and hundreds of volunteers responded.

At midday, officials at that hospital posted a list of the injured, with more than 200 names, so worried relatives could look for news about loved ones.

Mr. Keating said he toured what was left of the Murrah Building, built in the mid-1970s.

"It's Beirut, it's just incredible," he said. "One floor after the other, pancaked on top of each other."

Within an hour after the blast, authorities also ordered the evacuation of a northwest Oklahoma City office tower, about five miles from downtown, that houses the Oklahoma headquarters for the FBI.

"We've lost some of our innocence and we're now starting to accept the reality that terrorism has happened here," said Dr. Stephen Sloan, a University of Oklahoma professor and noted terrorist expert. He said he was not surprised that an interior metropolitan area such as Oklahoma City had become a target of terrorism.

"No area has ever been zoned against terrorism," he said. "There are softer targets here. It also sends a message of vulnerability that did not exist before."

AWAITING WORD

Hours after the explosion, about 250 people gathered at First Christian Church, 3700 N. Walker, to meet with ministers, funeral directors and counselors

98

and family members. Most were still awaiting word on the fate of loved ones.

Families waited in small groups and relatives were allowed to meet with counselors whenever one became available. Group counseling sessions were held for children.

The church began taking names of the missing at 2 p.m. and by 7 p.m. had gathered more than 150 names. Of those, only two people were found alive and well.

Women brought pictures of children and family members brought dental records. Relatives were asked to fill out forms to help identify bodies.

The bombing, the first outside a major metropolitan area in the United States, could represent a shift in terrorist strategy, experts said, away from population centers such as New York where previous bombings occurred, to the heartland where security is typically not as tight.

Former U.S. Rep. Dave McCurdy, a former chairman of the House Intelligence Committee, told CBS affiliate KWTV here that FBI sources told him the blast was similar to a 1992 attack on the Israeli Embassy in Argentina.

Dr. Sloan of the University of Oklahoma said the trend in terrorism is to plant multiple bombs, with some planned to detonate while rescue efforts from the first explosion are still going on. Such bombs would take lives while also preying on the psychology of victims, rescuers and citizens.

"It's too early to tell who did it," said Dr. Sloan, but if it were a terrorist attack "it implies a level of sophistication and it is a very, very serious potential to be considered."

Staff writers Gayle Reaves in Dallas and Todd Copilevitz, Tracy Everbach, Stephen Power, and J. Lynn Lunsford in Oklahoma City contributed to this report.

Lessons Learned

BY ARNOLD HAMILTON

It was 9:02 on a spectacular spring morning. My wife, Bev, and I had just returned from taking the boys to school. She was getting ready for work. I sat down to read the papers. The dog was snoozing in the living room.

An explosion shattered the calm. It was like nothing I ever heard. An electrifying surge of energy raced through the house. The dog, hair standing up on her back, leaped from her slumber and yelped, tucked her tail, and ran down the hallway.

There was a simultaneous "What was that?" from both ends of the house.

It seemed certain an airplane must have crashed in our neighborhood, about 12 miles north of downtown Oklahoma City. Or perhaps a nearby home had been leveled by a natural gas explosion. We ran outside to look for smoke, but saw nothing. Several neighbors also rushed out to see what had happened.

We went back inside and tuned into a radio news broadcast, which reported an explosion at the Oklahoma County courthouse. I flipped on the television just moments before a local news helicopter circled around the Alfred P. Murrah Federal Building downtown.

The northern one-third of the nine-story building was gone.

I immediately called my state editor, Rodger Jones, at the office in Dallas. "I think we've got a big one up here," I told him. I wasn't sure if it were a natural gas explosion or a bomb or what. But I knew that hundreds worked in that building. And I didn't see how very many could have walked out alive.

Rodger and I quickly mapped strategy. I would head to our bureau to gather as much information as quickly as I could, not only to begin the process of reporting the story, but also to help the editors dispatch other reporters and photographers to the appropriate venues, such as hospitals, rescue centers, and the blast site itself. Rodger quickly mobilized a team in Dallas: scheduling four reporters and a photographer on the next available Southwest Airlines flight; dispatching an editor, a graphic artist, and two other reporters on a Lear Jet, chartered along with CBS News.

As I quickly showered, I found myself shaking. I was used to parachuting into other cities where disaster struck. But I had no experience with an event of this magnitude in my town, the town where I grew up, where I chose to return and raise my kids.

Surely it wasn't a bomb. Not in Oklahoma City. The heartland? Terrorism? Here? Why? As I drove to work, I considered the possibilities: Must be a natural gas explosion. *Yeah, but this is the second anniversary of Waco.* There couldn't possibly be a connection...could there? *But wait, Bob Ricks, the FBI's chief spokesman during the 51-day standoff between federal agents and the Branch Davidians, is in charge of the field office here.* Yeah, but his office isn't even in the Murrah Building. *But...but...the ATF was headquartered there.*

Once I arrived at the bureau—and flipped on every communications device available, from computer to television to radio—I found my basic, yet most essential, link to Dallas inaccessible: I could not get through via telephone. "All circuits are busy...all circuits are busy...all circuits are busy." Cellular lines also were jammed.

I was able to make some calls within Oklahoma City, picking up information. Some in my office building dropped by to report what they had seen or heard when downtown earlier. I kept my finger on speed dial to Dallas....

Finally, I got through. We decided to leave the line open for as long as necessary. I used other phones in the office. Periodically, I would pick up the Dallas line and whistle or shout for an editor, anxious to pass along new information. I would listen for their efforts to get my attention. It was decidedly low-tech, but effective. I don't know what it cost, but the line was connected to Dallas almost all day.

Our deputy Washington editor, Bob Hillman, who just happened to be in Dallas that day, boarded the Lear jet, took the 45-minute flight to Oklahoma City, and set up a makeshift bureau in a motel about six miles southeast of downtown. He chose the location, figuring—correctly—that it might avoid some of the telephone headaches I had encountered.

I advised Rodger of the nearest hospitals, the most likely destinations for victims. He dispatched reporters to those locations. I helped advise him, and others, of the geography of Oklahoma City, the distances to key sites, their proximity to the Murrah Building.

It was an incredible team effort. I wrote the lead story on Day One, melding my reporting with dispatches from my colleagues who parachuted into town or worked the phones from Dallas and Washington and elsewhere. Assistant state editor Mark Edgar, with whom I work on a daily basis, edited the story brilliantly and shepherded it through the copy-editing maze.

What made this story particularly difficult for me to report and write was that I knew people who worked in and around the Murrah Building. I received periodic reports from my wife about friends who hadn't been accounted for. I tried in vain to reach a contact who had an office a block away in the old Post Office building. I later learned that he had been talking on the phone with his pregnant wife when the blast rocked his office. All she could hear over the phone line was voices shouting, "Where's Randy? Where's Randy?" He had been knocked out of his chair. Stunned, he dashed through the offices to see if anyone were seriously injured. He forgot he had been talking to his wife.

Emotions aside, it is a tremendous challenge to report a story the magnitude of the Oklahoma City bombing. There was so much false information circulating that first day. Some broadcasts in those first hours were rife with speculation, not hard facts. Professionally, two primary challenges emerged: 1) to tell the story as completely, concisely, and accurately as possible, and 2) to provide perspective that spectacular television video footage could not.

It was a monumental task, one that in retrospect seems like something of a blur. We were fortunate that the timing of the blast gave us nearly 10 hours to our first deadlines. We also were fortunate because we were able to marshal a veteran staff of reporters, editors, graphic artists, researchers, and photojournalists (all told, 125 people worked on the story). And we were fortunate both because of the proximity of Dallas to Oklahoma City and because *The Dallas Morning News* had committed nearly 15 years earlier to staffing a full-time bureau in the Sooner capital.

In the end, as it always does, it came down to execution. It was an international news story, but it was journalism at its most basic levels: Get the facts. Get them right. Get them quickly. Provide perspective. Tell the story with precision and flair. In essence, it was everything we train for.

Dazed family members gather to wait word on kin

APRIL 20, 1995

By J. Lynn Lunsford

OKLAHOMA CITY—They wandered, dazed and bleary-eyed, into a church with a tear-shaped dome.

And they waited for good news that would almost never come.

More than 250 people, the friends and relatives of those missing in Wednesday's explosion at a federal office building, came to wait in a building full of undertakers, doctors and clergy.

Only hours after the thunder of the bomb had subsided, a group of funeral home directors organized the session at First Christian Church near downtown to begin identifying the dead. For hundreds of people, it was here that the grieving began.

Those arriving at the church began filling out an "Identification Data Form: Presumed Decedent." They were asked to help identify the dead by providing photographs, driver's license numbers and dental and medical records.

Thirteen-year-old Elizabeth Luster came looking for her parents. She knew only that they had a 9:30 a.m. Wednesday appointment at the Social Security office in the federal building. She had failed to bring photos of her parents.

"All I know," said Elizabeth, who wore blue jeans and had straight red hair, "is that my mom was wearing a black dress with flowers on it."

The social worker didn't find her mother's name on the list of the living but offered encouragement nevertheless.

"That's a great start," she told Elizabeth. "We need to know that."

Laura Topel-Godfrey, a psychiatric therapist, spent the day talking to the confused and weary. She began by taking the names of the missing and looking for matches on a list of those treated in area hospitals. She found only one match.

"I actually got to tell somebody the person they were looking for was alive," said Ms. Topel-Godfrey, trying to accentuate a small victory in a long day of losses. "And it was so gratifying to see the relief in their face."

The family and friends waited in the church cafeteria as television sets blinked monotonously with live action from the explosion scene. Some sat alone, staring as if hypnotized. Others found consolation in the company of strangers.

The mood in the room was mostly hopeful, as voices on loudspeakers gently reminded them that all was not lost, that survivors might yet be found. But optimism gave way at about 6 p.m. when Dr. Dan Nelson told the crowd that none of the bodies recovered would be officially identified until Thursday.

"From the number of people in this room and the number of people that we still have no information on," Dr. Nelson said, "it's obvious that there will be many fatalities from this tragic event."

Funeral home directors helped the families fill out their identification forms. One funeral home director, Frank Parrish, said it was the worst day in his 27-year career.

Psychiatrists and social workers tried to talk to as many as possible, calling names from a list whenever a therapist became available. Special group therapy sessions were held for children.

As the day wore on, some of the waiting were treated for anxiety and hyperventilation. By night, they covered themselves in blankets and tried to sleep.

One man, who declined to give his name, said he already knew his two small children were crushed and killed in the day-care center. He came anyway, with photos of two tousle-haired boys, to fill out the identification forms so his children could be properly buried.

"I'd rather die than be going through this," he said.

Others, however, clung to the hope that their relatives might still be found.

"It's rough," said Tim Hearns, 27, whose mother Castine Deveroux, 48, was working on the building's seventh floor at the department of Housing and Urban Development. He said his mother was the sole support of his 12-year-old sister and 15-year-old brother.

"I don't know what to expect," Mr. Hearns said. "She worked right there where it's all torn up, and I really hope God was with her."

Sarita Redd came looking for her brother Woodrow Brady.

"He had an appointment down there today," Ms. Redd said, "and he never came home and nobody can tell us where he is."

Finally, there was Nancy Breman, 48, looking for her friend Susan Ferrell, an attorney for HUD. Ms. Breman dutifully filled out the undertakers' forms and waited two hours in the hope that she might hear something.

Then she went home to find a picture of Ms. Ferrell.

"It's so they can identify her as a survivor, of which I know she is one," Ms. Breman said, as she began to weep.

"She is, she is, I just know she is," she cried. "It just can't be any other way."

Lessons Learned

BY J. LYNN LUNSFORD

Sometimes the story that grabs your heart is the one that comes up when you think you've finished for the day.

That's what happened with the story about the families and friends of those who were killed in the bombing of the federal building. I was originally dispatched to Oklahoma City from Dallas that Wednesday morning with specific instructions to "stay out of downtown" and "get a feel for how this is affecting the people in the small towns."

I worked on that story throughout the day, calling in quotes and color to a rewrite back in Dallas. By 4:30 p.m., the piece was completed and I went to the hotel where the *Morning News* had set up operations. About an hour later, we learned from one of the local television stations that relatives and friends of the victims had been asked to meet at a church a few blocks away from the blast site. Because I was already finished with my assignment, I was the one sent.

When I arrived at the church, I was astounded at the number of cars in the parking lot. Looking toward the doors, I saw a steady stream of people going inside, some of them wearing bandages from wounds they had received in the blast. Inside a large meeting hall, several hundred people were gathered in clusters, talking or quietly crying. Several televisions continuously showed live scenes of what was going on downtown.

It was evident that most of these people believed that their missing loved ones would be found alive. Yet the people they were meeting with were funeral directors, who helped them fill out forms that bore the heading "Presumed Decedent."

I decided to mill around the room without talking to anybody, just to get a feel for what was going on and to get some idea of whose stories would be most compelling. Not knowing yet what my story would say, I wrote down everything I saw. What color the window shades were, how many workers, reactions to what was happening on the television. At some point, I knew it might be useful, and I knew that eventually the media would be tossed from the room. (We were, shortly after a swarm of television cameras showed up and surrounded anybody who stood still for more than a couple of seconds.)

One of the most poignant scenes occurred while I was sitting at a table near the front of the room. A 13-year-old girl came in with two adults and told the social worker that both of her parents were missing. She didn't have a photograph of her parents but she remembered that her mother was wearing a black dress with flowers on it.

"That's a great start," the social worker said. "We need to know that."

It was the social worker's job to try to match the names of the missing with people who had been identified and were in local hospitals. Throughout the evening, this social worker found only one match. To her, it was a single victory in a long day of losses.

It would have been very easy to just gloss over that information and call in a colorless story that was carried by the strength of quotes from relatives and friends.

On stories like this, I always try to drop in at least one passage where I take the readers to the scene and let them see some of the action play out. In this case, it was the conversation between the girl and the social worker.

Griff Singer, my college journalism professor, always stressed that clear, precise description of what you see, smell, and taste at a scene is crucial if you want to make a story come alive—especially on deadline. "If you don't tell me what you see, you might as well save the paper some money and do it by phone," he said.

I could hear his voice as I made my way around the room that day. He was right. Although you may be running on adrenaline and in a tremendous hurry, stop for just a minute and look around. Then write it down.

By the time I got what I needed, it was about 8 p.m. When I called Dallas to dictate, they transferred me to Jonathan Eig, who has to be one of the finest writers in this business. For the next 45 minutes—with me on a pay phone in the parking lot of an abandoned gas station—we worked on the story, paragraph by paragraph.

I would dictate a few lines and then I would describe the scene, to make sure that Jonathan understood what I had seen. He asked some questions that sent me back to my notes. (One of them was "What does the church look like?" It had white dome that, against the dark clouds in the distance, looked like a tear drop. That went straight into the lead.)

In retrospect, the story wrote itself once we decided where it was going. But the key was taking the reader there.

Rick Bragg
Non-Deadline Writing

Rick Bragg is a national correspondent for *The New York Times* who covers the South from the paper's Atlanta bureau. He previously won the ASNE Distinguished Writing Award in 1990 at the *St. Petersburg Times* where he was Miami bureau chief for three years. He began his career in his native Alabama, reporting for the Talladega *Daily Home, The Anniston Star,* and *Birmingham News.* At 17, he spent six months at Jacksonville State University, and he was a Nieman Fellow at Harvard University in 1992–1993. At *The New York Times,* he began on the metro desk in 1994 writing about the homeless, the poor, and, as he puts it, "the chronically weird," and he did a short tour in Haiti before moving to Atlanta for his current assignment. In addition to the 1995 ASNE award, Bragg's stories also won the Pulitzer Prize for feature writing.

Roaming the South, with a sidetrip to the horror of the Oklahoma City bombing, Bragg brings the story-

teller's art and craft to the news he covers. With an un-
erring eye for apt detail, an ear for the cadences and
metaphors of his native South, and the instinct of a
good street reporter, he introduces readers to people
and places that linger in the mind long after the paper
is folded.

Mardi Gras: Another battle of New Orleans

FEBRUARY 19, 1995

NEW ORLEANS, Feb. 18—The little shotgun house is peeling and the Oldsmobile in front is missing a rear bumper, but Larry Bannock can glimpse glory through the eye of his needle. For almost a year he has hunkered over his sewing table, joining beads, velvet, rhinestones, sequins, feathers and ostrich plumes into a Mardi Gras costume that is part African, part Native American.

"I'm pretty," said Mr. Bannock, who is 6 feet tall and weighs 300 pounds. "And baby, when I walk out that door there ain't nothing cheap on me."

Most days, this 46-year-old black man is a carpenter, welder and handyman, but on Mardi Gras morning he is a Big Chief, one of the celebrated—if incongruous—black Indians of Carnival. He is an important man.

Sometime around 11 a.m. on Feb. 28, Mr. Bannock will step from his house in a resplendent, flamboyant turquoise costume complete with a towering headdress, and people in the largely black and poor 16th and 17th Wards, the area known as Gert Town, will shout, cheer and follow him through the streets, dancing, drumming and singing.

"That's my glory," he said. Like the other Big Chiefs, he calls it his "mornin' glory."

He is one of the standard-bearers of a uniquely New Orleans tradition. The Big Chiefs dance, sing and stage mock battles—wars of words and rhymes—to honor American Indians who once gave sanctuary to escaped slaves. It is an intense but elegant posturing, a street theater that some black men devote a lifetime to.

But this ceremony is also self-affirmation, the way poor blacks in New Orleans honor their own culture in a Carnival season that might otherwise pass them by, said the Big Chiefs who carry on the tradition, and the academics who study it.

These Indians march mostly in neighborhoods where the tourists do not go, ride on the hoods of dented Chevrolets instead of floats, and face off on street corners where poverty and violence grip the people most of the rest of the year. The escape is temporary, but it is escape.

"They say Rex is ruler," said Mr. Bannock, referring to the honorary title given to the king of Carnival, often a celebrity, who will glide through crowds of tourists and local revelers astride an elaborate float. "But not in the 17th Ward. 'Cause I'm the king here. This is our thing.

"The drums will be beating and everybody will be hollering and"—he paused to stab the needle through a mosaic of beads and canvas—"and it sounds like all my people's walking straight through hell."

A man does not need an Oldsmobile, with or without a bumper, if he can walk on air. Lifted there by the spirit of his neighborhood, it is his duty to face down the other Big Chiefs, to cut them down with words instead of bullets and straight razors, the way the Indians used to settle their disagreements in Mardi Gras in the early 1900s. Mr. Bannock, shot in the thigh by a jealous old chief in 1981, appears to be the last to have been wounded in battle.

"I forgave him," Mr. Bannock said.

The tribes have names like the Yellow Pocahontas, White Eagles, the Golden Star Hunters and the Wild Magnolias. The Big Chiefs are not born, but work their way up through the ranks. Only the best sewers and singers become Big Chiefs.

By tradition, the chiefs must sew their own costumes, and must do a new costume from scratch each year. Mr. Bannock's fingers are scarred from a lifetime of it. His right index finger is a mass of old punctures. Some men cripple themselves, through puncture wounds or repetitive motion, and have to retire. The costumes can cost $5,000 or more, a lot of cash in Gert Town.

The rhythms of their celebration, despite their feathered headdresses, seem more West African or Haitian than Indian, and the words are from the bad streets of the Deep South. Mr. Bannock said that no matter what the ceremony's origins, it belongs to New Orleans now. The battle chants have made their way into popular New Orleans music. The costumes hang in museums.

"Maybe it don't make no sense, and it ain't worth anything," said Mr. Bannock. But one day a year he leads his neighborhood on a hard, forced march to respect, doing battle at every turn with other chiefs who are out trying to do the same.

Jimmy Ricks is a 34-year-old concrete finisher most of the year, but on Mardi Gras morning he is a Spy Boy, the man who goes out ahead of the Big Chief searching for other chiefs. He is in love with the tradition, he said, because of what it means to people here.

"It still amazes me," he said, how on Mardi Gras mornings the people from the neighborhood drift over to Mr. Bannock's little house on Edinburgh Street and wait for a handyman to lead them.

"To understand it, you got to let your heart wander," said Mr. Bannock, who leads the Golden Star Hunters. "All I got to do is peek through my needle."

I'm 52 inches across my chest
And I don't bow to nothin'
'Cept God and death

—from a battle chant by Larry Bannock

The more exclusive party within the party—the grand balls and societies that underlie the reeling, alcohol-soaked celebration that is Carnival—have always been By Invitation Only.

The origins of Carnival, which climaxes with Mardi Gras, or Fat Tuesday, are found in the Christian season of celebration before Lent. In New Orleans the celebration reaches back more than 150 years, to loosely organized parades in the 1830s. One of the oldest Carnival organizations, the Mystick Krewe of Comus, staged the first organized parade. Today, Mardi Gras is not one parade but several, including that of the traditional Zulus, a black organization. But Comus, on Fat Tuesday, is still king.

The krewes were—some still are—secret societies. The wealthier whites and Creoles, many of whom are descendants of people of color who were free generations before the Civil War, had balls and parades, while poorer black men and women cooked the food and parked the cars.

Mardi Gras had no other place for them, said Dr. Frederick Stielow, director of Tulane University's Amistad Research Center, the largest minority archive in the nation. And many of these poorer blacks still are not part of the party, he said.

"These are people who were systematically denigrated," said Dr. Stielow, who has studied the Mardi Gras Indians for years. So they made their own party, "a separate reality," he said, to the hard work, racism and stark poverty.

It might have been a Buffalo Bill Wild West Show that gave them the idea to dress as Indians, Dr. Stielow said, but either way the first "Indian Tribes" appeared in the late 1800s. They said they wore feathers as a show of affinity from one oppressed group to another, and to thank the Louisiana Indians for sanctuary in the slave days.

By the Great Depression these tribes, or "gangs" as they are now called, used Mardi Gras as an excuse to seek revenge on enemies and fought bloody battles, said the man who might be the biggest chief of all, 72-year-old Tootie Montana. He has been one for 46 years.

Mr. Bannock said, "They used to have a saying, 'Kiss your wife, hug your momma, sharpen your knife, and load your pistol.'"

Even after the violence faded into posturing, the New Orleans Police Department continued to break up the Indian gatherings. Mr. Bannock said New Orleans formally recognized the Indians' right to a tiny piece of Mardi Gras just two years ago.

Shoo fly, don't bother me
Shoo fly, don't bother me
If it wasn't for the warden and them lowdown
hounds
I'd be in New Orleans 'fore the sun go down

　　　　—Big Chief's battle chant, written by a
　　　　chief while in the state prison in Angola

They speak a language as mysterious as any white man's krewe.

In addition to Spy Boys, there are Flag Boys—the flag bearers—and Second Line, the people, sometimes numbering in the hundreds, who follow the chiefs from confrontation to confrontation.

They march—more of a dance, really—from Downtown, Uptown, even across the river in the poor black sections of Algiers—until the Big Chiefs meet at the corner of Claiborne and Orleans Avenues and, inside a madhouse circle of onlookers, lash each other with words. Sometimes people almost faint from the strain.

But it is mainly with the costume itself that a man does battle, said Mr. Montana. The breastplates are covered with intricate pictures of Indian scenes, painstakingly beaded by hand. The feathers are brilliant yellows, blues, reds and greens.

The winner is often "the prettiest," Mr. Montana said, and that is usually him.

"I am the oldest, I am the best, and I am the prettiest," he said.

A few are well-off businessmen, at least one has served time in prison, but most are people who sweat for a living, like him.

Some chiefs do not make their own costumes, but pay to have them made—what Mr. Bannock calls "Drugstore Indians." Of the 20 or so people who call themselves Big Chiefs, only a few remain true to tradition.

Mr. Bannock sits and sweats in his house, working day and night with his needle. He has never had time for a family. He lives for Fat Tuesday.

"I need my mornin' glory," he said.

A few years ago he had a heart attack, but did not have time to die. He had 40 yards of velvet to cut and sew.

Writers' Workshop

Talking Points

1) Rick Bragg is a Southerner whose beat is the South. Another Southern writer, novelist Eudora Welty, once observed that to know one place well is to know all places better. Discuss the various techniques that Bragg uses, including details, commentary, and history, to describe New Orleans.

2) Bragg's profile of Larry Bannock is more than a description of a man who has devoted much of his life to his yearly appearance as a Mardi Gras "Big Chief, one of the celebrated—if incongruous—black Indians of Carnival." It is an essay, Bragg's editor says, "on race and exclusion." Consider the passage in which he describes how blacks "march mostly in neighborhoods where the tourists do not go, ride on the hoods of dented Chevrolets instead of floats, and face off on street corners where poverty and violence grip the people most of the rest of the year." What are the celebrations that the news media in your community cover? Which ones merit a full story and photographs? Which ones are reported in a brief or get no coverage at all? Discuss the reasons behind such editorial decisions.

3) Other news outlets had covered the Mardi Gras chiefs before Rick Bragg. "The thing that was missing," he says, "was who these guys are." What is their motivation? Is getting dressed up and doing this fun or is there something deeper behind it? And there was something deeper: "It was the respect that they draw from the people in the neighborhood." As you read news stories written by yourself and others, consider how deeply they probe the reasons why people do things. Ask yourself if, in your own reporting, you are looking as hard as Rick Bragg does for motivations.

Assignment Desk

1) "Let place become a character in your story," advises Jeff Klinkenberg, a columnist for the *St. Petersburg Times*. On your next assignment, follow some of his suggestions to write more effectively about place: interview subjects in their natural habitat (their home or office instead of the newsroom or on the phone); find an expert who can identify

key landmarks for you, from buildings and trees to animals
and sounds; develop your eye by walking around your back
yard, looking around, closing your eyes, and recalling specific details.

2) Bragg says he is constantly searching for details that
"really register, that might make the reader say, 'OK, I can
see him now.'" In this story, a single image of Larry Bannock reveals a lifetime spent stitching elaborate Mardi Gras
costumes: "His right index finger is a mass of old punctures." During your next interview, search for a detail about
your subject (grease under a mechanic's fingernails, for instance) and use it in a single sentence.

In shock, loathing, denial: 'This doesn't happen here'

APRIL 20, 1995

OKLAHOMA CITY, April 19—Before the dust and the rage had a chance to settle, a chilly rain started to fall on the blasted-out wreck of what had once been an office building, and on the shoulders of the small army of police, firefighters and medical technicians that surrounded it.

They were not used to this, if anyone is. On any other day, they would have answered calls to kitchen fires, domestic disputes, or even a cat up a tree. Oklahoma City is still, in some ways, a small town, said the people who live here.

This morning, as the blast trembled the morning coffee in cups miles away, the outside world came crashing hard onto Oklahoma City.

"I just took part in a surgery where a little boy had part of his brain hanging out of his head," said Terry Jones, a medical technician, as he searched in his pocket for a cigarette. Behind him, firefighters picked carefully through the skeleton of the building, still searching for the living and the dead.

"You tell me," he said, "how can anyone have so little respect for human life."

The shock of what the rescuers found in the rubble had long since worn off, replaced with a loathing for the people who had planted the bomb that killed their friends, neighbors and children.

One by one they said the same thing: this does not happen here. It happens in countries so far away, so different, they might as well be on the dark side of the moon. It happens in New York. It happens in Europe.

It does not happen in a place where, debarking at the airport, passengers see a woman holding a sign that welcomes them to the Lieutenant Governor's annual turkey shoot.

It does not happen in a city that has a sign just outside the city limits, "Oklahoma City, Home of Vince Gill," the country singer.

"We're just a little old cowtown," said Bill Finn, a grime-covered firefighter who propped himself wearily up against a brick wall as the rain turned the dust to mud on his face. "You can't get no more Middle America than Oklahoma City. You don't have terrorism in Middle America."

But it did happen here, in such a loathsome way.

Whatever kind of bomb it was—a crater just outside the building suggests a car bomb—it was intended to murder on a grand scale: women, children, old people coming to complain about their Social Security checks.

The destruction was almost concave in nature, shattering the building from the center, almost front to back, the blast apparently weakening as it spread to both sides of the structure. Blood-stained glass littered the inside. So complete was the destruction that panels and signs from offices several stories up were shattered on the ground floor.

People could not stop looking at it, particularly the second floor, where a child care center had been.

"A whole floor," said Randy Woods, a firefighter with Engine No. 7. "A whole floor of innocents. Grown-ups, you know, they deserve a lot of the stuff they get. But why the children? What did the children ever do to anybody."

Everywhere observers looked, there were the discarded gloves, some blood-stained, of the medical workers.

There seemed to be very little whole inside the lower floors of the building, only pieces—pieces of desks, desktop computers and in one place what appeared to be the pieces of plastic toy animals, perhaps from the child care center, perhaps just some of those goofy little things grown-ups keep on their desks.

Much of it was covered in a fine powder, almost like ash, from the concrete that was not just broken, but blasted into dust. One firefighter said he picked through the big and small pieces almost afraid to move them, afraid of what he would find underneath. Here and there, in a droplet or a smear, was blood.

One woman, one of many trapped by rubble, had to have her leg amputated before she could be freed. Earlier in the morning, firefighters had heard voices drifting out from behind concrete and twisted metal, people they could hear but could not get to.

A few blocks away, Jason Likens, a medical technician, wondered aloud how anyone could have walked away unhurt. "I didn't expect to find anybody living," he said.

He was sickened by what he saw, but did not know who to hate.

"I would get mad, but I don't know who to get mad at," he said.

Next door, a group of grim-faced medical technicians, police and others gathered just outside the foyer of a church, not to pray, but to watch over the dead that had been temporarily laid inside in black body bags.

The stained-glass windows of the brick building had been partly blasted out, with a few scenes hanging in jagged pieces from the frames, but it was still the most peaceful place for blocks.

"I hope this opens people's eyes," Mr. Woods, the firefighter, said. What he meant was, it should show people everywhere that there really is no safe place.

A few blocks away, two elderly women slowly made their way up the street, their faces and clothes bloody.

They are retirees, living in an apartment building next door to the office building that was the target of the explosion. Phyllis Graham and Allene Craig had felt safe there. But this morning, as the glass went flying through their home, life changed forever.

"It all just came apart," Ms. Craig said. It was not clear if she meant her building, or something else.

Writers' Workshop

Talking Points

1) Study the opening paragraph of this story: "Before the dust and the rage had a chance to settle, a chilly rain started to fall on the blasted-out wreck of what had once been an office building, and on the shoulders of the small army of police, firefighters and medical technicians that surrounded it." Count the number of verbs and nouns and the number of syllables in each. What is the emotional impact of word choice that is so terse and vivid?

2) Notice how Bragg describes Oklahoma City as "...a place where, debarking at the airport, passengers see a woman holding a sign that welcomes them to the Lieutenant Governor's annual turkey shoot...a city that has a sign just outside the city limits, 'Oklahoma City, Home of Vince Gill....' " Discuss what these details convey about Oklahoma City. Do reporters run the risk of stereotyping a location by selecting single details to characterize people or places? How might such risks be avoided?

3) Writers on deadline must often work with incomplete information. Notice how Bragg deals with the as-yet unresolved question of how the federal building was destroyed: "Whatever kind of bomb it was—a crater just outside the building suggests a car bomb—it was intended to murder on a grand scale: women, children, old people coming to complain about their Social Security checks." Discuss the importance of his use of the word "suggests" and whether attribution, to an official perhaps, is necessary.

Assignment Desk

1) In *Feature and Magazine Article Writing,* Janet E. Ramsey describes color stories as those "that describe locations so clearly and precisely that those who read the descriptions feel as if they are there. Color stories are rich in the descriptions of physical things and rich in the description of atmosphere; they convey mood, as well as matter." Highlight every description in this story and catalog the moods they evoke.

2) Bragg had never been to Oklahoma City before the day of the bombing, yet he wrote with authority about its character. Visit a community that you've never seen before. Drive or walk around for a short time and then complete this sentence. "This is a place where...."

A killer's only confidant: The man who caught Susan Smith

AUGUST 4, 1995

UNION, S.C., July 31—The case of a lifetime is closed for Howard Wells. The reporters and the well-wishers have begun to drift away, leaving the Union County sheriff at peace. He will try to do a little fishing when the police radio is quiet, or just sit with his wife, Wanda, and talk of anything but the murderer Susan Smith.

It bothers him a little that he told a lie to catch her, but he can live with the way it all turned out. Mrs. Smith has been sentenced to life in prison.

Still, now and then his mind drifts back to nine days last autumn, and he thinks how it might have gone if he had been clumsy, if he had mishandled it. It leaves him a little cold.

For those nine days—from Mrs. Smith's drowning of her two little boys on Oct. 25 until she finally confessed on Nov. 3—he handled her like a piece of glass, afraid her brittle psyche would shatter and leave him with the jagged edges of a case that might go unsolved for weeks, months or forever.

"Susan was all we had," Sheriff Wells said, sitting in his living room the other day with a sweating glass of ice tea in his hand. If he had lost her to suicide, or to madness, because he had pushed too hard, there would have been nowhere else to turn. There had been no accomplices, no confidants, no paper trails.

The manhunt for the fictitious young black man she had accused of taking her children in a carjacking would have continued. The bodies of the boys would have continued to rest at the bottom of nearby John D. Long Lake, under 18 feet of water. The people of the county would have been left to wonder, blame and hate, divided by race and opinion over what truly happened the night she gave her babies to the lake.

Even if the car had been found, it would have yielded no proof, no clues, that everything had not happened just as she said, Mr. Wells continued. He would have been left not only with the unsolved crime but also with the burden of having driven a distraught and—for all anyone would know—innocent woman to suicide at the age of 23.

Mr. Wells says he has no doubt that he and other investigators walked a tightrope with Mrs. Smith's mental state and that as the inquiry closed around her, she planned to kill herself. For nine days she lived in a hell of her own making, surrounded by weeping, doting relatives she had betrayed in the worst way. "She had no one to turn to," he said.

So although he was her hunter, he also became the person she could lean on, rely on, trust. But unlike Mrs. Smith, he had no way of knowing that the boys were already dead, had no way of knowing that they were not locked in a car or a closet, freezing, starving.

Someday the Smith case will be in law-enforcement textbooks. The Federal Bureau of Investigation has already asked Mr. Wells to put down in writing the procedures he used in the case, as well as any useful anecdotes from it.

But the story of how he, with the help of others, was able to bring the investigation to a close in little more than a week begins not with anything he did but with who he is.

Mr. Wells, 43, is the antithesis of the redneck Southern sheriff. He has deer heads mounted on his wall but finished at the top of his class in the FBI Academy's training course. He collects guns but quotes Supreme Court decisions off the top of his head.

"I'm not a smart fellow," he said. But tell that to the people who work for him and around him, and they just roll their eyes. When the attention of the nation turned to Union in those nine days last fall, and in much of the nine months since, "we were lucky he was here," said Hugh Munn, a spokesman for the State Department of Law Enforcement.

People in the county say they like him because he is one of them. He knows what it feels like to work eight hours a day in the nerve-straining clatter and roar of the textile mills that dominate Union's economy: after high school, he worked blue-collar jobs until he was hired by the town's police force at the age of 23.

He went on to be a deputy in the county sheriff's department. Then, for several years, he stalked poachers and drug peddlers as an agent with the State Wildlife and Marine Resources Division.

When his brother-in-law quit as sheriff in 1992, Mr. Wells himself ran, as a 10-to-1 underdog. He promised not to operate under a good ol' boy system of favors gained and owed, and white voters and black voters liked his plain-spokenness and the fact that he was neither backslapper nor backscratcher.

He won, by just 10 votes.

His mother, Julia Mae, was then in the hospital dying of cancer. She had lain there unmoving for hours but opened her eyes when he walked in after the election.

"Who won?" she asked.

His father, John, has Lou Gehrig's disease, and every day Mr. Wells goes by to care for him. The sheriff went without sleep when the Susan Smith saga began on Oct. 25 but did not skip his visits to his father.

The Wellses have no children. Wanda suffered a miscarriage a few years ago, so they have become godparents to children of friends and neighbors. The Smith case pitted a man who wants children against a woman who threw hers away.

His investigation had to take two tracks. One, using hundreds of volunteers and a national crime computer web, operated on the theory that Mrs. Smith was telling the truth. The other, the one that would build a bond between a weeping mother and a doubting sheriff, focused on her.

Mr. Wells says Mrs. Smith never imagined, would never have believed, that the disappearance of her children would bring in the FBI, the state police, national news organizations. He thinks that when she concocted her story, she believed that the loss of the boys would pass like any other local crime.

Like other investigators, he was suspicious of her early on. As he talked to her only minutes after she had reported her children missing, he asked her whether the carjacker had done anything to her sexually. She smiled.

It would be months before the comprehensive history of her troubled life, of suicide attempts, sexual molestation, deep depression and affairs with married men, including her own stepfather, became known. But as bits and pieces of it fell from her lips during questioning, and as cracks appeared in her already unstable mental state, Mr. Wells began to realize that Mrs. Smith, and the case, could come apart in his hands.

He had to hold her together even as he and other investigators picked her story apart, had to coax and soothe and even pray beside her, until he sensed that the time was right to confront her and try to trick her into confessing.

And he had to shield her from others, who might push too hard. Once, on Oct. 27, a state agent accused her outright. She cursed loudly and stormed away.

After that, the people who had contact with her were limited. With the assistance of Pete Logan, a warm, grandfatherly former FBI agent now with the state police, Mr. Wells asked for her help in finding the boys, but did not accuse her.

The whole time, her family, her hometown and much of America were following her story, sharing her agony.

"She couldn't turn to her family, she couldn't ask for an attorney," said Mr. Wells. "She painted herself into a corner where no one could help her."

On Nov. 3, he told her, gently, that he knew she was lying, that by coincidence his own deputies had been undercover on a narcotics case at the same crossroad where she said her babies had been stolen, and at the same time, and that the officers had seen nothing. Actually there had been no such stakeout.

He prayed with her again, holding her hands, and she confessed. "I had a problem telling the lie," he said as his story unfolded in his living room the other day. "But if that's what it takes, I'd do it again."

After the confession was signed, as she sat slumped over in her chair, there was still one thing he had to know.

"Susan," he asked, "how would all this have played out?"

"I was going to write you a letter," she said, "and kill myself."

He feels sorry for her, and is disgusted by the men who used her and in their own ways contributed to the tragedy. But he is not surprised that a 23-year-old mill secretary could fool the whole nation, at least for a little while.

"Susan Smith is smart in every area," he said, "except life."

Writers' Workshop

Talking Points

1) Storytellers have "a talent for detail, image, drama, timing," Bragg says. Discuss how he weaves these elements throughout this retelling of how Sheriff Howard Wells persuaded Susan Smith to confess.

2) Bragg's portrait of Sheriff Wells begins with what Wells is not: "Mr. Wells, 43, is the antithesis of the redneck Southern sheriff." Analyze how he supports this statement with the next two sentences. Based on these details, discuss what qualities define the stereotype Bragg says his subject does not fit.

3) Spencer Klaw, a magazine writer and journalism teacher, preached that writers should use quotations only if they couldn't say it better than their subjects. In this profile of Howard Wells, Bragg quotes the sheriff just five times, and very briefly at that. Debate Klaw's "Law of Quotes."

Assignment Desk

1) Notice how, in the second paragraph, Bragg uses the device of foreshadowing—providing the reader with a hint of something to come later in the story—to heighten interest in his tale. Find the passage in the story where he delivers on the promise implicit in paragraph two.

2) "A good last sentence—or paragraph—is a joy in itself. It has its own virtues, which give the reader a lift and which linger when the article is over," William Zinsser says in *On Writing Well*. Bragg's haunting last line lends credence to Zinsser's claim that "a quotation often works best." Before you finish your next story, follow Zinsser's advice to "try to find in your notes some remark that has a sense of finality, or that's funny, or that adds an unexpected detail."

All she has, $150,000, is going to a university

AUGUST 13, 1995

HATTIESBURG, Miss., Aug. 10—Oseola McCarty spent a lifetime making other people look nice. Day after day, for most of her 87 years, she took in bundles of dirty clothes and made them clean and neat for parties she never attended, weddings to which she was never invited, graduations she never saw.

She had quit school in the sixth grade to go to work, never married, never had children and never learned to drive because there was never any place in particular she wanted to go. All she ever had was the work, which she saw as a blessing. Too many other black people in rural Mississippi did not have even that.

She spent almost nothing, living in her old family home, cutting the toes out of shoes if they did not fit right and binding her ragged Bible with Scotch tape to keep Corinthians from falling out. Over the decades, her pay—mostly dollar bills and change—grew to more than $150,000.

"More than I could ever use," Miss McCarty said the other day without a trace of self-pity. So she is giving her money away, to finance scholarships for black students at the University of Southern Mississippi here in her hometown, where tuition is $2,400 a year.

"I wanted to share my wealth with the children," said Miss McCarty, whose only real regret is that she never went back to school. "I never minded work, but I was always so busy, busy. Maybe I can make it so the children don't have to work like I did."

People in Hattiesburg call her donation the Gift. She made it, in part, in anticipation of her death.

As she sat in her warm, dark living room, she talked of that death matter-of-factly, the same way she talked about the possibility of an afternoon thundershower. To her, the Gift was a preparation, like closing the bedroom windows to keep the rain from blowing in on the bedspread.

"I know it won't be too many years before I pass on," she said, "and I just figured the money would do them a lot more good than it would me."

Her donation has piqued interest around the country. In a few short days, Oseola McCarty, the washer-woman, has risen from obscurity to a notice she does not understand. She sits in her little frame house, just blocks from the university, and patiently greets the reporters, business leaders and others who line up outside her door.

"I live where I want to live, and I live the way I want to live," she said. "I couldn't drive a car if I had one. I'm too old to go to college. So I planned to do this. I planned it myself."

It has been only three decades since the university integrated. "My race used to not get to go to that college," she said. "But now they can."

When asked why she had picked this university instead of a predominantly black institution, she said, "Because it's here; it's close."

While Miss McCarty does not want a building named for her or a statue in her honor, she would like one thing in return: to attend the graduation of a student who made it through college because of her gift. "I'd like to see it," she said.

Business leaders in Hattiesburg, 110 miles northeast of New Orleans, plan to match her $150,000, said Bill Pace, the executive director of the University of Southern Mississippi Foundation, which administers donations to the school.

"I've been in the business 24 years now, in private fund raising," Mr. Pace said. "And this is the first time I've experienced anything like this from an individual who simply was not affluent, did not have the resources and yet gave substantially. In fact, she gave almost everything she has.

"No one approached her from the university; she approached us. She's seen the poverty, the young people who have struggled, who need an education. She is the most unselfish individual I have ever met."

Although some details are still being worked out, the $300,000—Miss McCarty's money and the matching sum—will finance scholarships into the indefinite future. The only stipulation is that the beneficiaries be black and live in southern Mississippi.

The college has already awarded a $1,000 scholarship in Miss McCarty's name to an 18-year-old honors student from Hattiesburg, Stephanie Bullock.

Miss Bullock's grandmother, Ledrester Hayes, sat in Miss McCarty's tiny living room the other day and thanked her. Later, when Miss McCarty left the room, Mrs. Hayes shook her head in wonder.

"I thought she would be some little old rich lady with a fine car and a fine house and clothes," she said. "I was a seamstress myself, worked two jobs. I know what it's like to work like she did, and she gave it away."

The Oseola McCarty Scholarship Fund bears the name of a woman who bought her first air-conditioner just three years ago and even now turns it on only when company comes. Miss McCarty also does not mind that her tiny black-and-white television set gets only one channel, because she never watches anyway. She complains that her electricity bill is too high and says she never subscribed to a newspaper because it cost too much.

The pace of Miss McCarty's walks about the neighborhood is slowed now, and she misses more Sundays than she would like at Friendship Baptist Church. Arthritis has left her hands stiff and numb. For the first time in almost 80 years, her independence is threatened.

"Since I was a child, I've been working," washing the clothes of doctors, lawyers, teachers, police officers, she said. "But I can't do it no more. I can't work like I used to."

She is 5 feet tall and would weigh 100 pounds with rocks in her pockets. Her voice is so soft that it disappears in the squeak of the screen door and the hum of the air-conditioner.

She comes from a wide place in the road called Shubuta, Miss., a farming town outside Meridian, not far from the Alabama line. She quit school, she said, when the grandmother who reared her became ill and needed care.

"I would have gone back," she said, "but the people in my class had done gone on, and I was too big. I wanted to be with my class."

So she worked, and almost every dollar went into the bank. In time, all her immediate family died. "And I didn't have nobody," she said. "But I stayed busy."

She took a short vacation once, as a young woman, to Niagara Falls. The roar of the water scared her. "Seemed like the world was coming to an end," she said.

She stayed home, mostly, after that. She has lived alone since 1967.

Earlier this year her banker asked what she wanted done with her money when she passed on. She told him that she wanted to give it to the university, now rather than later; she set aside just enough to live on.

She says she does not want to depend on anyone after all these years, but she may have little choice. She has been informally adopted by the first young person whose life was changed by her gift.

As a young woman, Stephanie Bullock's mother wanted to go to the University of Southern Mississippi. But that was during the height of the integration battles, and, if she had tried, her father might have lost his job with the city.

It looked as if Stephanie's own dream of going to the university would also be snuffed out, for lack of money. Although she was president of her senior class in high school and had grades that were among the best there, she fell just short of getting an academic scholarship. Miss Bullock said her family earned too much money to qualify for most Federal grants but not enough to send her to the university.

Then, last week, she learned that the university was giving her $1,000, in Miss McCarty's name. "It was a total miracle," she said, "and an honor."

She visited Miss McCarty to thank her personally and told her that she planned to "adopt" her. Now she visits regularly, offering to drive Miss McCarty around and filling a space in the tiny woman's home that has been empty for decades.

She feels a little pressure, she concedes, not to fail the woman who helped her. "I was thinking how amazing it was that she made all that money doing laundry," said Miss Bullock, who plans to major in business.

She counts on Miss McCarty's being there four years from now, when she graduates.

Writers' Workshop

Talking Points

1) Rick Bragg believes his job as a national correspondent for *The New York Times* is to "paint Oseola McCarty as vividly as is true and let the readers make up their minds about what to think about her." Study how he uses details, quotations, and other voices to create this unforgettable portrait.

2) Good reporters listen for what they're *not* hearing as well as the sounds they can recognize: "Her voice is so soft that it disappears in the squeak of the screen door and the hum of the air-conditioner." What is the effect of such a sentence? How can you train yourself to hear what's *not* being said?

3) The writer waits until the fourth paragraph to deliver the news: "So she is giving her money away, to finance scholarships for black students at the University of Southern Mississippi here in her hometown..." His story, however, begins with the very first line: "Oseola McCarty spent a lifetime making other people look nice." What is the effect of such organization? Discuss other approaches Bragg could have used and debate the relative merits of each.

Assignment Desk

1) "Local heroes always make a good story," Bragg argues. Find a local hero and write his or her story.

2) Empathy is one of the most powerful emotions a writer brings to the task of capturing other people's lives. Rick Bragg's mother "took in ironing for a living." To write the story of Oseola McCarty, Bragg says he drew on his own personal experiences to bring a dimension of insight to the piece. Look for yourself in the lives of the people you are reporting about. Did the councilwoman you cover play field hockey like you did in school? When you go to interview the family of an accident victim, try to recall the grief you felt when a relative died.

3) Bragg relies on sensory details to convey mood and atmosphere, especially the sense of touch that he uses to con-

vey the weather. Find examples in this and his other stories. Add sense of touch to your reporting repertoire. What is the weather like at the parade you're covering? Remember Bragg's advice: "Just keep your eyes open, soak in how something smells or tastes or sounds."

Where Alabama inmates fade into old age

NOVEMBER 1, 1995

HAMILTON, Ala.—Grant Cooper knows he lives in prison, but there are days when he cannot remember why. His crimes flit in and out of his memory like flies through a hole in a screen door, so that sometimes his mind and conscience are blank and clean.

He used to be a drinker and a drifter who had no control over his rage. In 1978, in an argument with a man in a bread line at the Forgotten Man Ministry in Birmingham, Ala., his hand automatically slid into his pants pocket for a knife.

He cut the man so quick and deep that he died before his body slipped to the floor. Mr. Cooper had killed before, in 1936 and in 1954, so the judge gave him life. Back then, before he needed help to go to the bathroom, Mr. Cooper was a dangerous man.

Now he is 77, and since his stroke in 1993 he mostly just lies in his narrow bunk at the Hamilton Prison for the Aged and Infirm, a blue blanket hiding the tubes that run out of his bony body. Sometimes the other inmates put him in a wheelchair and park him in the sun.

"I'm lost," he mumbled. "I'm just lost."

He is a relic of his violent past, but Mr. Cooper, and the special prison that holds him, may represent the future of corrections in a time when judges and other politicians are offering longer, "true-time" sentences, like life without parole, as a way to protect the public from crime.

This small 200-bed prison in the pine-shrouded hills of northwestern Alabama near the Mississippi line is one of only a few in the nation specializing in aged and disabled inmates, but that is expected to change as prison populations turn gradually gray.

While the proportion of older prisoners has risen only slightly in recent years, their numbers have jumped substantially. In 1989, the nation's prisons held 30,500 inmates 50 or older; by 1993, that number had risen to almost 50,500, according to the American Civil Liberties Union's National Prison Project.

But experts say the major increases are still to come.

"Three-strikes" sentencing for habitual offenders and new laws that require inmates to serve all or most of their sentences, instead of just a fraction, will mean "an aging phenomenon" in American prisons, said James Austin, the executive vice president of the National Council on Crime and Delinquency in San Francisco.

"There are going to be huge geriatric wards," said Jenni Gainsborough, a lawyer with the National Prison Project.

The older inmates will fill beds needed for younger criminals who are more of a threat, said Burl Cain, warden at the Angola State Penitentiary in Louisiana, the nation's largest maximum-security prison. "We need our prison beds for the predators who are murdering people today," he said.

Locked away for good, inmates will need special medical care and will have to be housed inside separate cellblocks, or separate prisons like Hamilton, to protect them from younger, stronger predators, said W. C. Berry, the warden at Hamilton.

"What else can we do with them?" he said.

ONCE DANGEROUS, NOW HELPLESS

One Hamilton inmate, Thomas Gurley, has Huntington's disease. He sits in a chair all day and shakes and stares. He was a kidnapper, but now he has trouble holding a spoon.

It may seem cruel to lock a man away and watch him slowly die, Mr. Berry said, but most of the men in his care could not survive in the general population. Some are missing legs, some have misplaced their minds, some are just too old. They have heart, kidney or liver failure and need machines to stay alive.

Some victims' rights groups see the slow death of these men as poetic justice, and say they should take their chances in the general population, to see what it is like to live in fear. But Mr. Berry, who built a reputation as a no-nonsense police detective before coming here, has seen what men do to each other in prison. Inmates who are getting old write him letters and beg to transfer to his prison, which has been in operation since Federal lawsuits in the 1970s obliged the state to separate its weaker inmates.

"They sort of look out for each other here," he said. The inmates who can work strip beds and help clean up after the old, most helpless ones. When Mr. Gurley slips from his chair to the floor, other inmates lift him back in.

There are prison breaks, but the escapees do not usually get far. Two inmates, one blind, one mostly blind and unable to breathe on his own, made it as far as the town hospital. It is across the street.

"We had another one get out, and we found him at the end of the runway of the local airport," Warden Berry said. "He couldn't breathe that well. I told him that if he hadn't had to stop every fourth landing light to take a breath, he might have made it."

Mr. Cooper travels only in his mind. "I don't know if they'll ever set me free," he said, looking up from his bed, a pair of black-framed glasses sitting crooked on his face. "I don't know. I don't reckon so."

Some days, if he forgets enough, he already is.

LIFE AT THE END OF THE WHISKEY RIVER

All Jessie Hatcher's life, the devil in him would come swimming out every time a drink of whiskey trickled in.

"It was 1979, down in Pike County," he said, looking down some dusty road in his memory for the life he took. "Me and this boy was drinking. He thought I had some money, but I didn't have none. We took to fighting, and I killed him. Quinn. His name was Quinn. Killed him with a .32. I was bad to drink back then. I never drunk another drop."

Like Grant Cooper, he has a life history of violence. He shot a woman several times with a .22 rifle in 1978, but she lived and he served less than a year. He was drunk then. The murder of the man in Pike County sent him away for life.

He is 76 now and limps on a cane because of a broken leg that never healed right. He works all day in the flower garden, where he has raked the dirt so smooth you can roll marbles on it.

"My favorites are the saucer sunflowers," he said, "because they're so beautiful."

The young man, the one whose life was washed away on a river of whiskey, seems to have vanished inside this wizened little man on his knees in the mud, plucking weeds and humming spirituals.

"They could take the fences down and I wouldn't run," he said. "This is the right place for me.

"Lock me down in one of them other prisons, and I'd drop like a top," he said, referring to the practice in general prisons of locking aged or infirm inmates in cells to protect them.

HOW TO BEST USE PRECIOUS CELL SPACE?

The State of Alabama, often accused of taking prison reform in the wrong direction with its return to leg irons and breaking rocks, is part of a more progressive trend with Hamilton, said Ms. Gainsborough of the civil liberties union.

But while the prison is hailed as a humane answer, the practice of keeping old inmates until death is wasting crucial space, said Mr. Cain, the Angola warden.

"There comes a time when a man goes through what we call criminal menopause and he is unable to do the crime that he is here for," Mr. Cain said. "My prison is becoming an old folks' home."

He sees nothing wrong with letting an old killer die free after prison has taken most of his life from him. As politicians shout for life sentences, he watches helplessly as Angola, with 3,000 inmates doing life, fills beyond capacity.

"When the criminal is not able to commit that crime again, it's time to put someone in there who is killing now," said Mr. Cain, who keeps older inmates in a special ward. "As Jesus Christ said, 'Let the dead bury the dead.' We don't have room."

For some inmates at Hamilton, keeping them locked away for life is the only alternative. Jason Riley, 41, has been partially blind since a car hit him when he was 3. He killed two women by stabbing and strangling them, then cut his own arms to watch himself bleed. He has said he would kill again.

"I'll probably die here," said Mr. Riley, who carries a magnifying glass in his pocket to see with. One of his gray eyes looms huge behind it as he gazes at you. "I accept that, accepted it several years ago. Life would be easier for some of the other inmates if they would accept it, too."

THE REPERCUSSIONS OF A POLITICAL TREND

Sentences, especially life sentences, used to be like rubber bands. They stretched or snapped short depending on the inmate's record in prison, crowding and, sometimes, whether the inmate could convince the parole board that he had found the Lord. Inmates like the 76-year-old Mr. Hatcher could usually walk after 20 years, even with a murder conviction. But that was before it became popular for politicians to run on pro-death-penalty, throw-away-the-key platforms.

"I'd like to be free," Mr. Hatcher said, "for a little while."

He has a feeling he will be, he said, and winks, as if some higher power has whispered in his ear that this will happen.

Warden Berry, standing beside him, looks away. It is common for a man doing life without parole to have that feeling, even though he knows chances are he will leave on a hospital gurney, or with a blanket over his head.

"They think, 'I just want a few years at the end of my life, free,'" he said. "You'll see them, men in their 70s, suddenly start walking around out in the prison yard, trying to take care of themselves, to save themselves for it.

"And some we have who wake up in the middle of the night in a cold sweat, because the thought of going out terrifies them."

They know they have lived so long inside that everything they knew or loved outside will be gone, he said. So when they walk out the door, they will be completely alone.

The Birmingham jail was full of martyrs and heroes in the 1960s. The Rev. Dr. Martin Luther King Jr. made history locked behind its walls.

William (Tex) Johnson, who snatched $24 from a man's hand and got caught, was in fancy company. But as the civil rights heroes rejoined their struggle, a white judge gave him 50 years.

He escaped three times. "You can't give no 21-year-old boy 50 years; I had to run," he said. While he was out, he committed 38 more crimes. Now he is at Hamilton, finishing his sentence. He will be released in 1998, but two strokes have left him mostly dead on one side. "I believe I can make it," he said. "I believe I can."

There will be nothing on the outside for him. Warden Berry said that when an inmate reached a certain point, it might be more humane to keep him in prison. Wives die, children stop coming to visit.

"We bury most of them ourselves" on state land, he said. The undertaking and embalming class at nearby Jefferson State University prepares the bodies for burial for free, for the experience.

"They make 'em up real nice," the warden said.

Writers' Workshop

Talking Points

1) In *The American Conversation and the Language of Journalism,* Roy Peter Clark celebrates what scholars of writing call "right-branching sentences," those that begin with a subject and verb, followed by other subordinate elements. In his stories, Rick Bragg relies on this form to deliver information and convey emotion. Notice the lead of this story: "Grant Cooper knows he lives in prison, but there are days when he cannot remember why. His crimes flit in and out of his memory likes flies through a hole in a screen door, so that sometimes his mind and conscience are blank and clean." Discuss why this form is so effective for the reader and the writer.

2) Like sunlight through a magnifying glass, the focus of a story concentrates the power of a story. What the story is about determines everything from the lead to the ending. As succinctly as possible, summarize the point of this story. Then study how Bragg's lead and ending are determined by its focus.

3) Bragg doesn't outline his stories, but he does preach the value of the "five boxes" method of story organization. The first box, the lead, contains the image or detail that draws people into the story. The second box is a "nut graph" that sums up the story. The third box begins with a new image or detail that resembles a lead and precedes the bulk of the narrative. The fourth box contains material that is less compelling but rounds out the story. The fifth, and last, box is the "kicker," an ending featuring a strong quote or image that leaves the reader with a strong emotion. Study how this and his other stories follow this organizational scheme.

Assignment Desk

1) Focusing your story is the most important task you face as a reporter and writer. Every time you read or write a story, ask yourself two questions: "What's the news? What's the story?"

2) The clearer you are about your story's focus, the better off you will be when it comes time to report, plan, organize,

draft, and revise. Try to summarize every story you work on in six words. Avoid stock phrases ("Boy Saves Girl, Hit by Train"). Strive for poetry ("Lost, Then Found, on the Tracks").

3) The next time you're stuck on a story, employ the "five boxes" method of story organization. Don't feel bound to stick with it. "Even if you just completely scramble it later on," Bragg says, "at least it got you rolling."

A conversation with
Rick Bragg

CHRISTOPHER SCANLAN: You won this award in 1990. Are there new things you've learned about writing since then?

RICK BRAGG: One thing I learned from Bill Kovach at Harvard during my Nieman year. One day, we were sitting in his office and he pushed a postcard across the desk at me. I'm not up on my classical painters, but it was a beautiful landscape. It was very stark. He asked me, "What's pretty about this?" Kovach is from east Tennessee, so it came out, "What's purty about this?" He and I speak the same language in that way. I said, "Well, it's not so much what's in it, but what's *not* in it." I don't remember exactly what he said, but it was the equivalent of, "Bingo."

He had been saying for a long time I should pull back just a little—in other words, I was overwriting.

Instead of having three good phrases in a paragraph or a section, one really good line is enough. He wasn't saying I should leave out any of the detail or the images. He was just saying I don't need to be fancy in every line and that the details and the images and the color can often be very simple things. He said it was the football equivalent of "piling on" sometimes in my stories. He was right about that. And I think what I've tried to do is to just not pile on as much as I used to. I think it's helped me a lot.

How do you keep from "piling on"?

In the first paragraph of a story, you want to have a good strong image, a good strong detail, but you don't necessarily want another one in the sentence next to it. You want a rhythm or a cadence. It's almost like having your iced tea too sweet. I've learned not to put that extra tablespoonful of sugar in there.

In the story about the prisoners...

"Grant Cooper knows he lives in prison, but there are days when he cannot remember why. His crimes flit in and out of his memory like flies through a hole in a screen door, so that sometimes his mind and conscience are blank and clean."

The combination of those two sentences: one is very simple, the other one isn't fancy, but I thought it really captured the way his mind drifted. The scenes and the images in his prison room were full of evocative details and I was tempted to just...

Pile on.

Exactly, and it was really hard. I left out a couple of pretty lines, but I thought that the simple image of the flies on the screen door was about as much as anybody would want.

It was also one of those very Southern images where I think anyone who's ever seen a screen door would know what I was talking about. But it was also clear enough that even people in Secaucus could figure it out.

Usually, I think it's done sort of pre-emptively. I don't fill it up full of color, detail, and then go through and strip it out. I make the decision paragraph by paragraph as I go.

How do you make a story come to life?

God knows, we've got a hard enough job sometimes just getting the names spelled right. I think we sometimes forget that we can convey quickly and effectively the notion, the idea of the story, without having to get six college professors to tell us how to think.

I tell people to always be looking. I know that sounds a little absurd, but you just keep your eyes open, soak in how something smells or tastes or sounds.

Or the fact that the Oldsmobile in front of his house is missing a rear bumper.

You have to go into the story with your eyes open, looking into the corners. If there's a car parked in front of the house, you've got to know what it looks like.

Oftentimes, you can read a person's whole economic story, their loves and their dislikes, by what they've got parked in their driveway. Cars are not just a conveyance. They're part of our character and our personality. So is the music that's playing when you walk in the door, or the show on the television, or the paintings on the wall, or the clothes a person wears. You have to be making these notes. They're not necessarily something you write down in your notebook; they're things that you catalog in your head.

I'm talking about things that register, really register, that might make the reader say, "OK, I can see him now," or, "I can see her now."

"The little shotgun house is peeling and the Oldsmobile in front is missing a rear bumper, but Larry Bannock can glimpse glory through the eye of his needle. For almost a year, he has hunkered over his sewing table, joining beads, velvet, rhinestones, sequins, feathers and ostrich plumes into a Mardi Gras costume that is part African, part Native American."

That's a perfect example of leaving something out. The original lead I'd written had been exactly the same, except that it was, "...part African-American, part Native American, and part Liberace," because it is so glittery. When I went back and looked at that, I thought, "No, this cheapens it," you know, "This is a gimmick here."

How long did you spend on this story?

A couple of evenings with him, a day writing. I wrote it overnight.

But you went back more than one time to him?

Oh, yeah. You always find something new the second time.

He also informed me that you did not come and visit the big chief unless you bring a present. And I told him it is customary in our profession not to be bearing gifts to our interview subjects; it is unethical.

And he said, "Well, I don't know about ethics, but I know about New Orleans and if you're going to come visit me, you'd better bring some root beer." (They make great root beer down in New Orleans called Barq's.)

So I did, and in return, instead of just giving me the obligatory interview, he sang for me. He has a very soft voice with a little bit of a lisp, but when he sings, it gets deep and strong, and I just truly enjoyed being with him.

I do a lot of bad news, I do a lot of stories with people in trouble. But this was just a very fun time. The bottom line is that local heroes always make a good story.

How does a story like this take shape? At the keyboard? In the shower? Do you outline? Tell me about how you write.

I've never outlined anything in my life. But I do have a good plan for outlining that I sometimes share with young reporters who kind of get stuck on a story.

I just draw five boxes in the air and say, "OK, in the first box, you're going to have your lead, the image, the detail that you want to draw people into the story by using. It can be as many paragraphs as you want it to be. In the second box, you're going to have your nut graph. An editor at the *Birmingham News* used to call it the "bring on the bears graph," which is just to sum it all up for you.

The third box is the beginning of the retelling of the story, almost a second lead. And this will work in a story that's 15 inches or 50 inches long, but the third box would be almost a new lead, a new detail, a good, strong, solid image that will draw you into the bulk or the meat of the story. This is not an inverted pyramid. You may have some numbers in there, if it's that kind of story. This is where you put the best, the good, strong stuff.

In the fourth box, you put stuff that is less compelling, but still rounds out the story, makes it a complete piece. And then the fifth one is the kicker. I'm a strong believer that you can't have a decent story if it doesn't leave you with a strong feeling or sense or image.

On long pieces, you can use the boxes as a way of a chronology, you know. Pat Farnan, a city editor at the *St. Petersburg Times,* told me that once when I was kind of stuck. If you just sketch out five rough boxes, even if the items within them change or merge, it's still got you thinking about the progression of the story. And even if you just completely scramble it later on, at least it got you rolling and getting stuff down.

In the Mardi Gras story, the fourth box is where Dr. Frederick Stielow comes in.

Larry Bannock is the most important part of this, and I wanted to give people a good, strong, rounded image of him. But I also needed some historical perspective. The best stories are the stories in which you don't necessarily need that kind of backup, but I think in this story, you needed an idea of who these folks were and where they came from.

Tell me about writing the Oklahoma City story.

I was in the Atlanta bureau and the phone rang and it was our deputy national editor, Bill Schmidt. And he said, "There's a flight leaving Atlanta in one hour. Can you be on it?" And of course, you know, the answer is, "Certainly." We knew about the bombing at that point, but had just found out. I don't think anyone really knew the magnitude of it, I don't think anyone really understood how many people were dead. I don't think we knew the horror of it yet, but we knew it was bad.

So I got lucky and I caught the flight literally running to the gate, got on it, rented a car, the last car there, and drove as fast as I could, breaking the law to get to the scene. I was lucky in that I got there before they were able to seal off everything. And they had already pushed the reporters outside of the cordoned off area, but it was a loose area.

I had left Atlanta wearing a pair of jeans and a pair of work boots and just a T-shirt. That's what I wear if I know I'm going to get dirty doing a story. It just makes common sense not to wear a necktie and a pair of penny loafers. Some editors may disagree with this;

they want their reporters to look like reporters. Well, sometimes you look like whatever you look like. And this time I think it helped me because instead of 45 cops grabbing me and pushing me away, I just walked right in. I didn't sneak in, I didn't represent myself as anything. I just walked in.

I walked through the cordoned off area and around to the back of the building where obviously, it was shaky, but it was still more or less intact, at least the facade was. The windows were blown out and I walked right in.

I did not stay long, but I just wanted to see the inside of the building. That's my job, you know, my job is to report it. I had my notebook in my hand. If anyone had challenged me, I would have turned around and walked out. This is not something, as a human being, you want to be part of. I've never developed that voyeuristic side. I didn't want to see pieces of children in there and fortunately I didn't. But I saw some blood, I saw some toys on the floor, because apparently this was part of the level that the nursery had been on. They were still trying to get people out. I was determined to not be in the way, so I looked hard and tried to register as much as I could, and then I had to get out. I didn't want to be in the way.

All the way through I had talked to people. These were not the kind of interviews where you're going to be able to develop a character. You just had to grab someone's words almost on the run. And the firemen I talked to were just absolutely exhausted, leaning against a brick wall. The medical worker I talked to was smoking a cigarette, trying to keep it lit in the rain and, as they were seeing this horror, they didn't lose their humanity. One fella, he looked a lot tireder than anybody there, came over and gave me a yellow slicker so I wouldn't get wet. I helped tote a little coffee urn, because this guy needed help toting it.

A reporter at *The New York Times* had a very good point. He said that if you cannot feel in the story, then you shouldn't be writing about it. That's kind of contrary to what a lot of us were taught when we were real young, to keep an aloof distance. But you have to feel it.

What was your deadline?

The story was planned to be a little inside piece. I don't want to call it a color piece, but it was designed to just give a personal glimpse of the people involved. I called the national desk and they told me I had about an hour to write. And then, of course, my computer crashed as I turned it on and I wasted 15 minutes just trying to get it back up, and I had about 45 minutes' writing time.

You don't really have time to think. That's when it's good that you're 36, instead of 26. If I had been 26, I'm sure I would have wasted 30 minutes staring at the computer screen, not knowing what to do. But I knew I couldn't waste time being fancy on the lead. It just came to me that as the rain fell, people were still enraged. And that was my lead, that the rain started to fall even before the dust and the rage had settled.

On a story that was less important than this one, that might have been a little excessive, but it was absolutely true. I knew that I was only going to be able to weave at the most four or five people into it, which simplified it for me. Only having 45 minutes or so to write was a damned fine way to get you to think in a linear way. I knew that the two firemen were important because they backed up the premise, which is that any other day, these people would have been answering the grease fires, helping a guy who slipped on the sidewalk, even getting cats out of a tree.

Had you ever been to Oklahoma City before?

No, as a matter of fact, the heartland is probably the part of the country I know least about. But I knew some things. I knew that if you see a woman holding a sign that says, "Welcome to the Lieutenant Governor's Turkey Shoot," then you are probably not on Staten Island. I knew that if you see a big sign proclaiming proudly that this is the home of Vince Gill, you know this is a real place, this is a place very similar to the cities that I knew well: Birmingham, Montgomery, cities in my state where I grew up. And it was.

When I was talking about keeping your eyes open, I knew that I wouldn't have time to call the Chamber of Commerce and find out what kind of town Oklahoma City was, so I had to go with common sense.

I didn't really have any plan in my head as I did the interviews. I was just trying to get as much information in my notebook and in my mind as I could and then run back to the hotel to write, and that's what I did.

And when I got back and sat down, you do what is most obvious, you write what is most obvious because those are the things that are going to come to your mind the quickest. And fortunately, those things were compelling, too.

It took about an hour probably from the time I filed it until I heard back from them that I had written it onto Page One.

One thing that puzzled me a bit is, I've been doing this a long time. I've been a full-time reporter since I was 18 years old. But for some reason, I couldn't get it all out of my notebook. Some of what I saw inside that building was so horrible that, rushed the way I was, I might have made it blander than it was.

I think this really had more to do with the fact that it was personal. It hurt me to look into that building.

A reporter I knew once said that the greatest compliment to a reporter is if you sit there and blood pops out on your forehead and you strain and strain and strain and you kind of just sandblast it together, and then the next day, you go back and you can't really see the seams. That's a great compliment.

I've never met anybody who really, really loved this business who looked at something and said, "Boy, I kicked that in the ass." I think they always are saying, "Well, I didn't get that right," or, "I didn't get this smooth enough," or, "I didn't spend enough time," or, "If I had spent another hour, I could have gotten it," that kind of thing.

What's the value of what you're doing?

I think the only real depth left in this country in news is in newspapers and maybe a handful of the news magazines, although I think even some of them have gone to...you know that old phrase, "Give people what they want."

Well, sometimes you don't do that; by God, sometimes you give them what they need. If you gave people what they wanted every time somebody went to the dentist, they'd be told their mouth looked fine. If you gave people what they wanted, instead of what they needed, hell, we'd all be eating peach ice cream and sitting around singing "Kumbaya." You can't do that; sometimes you've got to give people what they need. And those decisions are made by smart people who work for newspapers.

In Oklahoma City, we knew that we could not give them too much depth, too much detail. Over days, we did that. We put a human face on it. We explained the thing.

People can run around carping about how print is dead all they want to. I do know this, that you log onto the Internet for information, and certainly you can read every story in every newspaper on a screen. I call it reading on the light bulb. And that's fine, except that I believe whether you're reading it on a light bulb or whether you're reading it in your hands sitting on your couch with your feet propped up or at your breakfast table, you're reading. You're not just soaking up information, but you are reading. There's a difference.

And newspapers have to continue to change and I think they are changing. You look at *The New York Times*. Joe Lelyveld and Gene Roberts have put a huge premium on writing. They want the paper to be one of voices. And I think it is. I think they have gotten some real good people there who can tell a great story, not just explain the world, but can tell it the way a story-teller tells a story.

How does a storyteller tell a story?

A storyteller has a talent for detail, image, drama—not melodrama, that's false drama—but a talent for timing. A storyteller is exactly like a painter, there's absolutely no difference. You know, I learned how to tell a story by watching the men in my family sit on the front porch. And these are men that never read a book in their whole life, but they sat on the front porch and told long, beautiful stories with drama and danger and great detail. And I think that blessed me in some ways. I knew how to tell a story long before I ever sat down to write one.

What was the story behind "A Killer's Only Confidant"?

I was sent to Union thinking that we would only hit the high spots. We would only do the curtain-raiser story and then we would do the opening arguments and then the closing arguments and both jury phases of the trial.

But it turned out to be the kind of story that you could not leave, because every day was just a fascinating turn.

Sheriff Howard Wells—when you talk about people that are almost too good to be true, well, he's one of them. Here was a smart man, completely unassuming, who was just trying to do the right thing, given an impossible job. He could not win, no matter what he did. Babies were still dead; he could not save them. He had to try to catch the killer and keep her from destroying herself.

During the trial, you know how the reporters are, we're often a godless back slapping, back stabbing horde, and the people of Union had never seen this before. They obviously got a big taste of it when the children were missing. They saw reporters, as we are wont to do, grinning and joking, not out loud necessarily and disrupting the courtroom, but, you know, we're doing our work.

I've always kind of treated courtrooms a little bit like church. Maybe it's because I'm afraid of winding up in one one day, but I was quieter I think. I talked, but I didn't act "a fool," as my grandma used to say. And Howard Wells was watching, as it turned out. He had been besieged by reporters and he sat in the courtroom every day in one of those auxiliary little jury boxes and watched. He actually contacted me through a third party and said, "I've been watching you in the courtroom. You seem to be respectful of what is going on. When this is all over, I'd like to talk to you." I guess I got the story because I was well mannered.

So I went back and I interviewed him the Sunday before I left town and just went and sat in his living room and listened to him talk. I watched his kind of quiet intelligence; he showed me his gun collection. Then, as I said in the story, then he'd pop off a

Supreme Court decision off the top of his head. And I knew that this was a complicated and smart man, obviously a caring man because of his devotion to his father. The fact that even as all this was going on, he went without sleep rather than go without seeing his father, who was very sick at the time, still is.

I've never been a wallflower, but I do think there are times when life and death are being weighed in front of you, you ought not to be laughing out loud.

Every now and then, it helps to talk like you just fell off a turnip truck, you know. I have a Southern accent, a profound one, and I think sometimes it helps me, I think that people are not afraid of me the way they are of some reporters. There's something maybe almost reassuring about it, and I think this might have been one of those times.

I once had this young woman from Indiana tell me, "Well, that's fine for you to talk about your voice and all that. But I grew up in Indiana next to a Kmart, so where's my voice?" And I said, "Everybody's got a voice; everyone has a distinct writing voice," and my reporting techniques are just part of that, just part of who you are. You know, you use what works for you.

I will not play dumb to get a story. Of course, the blessing is that I don't have to play dumb. Most people just figure I am. That's fine, too.

What's your aim for this story?

I wanted this story to be the long breath after the excitement. The lead was almost entirely different from what I usually do. The lead was designed to get the reader to think, take a deep breath, sit back with Howard Wells, and just listen.

Where did you write the story?

We rented the second floor of a machine shop from a fella named Gus. In Union, South Carolina, it was the only real lodging we could find because all the hotel rooms were taken and many of the houses were rented, so we didn't have much choice. We rented a second floor of a machine shop that had yellow and green and brown speckled shag carpeting and yellow naugahyde couches. I loved it. It had a good air-conditioner that worked most of the time and it had a phone and outlets and a refrigerator. I lived on Kentucky Fried Chicken and Dr Pepper for about two weeks.

I didn't realize the life of a national correspondent was so...

Glamorous? Hell, sometimes we even have Ding Dongs. The ants were bad; they'd come in and eat anything you left out.

What role does an editor play in your stories?

They have saved me a whole lot more times than they have hurt me, let me put it that way.

How have they saved you?

You do something stupid in there. You're sitting there, worn out from the plane ride, and you file your story at 3 a.m. and the calendar says it's Friday, but you've got it in your head it's Tuesday. And most of the time, they have saved me from myself.

How long have you been at the *Times?*

I've been there over two years. I started out as a metro reporter, a general assignment reporter. I didn't have a beat. I was just told by the metro editor, Michael Oreskes, that I should go out and find the best damned stories I could find.

I think the best stories in any newspaper are the ones that deal with life and death. Sometimes that might not necessarily be killing. A paper I worked at when I was a young man, called the *Anniston Star,* used to have a little note on it that said it's a newspaper's responsibility to be an attorney for the weakest of its readership. I've always believed that's true.

I think the most important stories in the paper are the ones that involve people who are being victimized by life itself, by circumstances, not necessarily by other people. I've always thought the best stories in any newspaper were about people in trouble.

Are there writers who have shaped you, made you the writer you are?

Robert Penn Warren or Tennessee Williams. I admit I've read a lot of Faulkner and in between the kind of fatness of his phrases are some remarkable words, beautiful, beautiful phrases.

Obviously you cannot steal their lines because that's plagiarism. It doesn't matter if they've been dead 30 years; you're still stealing from them. But you soak up the rhythms and the flavors of it. Just like eating good food. You remember the taste.

I like your use of detail. It's not just a "...man at a bread line," it's a "...man at a bread line at the Forgotten Man Ministry in Birmingham, Alabama."

That's the difference between writing and just typing words in. In another story, the fella drove home on the expressway. I could have used the number of the expressway, but it turned out to be the Ronald Reagan Expressway. And here's a laid-off guy driving a Mercedes with a slipping transmission. Reagan has come to stand in many ways for this failed dream of the '80s, and what a great image. It just added a little something to the story.

Let's be honest here. One of the reasons that the details and the images are so rich is because I write about things that are rich. You know, I'm truly blessed that way, in that most of what I write, most of what I've written in my whole life were not boardrooms or city council chambers, but stories that had to do with living and dying and suffering. I lived in Miami for three years. How can you not write great stories about Miami? I've walked through welfare hotels in Manhattan. I've always been able to go to the places where the stories were the darkest and the richest.

Where are they the darkest and the richest?

They're always the darkest and the richest where life is at its most tenuous. I am more likely to find these stories in a wretchedly poor neighborhood, in a violent neighborhood. But the fact is, that is where the dying happens. That is where the killing happens, that is where the fear is. But I'm sure that there are private little agonies going on in places that are neat and clean.

Where do you find your stories, where do you look for your stories?

The stories come in two ways. The first way is that it is of a national significance or of a broad significance and we just have to go write about it. That often is not necessarily breaking news, but it will be an issue story.

I have the luxury of traveling to the ones that I think are the most compelling. And that word, "compelling," is what gets me out of bed in the morning. I don't think that is necessarily the best way to go about it, it's just my way of going about it.

The piece about Osceola McCarthy was proposed by a very good assistant national editor named Paul Haskins, who asked me if I had heard about this story. I was on the road just as soon as I could. It was not a hopeless story, like a lot of the stories I write. A lot of the stories I write are fairly hopeless, but she was hope incarnate. After a year where I had seen a lot of bad things, killing and dying, I sat in her living room and listened to her explain why she wanted to take her life savings and give it away. My own mom had taken in washing and ironing for people. I know what went through her mind. She did these clothes for people who went away to parties and things she was not part of, and I had some insights. I mean, we've all got living stored up inside of us, years and experiences. And this was one case where I could draw on that, use that, and find some parallels and some deeper insight into it.

Do you think reporters need to do more of that? Do you think we're leery of it?

We're scared to death of it. We've been ordered not to inject ourselves into our stories by a lot of folks. Make it quick and clean. Well, that ain't right. People ask me why my stories are so personal. Well, how can they not be personal? Living is personal. You can't treat it like you're handling life in one of those germ-free suits in a laboratory. You've occasionally got to reach

out and get a good grip on it, even if you don't necessarily want to touch it sometimes.

What is it that makes them personal?

When I say personal, I don't mean personal from my
standpoint. Obviously, my voice is in those stories.
But personal in that there is a connection, and not in
some bullshit "get in touch with your feelings" way,
but there is a very real emotional connection between
an emotional event, between people, between Miss
McCarthy and the readers of *The New York Times.*
That can be accomplished.

My job is to paint her with as many appropriate colors and other senses as is true, as is appropriate, and
let the readers make up their minds about what to
think about her.

If you do that right, if you show someone as flesh
and blood, as having failed dreams and hopes, and if
you talk about a woman in her 80s anticipating her
own death, how can that not be personal? How can
you not, if you do it well without any artificial con-
trivance, make readers care about it, think about it?

It's not my mission, obviously, to make people like
her or dislike her. It is my mission to give them
enough information to where they can make up their
own minds.

**In the piece about Howard Wells, you write, "His
mother, Julia Mae, was then in a hospital dying of
cancer. She had lain there unmoving for hours but
opened her eyes when he walked in after the election. 'Who won?' she asked." You take up six lines
in *The New York Times* to tell a bit about a dying
woman no one has ever heard of and about the love
she has for her son, who some people have heard of.
That's personal.**

Right. And it was absolutely appropriate.

I think he trusted me because I talked with him a little
bit about who I was. I've sat with reporters, particularly
young reporters—and please don't make me sound ancient; I'm just 36—who treated their interview subjects
as though they were mining gold with all the subtlety

of a pick, and just sort of kept slapping at them with it until they got what they were looking for.

Howard Wells was gracious enough to invite me into his home and give me a glass of iced tea and let me meet his wife and sit on his couch and just talk about living for a long time before we talked about Susan Smith. And we talked about who he was and where he was from, and I told him who I was and where I was from. And I told him that my mom had picked cotton for a living and that I grew up in Alabama, and I let him get an image of who I was. After a while, he felt comfortable telling a stranger about his mom's dying.

If you're a new reporter in town and it's not your town, what would you do to find the kinds of stories that you do so well? What would you do as a reporter?

The first thing you do is operate on the assumption that the most compelling stories are going to be about people who have the most to lose. I don't think what I have to say is usually that damned important, but I do think this is worth adhering to. Most reporters tend to be from a particular caste of society, fairly well educated—this doesn't include me—but they tend to be fairly well educated, they tend to be curious about life, but often they haven't lived a whole lot of it, if you know what I mean. They haven't been in too many fist fights, they have never had to crawl under a 1969 Mustang Mach 1 to keep Howard Higginbotham from beating the mortal hell out of you.

If you're looking for stories, you can't go to dinner every night at the neatest, cleanest, most funkily avant garde restaurant in town. Go eat outside the mill. Have some macaroni and cheese and lima beans and cornbread sticks. You cannot treat your beat as though you were on safari; you have to go out and soak it up. Go to church. You might want to sit in the back pew if you feel self-conscious, but go to a church and just listen to what people are saying on the podium, the pulpit. It doesn't matter what color people are, just go and be part of it. It's OK if you stand out like a sore thumb; it's fine to do that.

Take a walk through the Kmart. That's where people are living, that's where real people are. Strike up conversations, sit at lunch counters.

If your life basically consists of tapping into the Internet, going to eat dinner at a place that has anything to do with foie gras, or taking your designer dog for a walk with a silly assed bandanna tied around his neck, then no, you're probably not going to get a real good taste of a place. You have to go out and see people. If you're covering city hall, follow the people back to their neighborhoods.

If you're writing about an intersection that's supposed to get a new stop light, then find out who got killed there and go out and talk to people about it, why it's important. The next thing you know, a story about someone voting money to put up a new stop light, which would be, what, not even a paragraph in a city council story, can give you a front page story because it matters all of a sudden.

What advice would you give others about reporting and writing?

Clarity is probably the most important foundation, figuring what's important and where it should go. But after that, I think they need to just make it compelling, make it a read. Think about what editor Clarke Stallworth at the *Birmingham News* told me a long, long time ago. It's the biggest cliché in the business, but it's still applicable: "Show me. Don't tell me." Put flesh and bones and blood on the people that you write about. If there is honest emotion there, use it. Don't write about the sunset if it doesn't have a damned thing to do with the story; but if the place is important to it, then bring it to life, put paint on the walls, let people know what it's like.

If you're writing about a school that needs renovations, then you've got to find every crack in it and talk about what it needs. Don't let the principal tell you why he needs this money. Get him to show you, and then you show the reader. The only way to draw people into the story is to take them by the hand and lead them with you through it. If you've done that, then you've won.

The Des Moines Register

Ken Fuson

Finalist, Non-Deadline Writing

Ken Fuson is a general assignment reporter for *The Des Moines Register* where he has worked since 1981. Born in Granger, Iowa, he began his career making $1.50 an hour as a high school sportswriter for the *Woodward* (Iowa) *Enterprise.* He attended the University of Missouri and interned at the *St. Louis Post-Dispatch* where he wrote a story about a woman who saved a dog's life by giving it mouth-to-mouth resuscitation. From 1978–1981, Fuson worked as a reporter and editor at the *Columbia* (Mo.) *Daily Tribune.* He was a finalist three times for the Livingston Award for Young Journalists and this marks his third time as a finalist in the ASNE's non-deadline writing category.

The best writers aren't afraid to take risks, whether it's writing a weather story in one luxurious sentence or tackling a potentially sentimental subject like the death of a child. In both of these stories, Ken Fuson displays a command of language and emotion that produces reading experiences that touch the heart and stimulate the imagination.

Ah, what a day!

MARCH 16, 1995

Here's how Iowa celebrates a 70-degree day in the middle of March: By washing the car and scooping the loop and taking a walk; by daydreaming in school and playing hooky at work and shutting off the furnace at home; by skateboarding and flying kites and digging through closets for baseball gloves; by riding that new bike you got for Christmas and drawing hopscotch boxes in chalk on the sidewalk and not caring if the kids lost their mittens again; by looking for robins and noticing swimsuits on department store mannequins and shooting hoops in the park; by sticking the ice scraper in the trunk and the antifreeze in the garage and leaving the car parked outside overnight; by cleaning the barbecue and stuffing the parka in storage and just standing outside and letting that friendly sun kiss your face; by wondering where you're going to go on summer vacation and getting reacquainted with neighbors on the front porch and telling the boys that—yes! yes!—they can run outside and play without a jacket; by holding hands with a lover and jogging in shorts and picking up the extra branches in the yard; by eating an ice cream cone outside and (if you're a farmer or gardener) feeling that first twinge that says it's time to plant and (if you're a high school senior) feeling that first twinge that says it's time to leave; by wondering if in all of history there has ever been a day so glorious and concluding that there hasn't and being afraid to even stop and take a breath (or begin a new paragraph) for fear that winter would return, leaving Wednesday in our memory as nothing more than a sweet and too-short dream.

Life is more than a game

JULY 9, 1995

GRINNELL, Iowa—The game is over. The South Des Moines junior team—the JTs—have fallen in the second round of the state softball tournament for girls 12 and younger.

Lisa Birocci, the team's leader and one of the best young pitchers in Iowa, walks to the bleachers, hangs her head and cries.

"Leave her alone," Pete Vivone says. "She'll be OK."

How typical of Vivone to spot her first. He's the assistant coach who consoles the girls when they strike out, who reminds them to choke up with two strikes, who performs the last-minute repairs on lucky batting gloves.

A few minutes later, Vivone takes Lisa by the hand.

"I want to show you something," he says.

He leads her away from the bleachers, away from the fresh defeat. Holding hands, swinging their arms like school buddies, they walk down a gully, up a hill and sit on a wooden bench.

"Look around you, Lisa," he tells her. "The grass is still green. The sky is still blue. The clouds are out and it's a beautiful day. There are worse things that can happen in life than losing a softball game."

He doesn't mention Diana. He doesn't have to.

* * *

When his daughter died, Vivone quit coaching. Fathers coach their daughters. Now that Diana was gone, he no longer had a daughter on the team.

Besides, how could he and his wife, Sue, go to games and look out in left field or behind home plate and not see Diana there? How could they look into the faces of their daughter's teammates and not be reminded of what had been lost? How could they stay strong when their hearts were broken?

That was the thing that everyone noticed at the prayer service the night before Diana's funeral. All those kids—neighborhood pals, school classmates, softball teammates—collapsing in loud sobs at the casket. There stood Pete and Sue, patting their backs, whispering, "We'll be OK."

"It was the saddest thing I've ever been through in my life," says Sonja Gonzalez, whose daughter was a friend of Diana's. "Pete and Sue were just so strong for them. I'll never forget that."

The accident happened last August in Des Moines. Diana and her sister were headed to a south-side bank to pick up another sister. Their car turned and a truck slammed into the passenger side, where Diana was sitting. She was 11 years old.

At the prayer service, Michael Tonini, the funeral director and a family friend, played the song "Centerfield" ("Put me in, Coach..."). Diana's teammates on the JTs wore their uniforms—the red-and-white shirts and the red, pinstriped shorts. Their arch-rivals, the West Des Moines Panthers, came in their uniforms, too. Girls on the two teams, fierce competitors only weeks before, now hugged and wept.

What a summer it had been. Diana was so excited when she made the JTs. Only a few 11-year-olds are good enough to play with the 12-year-olds on the South Des Moines all-star team. Diana, Lisa Birocci and Sarah Miller were the 11-year-olds invited.

Diana and Sarah called themselves "The Bench Buddies" because that's where they usually sat during games. They made up cheers and laughed when Diana called out, "Moooove over, butter!" Don't ask why.

"When she bumped into you, she'd say, 'Quit giving me love nudges,'" Lisa says.

Diana was known for her naturally curly, dark brown hair. She wore it in a ponytail during games; it flipped up when she swung.

She loved to tease. Everyone remembers the time when she got on all fours at a softball tournament, searching the ground as if she had misplaced a contact lens.

"What did you lose?" a man asked her.

"My money," she joked.

"Well, here you go," the man said, handing her a $5 bill. Friends say Diana was too stunned to respond, so she pocketed it.

"Don't tell her dad," Lisa says.

Her dad laughs when he hears the story. Pete Vivone is 48, an underground cable splicer for Mid-American Energy Co., and has coached softball and basketball for about 10 years. Each of his four daughters played softball. Diana, the youngest, improved steadily.

So did her team. Last year the JTs finished fourth in the state tournament—the West Des Moines Panthers beat them twice to knock them out—and fourth in the Midwest regional tournament. They went on to tie for 25th place in the national tournament in Indianapolis— pretty good, considering that 6,000 teams started the season.

After the JTs were done, Diana joined a Police Athletic League team for the fall season. Her father was the head coach. They had played four games when the accident happened.

At first, the players wanted to quit, then reconsidered. Pete Vivone stayed away for two weeks, until one of his players, a friend of Diana's, visited him.

"We need you at third base," she said. "We miss you."

So Vivone returned to the softball field, to the coach's box at third, and the team went on to win the Des Moines metro fall championship. But would he return to the JTs as an assistant coach this year? When Francis Miller, the head coach, called to find out, Vivone asked for a few days to think. Then he decided.

"It's tough going out there on that field every day," he says, "but I think these girls are worth it."

PLENTY OF CHATTER

You gotta want it,
To win it,
AND WE WANT IT MORE!

The JTs cheer, chant and chatter more than English soccer fans. They warm up with a song that includes the phrase, "Boogie woogie woogie a boogie down." When the opposing pitcher walks someone, they chant, "Pit-CHUR's getting tired—OH, so very tired." When Sarah "Bullet" Miller is up at the plate, they sing, "I see a hole and Bullet's gonna find it."

That's the other thing about the JTs. You've got to have a nickname. The last names on the lineup card

represent the ethnic stew that is the south side of Des
Moines—Birocci and Crivaro, O'Donnell and McAn-
inch, Aguilar and Vaughan. But it's the nicknames that
go on the backs of the uniforms—Kirby, Rocket and
Taz; Lightning, Lefty and Yogi. One sleeve carries
their first names; the other sleeve carries the initials
"DLV."

The initials stand for Diana Lee Vivone. Every girl
who plays for the South Des Moines Girls Softball Association wears those initials on her uniform this year.

It says "Pete" on the back of Pete Vivone's uniform. If the JTs had their way, it would say "Chicken
Legs" or "Peanut Butter" or "Melon Head" or any of
the other goofy names the girls call him.

They like the way he yells, "Hit the stupid thing,"
when they're in a slump. Or how he claps his hands
real fast when they rip a hit. Or the way he and Sue
just laughed earlier this summer, at a tournament in
Sioux City, when three girls sneaked into the Vivones'
hotel room and decorated it with toilet paper.

"He's kind of a second father to anybody who
needs him," says Lisa "Kirby" Birocci. "He's there
for us."

The Sioux City tournament was a good trip. The
JTs lost once, then clawed their way through the losers' bracket and beat the same team twice to claim the
championship.

After the exciting finale, when the girls and fans
were crying and celebrating, Sue Vivone said to a
friend, "It's not fair. It's just not fair."

She knew how Diana would have loved this team.
These were girls she went to school with or played
softball with when she was 10. Last year, Petie—that
was the nickname on her uniform—warmed the
bench. This year, she could have starred.

Imagine how Diana would have taken to Mr. Man.
That's what the girls call Jesse Gonzalez, whose step-
daughter, Tanya "Lightning" Miller, plays second
base.

Mr. Man wears tennis shoes with the players'
names on them. He had "JTs" signs printed that he
sticks on his red van. When the team wins, he and
Jesse Hart, the catcher's father, run around beyond the
outfield, waving the signs over their heads. Before

each game, Mr. Man leads the players and the fans as they twist their bodies to spell out the initials "SD-MJTS," for South Des Moines JTs.

All the girls and the parents tell Sue Vivone how often they think of Diana during the games and how deeply they feel her spirit.

"They tell me, 'She's here with us,'" Sue says. "I feel that, but I feel her missing, too."

REMEMBERING PETE

On Father's Day, the JTs won a tournament in St. Joseph, Mo. Between games, the girls called their fathers to the playing field and presented each with a red rose. Then each girl walked over to Pete Vivone and handed him a rose, too.

"He was crying," Lisa Birocci says.

Birocci is a 5-foot-6-inch pitcher with a buggy whip for an arm. She once pitched five games in one day and is so talented that fans of Lincoln and Dowling high schools already are arguing over which school she should attend. She's also a 12-year-old girl who dances in the dugout between innings—the JTs' fans bring taped music—and keeps a picture of Diana Vivone in her equipment bag.

"I think of her all the time," she says. "When I strike somebody out, I'll raise my hand in the air to show how many outs there are, but I'm also pointing at Diana."

There are so many symbols on this team—the initials on the uniform sleeve, the tiny gold angel pins that the Vivones wear during games, the way Heidi Hart, the catcher, sometimes uses Diana's glove to warm up.

But it's all unspoken. Nobody yells, "Let's win this for Diana." When Pete grabbed Lisa's hand and walked up the hill after the state tournament loss, he didn't have to tell her that life's too short to fret about a softball game. It's as if the coach and his players know each other so well that words have become unnecessary.

"They understand," Pete says. "You don't have to say anything to them. It's just there."

His wife agrees: "I know it's hard for them. They're trying to get through this, too."

So they stuff their thoughts and feelings and grief into their matching equipment bags and head for the respite promised by a softball game.

"I told Pete, 'Each one of these girls loves you like a father,'" says Linda Birocci, Lisa's mother and an assistant coach. "They know they can't replace Diana. They're just doing the best they can."

SEEKING THE STATE TITLE

With a record of 34-4 and three tournament championships, the JTs stroll confidently into Grinnell for the Amateur Softball Association's 12-and-under tournament. This is the state championship; the top four teams advance to the Midwest regional tournament in Kearney, Neb.

The JTs want to do more than advance. They want that giant first-place trophy.

But so does Ankeny. Their pitcher is as unhittable as Birocci. One bad inning for the JTs and it's over: Ankeny wins, 2-1, sending Birocci and Pete Vivone on their walk up the hill.

"You've got nothing to worry about," he tells her.

Because this is a double-elimination tournament, the JTs have another chance. All they have to do to advance to the title game is run the table and win six straight games over the next two days.

Which, of course, is exactly what they do. Birocci is phenomenal. About the only way opposing players get on base is if the third strike squirts away from the catcher.

In the championship game, the JTs face the Jack Pinney Royals from Sioux City. The score is 1-1 when Mr. Man decides it's time to swing into action.

He sees that the JT fans are dragging, and he knows that the players must be exhausted. They have been playing for almost five hours on a shadeless field in the middle of a hot afternoon. Mr. Man walks to the dugout and brings forth a special cheer. He yells a line and the girls yell it right back at him:

I don't know but I've been told,
JT girls are as good as gold.
Call me mean, call be bad,
I don't listen to Mom and Dad.

The giggles that follow loosen the team. The JTs explode, winning 11-1. Birocci has pitched nine games in three days, striking out 53 of the 105 batters she has faced.

"Special team," Pete Vivone says.

SPECIAL VISITS

It started this summer when the JTs won their first tournament. Jesse and Sonja Gonzalez took their family to Glendale Cemetery to visit Diana Vivone's grave.

They returned after the JTs won their second tournament, this time bringing another player with them.

By the time the JTs won their third tournament, the whole team wanted to go.

"The girls had a real hard time," Gonzalez says. "That was the first time a lot of them had been there since the funeral."

On Wednesday, three days after they captured the state championship, the JTs load into vans for another trip to the cemetery. They find Diana's grave by a tree.

Each girl places a red and white carnation on Diana's grave. They attach two balloons on either side—the red one contains their names, the white one says, "State Champs" and "We did it for you, Diana."

They recite the Lord's Prayer and a Hail Mary. On the field, the JTs always look older than many 12-and-under teams. Now, as the girls cry and hug each other, you understood why. Whatever feelings they had stuffed in those equipment bags come rushing out.

Pete and Sue Vivone do not attend this ceremony; they don't even know about it. This is something the girls must do by themselves. The Vivones will see the flowers and balloons the next time they visit.

"I don't know how we would have made it this far without those girls," Pete says.

After the final state tournament game, those girls stood in the middle of the diamond and sang "Happy Birthday" to Vivone (it was a few days earlier) and then presented him with the championship trophy. If they could, the JTs would take him and Sue by the hand and start walking, down gullies and up hills, as long and as far as it took, out beyond the pain and the hurt.

But they can't. As much as the JTs care, the car still is empty when the Vivones return home after games. All the girls can do is what Lisa Birocci did after the last out. She tossed her glove 10 feet in the air, joined her teammates in a celebratory heap and then searched for Pete Vivone.

Her face red from the heat, her eyes red from the tears, she grabbed him and hugged him and then hugged him some more.

"You know who that trophy is for, don't you?" she asked.

He nodded but said nothing.

He didn't have to.

Lessons Learned

BY KEN FUSON

AH, WHAT A DAY!

Before I explain the weather story, let me tell you about living in Iowa. Each year we are guaranteed 10 tolerable days; it's in our contract. The rest of the year we function as a meteorological theme park inspired by the Book of Revelation.

So you must understand what it's like to receive a bonus 70-degree day in the middle of March. It's a gift—a wonderful, delightful, unexpected present. If Sally Field lived here on such a day, she would shout, "God likes us! He really, really likes us!"

I wanted to capture that glorious feeling. I wanted a story that reflected Iowa's breathless attempt to savor a day we knew was too good to last. I wanted a story as unique as the day itself.

The result is a six-inch, one-sentence, one-paragraph story that contains exactly one hard fact: the temperature. But it's stuffed with emotional facts—observations collected from walking through downtown Des Moines at lunch hour and driving around town later. I decided it was more important to describe what this special day *felt* like than to quote people waiting in line at the car wash.

When I returned to the newsroom, I told Randy Essex, a deputy editor, that I wanted to try something different. He didn't roll his eyes. He read it and liked it. When it was time for the news meeting, he put the entire story on the budget. That's what they call "closing the sale," and I appreciated it.

This is a lark of a story, the surprise in the Cracker Jack box, but I enjoy surprises in my newspaper and I assume others do, too. When Neil Armstrong walked on the moon, I couldn't wait to see how the *Register* would handle it—it would be special, I was certain. The next morning, I raced to the milk box (we had milk boxes then) and there was my newspaper and this headline: MAN WALKS ON MOON! In blue ink! I loved it.

Extreme risk-taking in the pursuit of readers is no vice. Try anything. And cultivate editors who will let you try.

By the way, if I had a fresh shot at this, I would cut an inch or so of observations to get to the punch line—or begin a new paragraph—quicker, and instead of my "yes! yes!" interjection, I would have stolen James Joyce's famous "and yes I said yes I will Yes" from the end of *Ulysses.*

Alas, a rare opportunity to add humor and an oblique literary reference was squandered.

LIFE IS MORE THAN A GAME

The lesson is simple: Be there.

I cheated to get this story. My editor, Randy Evans (as a matter of fact, all our editors are named Randy), had a daughter who played on the team the year before. He knew the coach, Pete Vivone, his daughter Diana, and the other players.

One night, as Randy and I were chatting about kids and sports, he told me how Pete Vivone had continued to coach the team after Diana was killed in a car wreck and how the girls had gone out of their way to embrace him—giving him a rose on Father's Day, for example.

The more he talked, the more we both realized that we should be writing this. We also realized that to do it right would take time. The more emotional the story, the longer you need to earn the trust of the people involved.

From the start, my goal was to get to know the girls on the team. This was a lesson learned the hard way. Several years ago, I followed a small town baseball team's final season; the tiny school would be gobbled by a larger district. To me, the situation had everything—drama, history, changing times in rural America, and a proud town's acute sense of loss.

But the finished product just didn't connect with readers. The reason, I decided, was that I had made the town itself my main character, when I should have focused on the players and what they were feeling. I didn't want to make the same mistake this time.

So how does a 40-year-old man gain the trust of 12-year-old girls? By being there. I went to practices, games, the state tournament (my sunburn became a running joke). I learned the goofy cheers and asked for the stories behind their nicknames. When they went to Diana's grave, I tagged along, staying out of sight while they cried, asking them afterward to share their favorite stories about Diana. The girls believed I cared about them. They were right.

Writing the story was simply a matter of getting out of the way and introducing my readers to these special kids. (And, of course, it helped tremendously that they won.)

Two months after the story appeared, Lisa Birocci, the star pitcher, invited me to the team's end-of-season party. No home run ever felt sweeter.

The Oregonian

Tom Hallman Jr.

Finalist, Non-Deadline Writing

Tom Hallman Jr. has been a reporter at *The Oregonian* for 16 years. A former police reporter, he now writes features as part of the Living in the '90s team. He graduated with a degree in journalism from Drake University in Des Moines, Iowa. He won the Livingston Award for Young Journalists in 1985, was a member of the team that won the National Sigma Delta Chi award for non-deadline reporting in 1989, and was a Pulitzer finalist in beat reporting in 1994.

In "Life of a Salesman," Hallman displays the characterization, evocative scene-setting, and compelling prose that come from in-depth reporting and skillful writing. The result is an inspiring and enduring profile of one courageous man's triumph over physical infirmity and a masterful display of the power of narrative nonfiction.

Life of a salesman

NOVEMBER 19, 1995

The alarm rings and he stirs. It's 5:45. He could linger under the covers, listening to the radio and a weatherman who predicts rain. People would understand. He knows that.

A surgeon's scar cuts a swath across his lower back. The medicines and painkillers littering his night stand offer help but no cure. The fingers on his right hand are so twisted that he can't tie his shoes.

Some days, he feels like surrendering. But his dead mother's challenge reverberates in his soul. So, too, do the voices of those who believed him stupid or retarded, incapable of being more than a ward of the state. All his life he's struggled to prove them wrong. He will not quit.

And so Bill Porter rises.

He takes the first unsteady steps on a journey to Portland's streets, the battlefield where he fights alone for his independence and dignity. He's a door-to-door salesman. Sixty-three years old. And his enemies—a crippled body that betrays him and a changing world that no longer needs him—are gaining on him.

With trembling hands he assembles his weapons: black wingtips, dark slacks, blue shirt and matching blazer, brown tie, tan raincoat and pinched-front, brown fedora. Image, he believes, is everything.

He stops in the entryway, picks up his briefcase and steps out onto the stoop of his Northeast Portland home. A fall wind has kicked up. The weatherman was right. He pulls his raincoat tighter.

He tilts his hat just so.

* * *

On the 7:45 bus that stops across the street, he leaves his briefcase next to the driver and finds a seat in the middle of a pack of bored teenagers.

He leans forward, stares toward the driver, sits back, then repeats the process. His nervousness makes him laugh uncontrollably. The teenagers smirk. They don't realize Porter's afraid someone will steal his briefcase, with the glasses, brochures, order forms and clip-on tie that he needs to survive.

Porter senses the stares. He covers his mouth, stifles a laugh and regains his composure. He looks at a boy next to him. He smiles. The kid turns away and makes a face at a buddy.

Porter looks at the floor.

His face reveals nothing. In his heart, though, he knows he should have been like these kids, like everyone on this bus. He's not angry. But he knows. His mother explained how the delivery had been difficult, how the doctor had used an instrument that crushed a section of his brain and caused cerebral palsy, a disorder of the nervous system that affects his speech, hands and walk.

Porter came to Portland when he was 13 after his father, a salesman for a neon sign company, was transferred here. He attended a school for the disabled and then Lincoln High School, where he was placed in a class for slow kids.

But he wasn't slow.

His mind was trapped in a body that didn't work. Speaking was laborious, as if words had to be pulled from a tar pit. People were impatient and didn't listen. He felt different—was different—from the kids who roughhoused in the halls and planned dances he would never attend.

People like him were considered retarded then. What could his future be? Porter wanted to do something and asked the State Vocational Rehabilitation Division for help. They sent him to several social service agencies, but it did no good. He couldn't use a cash register, unload trucks or solicit funds on the telephone. "Unemployable" is what they called him. He should collect government disability checks for the rest of his life.

His mother was certain, though, that he could rise above his limitations. She helped start a workshop for people with cerebral palsy, and Porter sold redwood planters to raise money for it.

People listened.

With his mother's encouragement, he applied for a job with the Fuller Brush Co. only to be turned down.

He couldn't carry a product briefcase or walk a route, they said.

Porter knew he wanted to be a salesman. He began reading help wanted ads in the newspaper. When he saw one for Watkins, a company that sold household products door-to-door, his mother set up a meeting with a representative. The man said no, but Porter wouldn't listen. He just wanted a chance. The man relented and offered Porter a section of the city that no salesman wanted.

It took Porter four false starts before he found the courage to ring the first doorbell. The man who answered told him to go away, a pattern repeated throughout the day.

That night Porter read through company literature and discovered the products were guaranteed. He would sell that pledge. He just needed people to listen.

If a customer turned him down, Porter kept coming back until they heard him. When apartment managers refused to admit him, Porter waited until someone else was buzzed inside and then walked in behind them.

And he sold.

He was rewarded with the Laurelhurst sales route in Northeast Portland. His parents made deliveries because he couldn't drive. He prospected the area for 13 years before concentrating solely on Portland's westside, a bigger market.

For several years he was Watkins' top retail salesman in all of Oregon, Idaho, Washington and California. Now he is the only one of the company's 44,000 salespeople who sells door-to-door.

He's headed back to his route today. The bus stops in the Transit Mall, and Porter shuffles off.

His body is not made for walking. Each step strains his joints. Migraines and other aches are constant visitors. His right arm is nearly useless. He can't fully control the limb, and it's pressed close to his body and thrust backward as if he's pushing off with a ski pole. His torso tilts at the waist; he seems to be heading into a strong, steady wind that keeps him off balance. At times, he looks like a toddler taking his first steps.

He walks 10 miles a day.

His first stop today, like every day, is a shoeshine stand where employees tie his laces. Twice a week he pays for a shine. At a nearby hotel one of the doormen buttons Porter's top shirt button and slips on his clip-on tie. He then walks to another bus that drops him off a mile from his territory—a neighborhood near Wilson High School.

He's been up for nearly five hours.

He left home nearly three hours ago.

* * *

The wind is cold and raindrops fall. Porter ignores the elements and the sluggishness in his thighs. He trudges up one hill and down another until he reaches the edge of the neighborhood.

He stops at the first house. This is the moment he's been preparing for since 5:45 a.m. He rings the bell.

A woman comes to the door.

"Hello."

"No, thank you, I'm just preparing to leave."

Porter nods.

"May I come back later?" he asks.

"No," says the woman.

She shuts the door.

Porter's eyes reveal nothing.

He moves to the next house.

The door opens.

Then closes.

He doesn't get a chance to speak. Porter's expression never changes. He stops at every home in his territory. People might not buy now. Next time. Maybe. No doesn't mean never. Some of his best customers are people who repeatedly turned him down before buying.

He stops again.

"No, I'm babysitting for friends, and I have three toddlers in here. I can't talk now."

The door shuts.

He makes his way down the street.

"I don't want to try it."

"Maybe next time."

"I'm sorry. I'm on the phone right now."

"No."

He makes his way up and down the hills. His briefcase is heavy. He stops and shifts it to his bad hand, forcing the handle between his fingers. He walks 15 feet and stops.

His hand hurts.

He catches his breath.

He walks on.

Ninety minutes later, Porter still has not made a sale. But there is always another home.

He walks on.

He knocks on a door. A woman wanders out from the back yard where she's gardening. She often buys, but not today, she says, as she walks away.

"Are you sure?" Porter ask.

She pauses.

"Well..."

That's all Porter needs. He walks as fast as he can, tailing her as she heads to the back yard. He sets his brief-case on a bench and opens it. He puts on his glasses, re-moves his brochures and begins his spiel, showing the woman pictures and describing each product.

Spices?

"No."

Vanilla?

"No."

Pasta toppings?

"No."

Jams?"

"No."

Potpourri?

"No. Maybe nothing today, Bill."

Porter's hearing is the one perfect thing his body does. Except when he gets a live one. Then the word "no" does not register.

Cinnamon?

"No."

Pepper?"

"No."

Laundry soap?

"Hmm."

Porter stops. He's a shark smelling blood. He quickly remembers her last order.

"Say, aren't you about out of soap? That's what you bought last time. You ought to be out right about now."

"You're right, Bill. I'll take one."

Because he has difficulties holding a pen, Porter asks his customers to complete their order forms. The woman writes him a check, which he deposits in his briefcase.

Then he is on his way.

No sale.

No sale.

No sale.

Finally, a woman and her daughter invite Porter inside. The woman and Porter talk about the neighborhood—who's moved away and who's sick. After a few minutes of small talk, Porter takes off his hat and raincoat and sets them on a chair. Out come the glasses and the brochures.

"A good buy on detergent. No phosphates. Do you have a brand you already buy?"

"Yes, the biggest one Costco sells."

"Oh."

"We have a new kind of pepper."

"I don't do much with those kinds of things."

"Hot spices?"

"No."

"All natural, pure pasta toppings."

He glances at the customer. She's teetering and just needs a push.

"Sure would make a nice gift."

He studies her face, searching for clues as to what she needs to hear.

"Nothing synthetic."

"Really?"

Touchdown!

"How much is a set?" she asks.

"$22.99, and they go a long way."

"OK, I'll give it a try."

"I think you'll like those toppings. They have a good flavor."

As the woman fills out her order form, Porter suggests another item.

"How about some vanilla."

"How much?"

"$10.19."

She added it to the form. Porter removes his glasses and places everything in his briefcase. He pulls on his coat, replaces his hat and follows the woman to the front door.

He turns to her.

His bent body makes it appear as if he were bowing. He struggles to get out one final sentence.

"And I thank you."

* * *

He arrives home, in a rainstorm, after 7 p.m. Today was not profitable. He tells himself not to worry. Four days left in the week.

At least he's off his feet and home. He and his parents moved here more than 30 years ago. They're both gone now. Not a day goes by that he doesn't silently thank them.

After his father died, his mother lived off a small pension with help from Porter's income. When she passed on eight years ago, she left only the house and a voice he still hears.

Inside, an era is preserved. The telephone is a heavy, rotary model. There is no VCR, no cable. His is the only house in the neighborhood with a television antenna on the roof.

He leads a solitary life. He's met a couple of women over the years, but nothing serious developed. Most of his human contact comes on the job. Alone, he does paperwork, reads and watches television, especially sporting events.

Now, he heats the oven and slips in a frozen dinner, a staple because they're easy to fix.

As his food warms, he opens his briefcase and stacks the order forms. In two weeks, he will use a manual typewriter to write detailed directions to each house so the women he hires to make deliveries won't get lost. He can use only one finger and one hand to type.

The job usually takes him 10 hours.

He's a weary man who knows his days—no matter what his intentions—are numbered.

He peddles his goods in downpours, snowstorms, and sweltering heat. He does not know how much longer his body can take the pounding. In quieter moments, he wonders if the day is fast approaching when the world will no longer answer his knock at the door.

At many homes, the woman of the house is off working. And if someone is there, they buy in bulk at superstores. They'd rather save a dollar than deal with a stranger who talks about money-back guarantees.

He works on straight commission. He gets no paid holidays, vacations or raises. Yes, some months are lean.

In 1993, he needed back surgery to relieve pain caused from decades of walking. He was laid up for five months and couldn't work. He was forced to take a loan on his house to eat, consolidate past debt and pay three years of back property taxes.

When he returned to the street, business was slow. He fell further behind. Eventually, he sold his home, cleared the books and started over. The new owners, familiar with his situation, froze his rent and agreed to let him live there until he dies.

He doesn't feel sorry for himself.

The house is only a building. A place to live, nothing more.

His dinner is ready. He eats at the kitchen table and listens to the radio. The afternoon mail brought bills that he will deal with later this week. The checkbook is upstairs in the bedroom.

His checkbook.

He pays a gardener. He pays his medical insurance. He pays a woman to shop for him, clean his house, do his laundry and make his lunch when he knows his daily route will take him far from a fast food restaurant.

He types in the recipient's name and signs his name.

The signature is small and scrawled.

Unreadable.

But he knows.

Bill Porter.

Bill Porter, salesman.

From his easy chair he hears the wind lash his house and the rain pound the street outside his home. He must dress warmly tomorrow. He's sleepy. With great care he climbs the stairs to his bedroom.

In time, the lights go off.

Morning will be here soon.

Lessons Learned

BY TOM HALLMAN JR.

PERSISTENCE

My wife, Barbara, was the person who suggested I write this feature. While driving in Portland's West Hills one morning she spotted a salesman she remembered from childhood. Although she didn't know much about him, she thought he'd make an interesting story.

But she didn't know his name, where he worked, or where he lived. I called the Fuller Brush Co., but they said they didn't have any door-to-door salesman in Portland.

So I went back to the street where my wife last saw this man. I walked house to house, knocking on doors until I found someone who had purchased something from him. I asked to see the order form and learned the salesman's name was Bill Porter. He worked for the Watkins Co. and was listed in the telephone book. I called him.

Our conversation lasted all of 10 seconds.

He was not interested in a story.

I waited a few days and called again.

No.

Again.

He reluctantly agreed to meet.

Then he called to cancel the appointment.

I tried once more.

Just a few minutes of your time, I asked.

We met.

I sold the salesman.

REPORTING

We sat in his living room and I conducted one of the most difficult interviews of my career. His responses were limited to a few words. It was clear he wanted me to leave.

He couldn't understand why I wanted to talk with him. There was no story. Once there, though, I wasn't budging. We talked for nearly an hour that day—about sports, about the weather, his neighborhood, and, finally, about his life. With some hesitation he told me something of his background: when his family moved to Portland, his parents' names, and where he had attended high school.

That was all I needed. Now I approached the story as I would an in-depth news story. I talked to anyone who knew Porter's mother or his father, going back to when they moved to Portland. I talked with old classmates. I walked his sales route and talked with customers. I even tracked down the eulogy a priest had written for his mother's funeral. In short, I learned as much as possible about this man and the forces that shaped his life.

And then I went back to Porter.

Now he couldn't get away with just two-word responses. I knew too much. I could ask a hundred questions, each one more probing than the last.

FLEXIBILITY

I originally envisioned this story as a funny tale. The last salesman, tired feet. All the clichés.

But as I talked with Porter—and continued to interview the people who had known him over the years—I realized there was a much more powerful story here.

I forgot about being funny and worked at getting Porter to open up, knowing that the true story wasn't out on the streets, but in here, in this house.

But Porter was not forthcoming.

So I set the story aside.

I worked on other stories, but continued to keep in touch with Porter to build his trust.

This man had never opened up to anyone in his life. That's what I wanted him to do, but it would take time. As much time as it takes to put together a good investigative story.

If the Porter story had been on an editor's budget, I could have written a standard Sunday feature. But there was no such pressure because I controlled the timing of the story that I wanted to write by working on other stories.

PRE-WRITING

What is this story about?

If you look carefully, you'll see that it is not a story about a disabled man. It's a story about a man who refuses to see himself as disabled.

We've all seen features about disabled people, but they usually highlight the disability.

Not once in this story do I use the word "disabled."

Instead, I focus on the man. That allowed readers to relate to him in a way they wouldn't have if this had been a story about a man with cerebral palsy. It's a subtle thing, but it's critical.

I received more than 2,000 calls and letters from readers. Porter received another 500. The last I heard, *CBS Morning News* is planning to come to Portland to do a story on the story, the reaction it generated, and follow Porter around for a day.

I don't believe that would have happened if the focus of the story had not been honed before I began writing.

FINAL REPORTING

I wanted to build my story around one of Porter's days— follow him as he sold and then tell his larger story within that structure.

A week before we went out, I walked his route, interviewing some of the people I knew he'd come in contact with: the bellhop who buttons his shirt, the shoe shine man who ties his shoes. I did this early because I wanted to be in the background when I was with Porter. I didn't want to break the mood by asking anyone to spell their name, or get caught up in being a traditional reporter. I wanted only to observe.

WRITING

This is never easy.

But in many ways, the hard work was done in the pre-writing stage. I knew exactly what elements I needed for this story. There were about 10 different stories. I picked one of them. Someone else may have focused on something else.

During the reporting stage, I had talked with more than 25 people about Porter and his life. None were quoted or referred to in this story. So was all that reporting a waste?

Not at all. Good writing can't happen without great reporting. Every one of those people is in the story. The reader doesn't see them. But they're there.

EDITING

Good writers want good editors. My editor, Kay Black, understood the heart of this story. That happens on most of my stories she edits. Writers need editors who see the potential in a story that is summed up in a budget line that reads: "Profile of a door-to-door salesman."

Looks pretty lame. Someone other than the reporter has to see the story.

Black was also enthusiastic and encouraging, two things writers need when they attempt anything other than a standard news story. Reporters can take risks when they have a safety net.

Finally, Black also understands the elements that go into a story. That made the actual editing easy. There were only minor changes. But the ones that Black suggested were perfect.

Peter H. King

Commentary

Peter H. King is a columnist for the *Los Angeles Times.* He attended California Polytechnic State University, worked as a staff writer and copy editor at the San Luis Obispo *Telegram-Tribune,* and held summer internships with the Associated Press and *The Fresno Bee.* From 1977–1978, he was a general assignment reporter in the AP's San Francisco bureau and then spent three years reporting for the *San Francisco Examiner.* He joined the *Los Angeles Times* in 1982 as a reporter and has held a variety of writing and editing jobs there including city editor and metro staff writer. He wrote the "On California" column, where these columns appeared, from 1991 until 1996 when his statewide focus was expanded to a national one.

You think you've got the news all figured out—welfare reform, the Unabomber's manifesto, corporate downsizing, the undeserving poor—until you read Peter H. King. He consistently challenges readers' assumptions and prejudices with pointed commentaries and graceful prose that make them see the news and the world in a fresh, new light. His columns glitter with evocative images and echo with sharply honed insights.

A story of the season

FEBRUARY 26, 1995

Where were the Cadillacs? This was Hunters Point, the projects. This was San Francisco's contribution to that part of the country known as "inner-city" America, where the fear and the stereotypes play. Welfare Queens luxuriate in such places. They drive Cadillacs, crank out children, buy good whiskey with food stamps. It's a swell life, underwritten by taxpayers who have fallen prey to the Compassion Crowd and who themselves can no longer afford good whiskey, not to mention Cadillacs.

I know these things.

I listen to talk radio.

And yet, somehow, standing beneath the burned-out unit where Nina Davis lived, it all didn't seem so swell. The cars were junkers, some stripped, tires flat. The housing units were sagging, dilapidated, the pastel paint chipped and scarred with graffiti. Faded orange bedsheets hung in the windows, blocking out the sun and everything else. The faces peeking out from behind the bedsheets seemed less than royally content. Although there was no chance to inquire. Here, they don't open doors to strangers. Here, Nina Davis, in her brother's phrase, "was a prisoner in her own home," staying indoors, not letting her children wander. Trapped.

"Sometimes," the brother said, "you can only move where your money lets you."

Well, she has escaped now. They buried her Saturday, five weeks after a still-unexplained fire gutted her unit. While such tragedies are commonplace in city-land, the ordeal of Nina Davis would evolve into something remarkable. Hers is a story of this meanest of seasons.

* * *

The fire erupted on a Saturday afternoon. Davis, pregnant, unmarried, was in the shower. Three of her children were away for the afternoon. Three others were home. Davis plunged into the smoke, found her terrified youngsters and shepherded them to a third-story window. Flames were everywhere. She shielded her children with her body—"like a mother in her den," a doctor would say later, "protecting her puppies." Passersby gathered down below. One by one, Davis hurled her babies down to waiting hands. Then, half her body scorched, she jumped. Everyone made it out alive—even the fetus, delivered later by emergency C-section.

Afterward, the mayor wanted to pin a medal on someone. A press conference was called to honor the one man said to have caught the babies. Then two others came forward, claiming they had been the heroes. Then a fourth. Amid the embarrassment and confusion at City Hall, it was declared finally that Davis herself was, as someone put it, "the real hero."

That did it. When those words saw print in the *San Francisco Examiner,* the gates of public opinion hell swung open. Annie Nakao, the reporter who covered the story, was broadsided with letters, calls, faxes, all bubbling with pure white hatred and self-righteous indignation.

"Where do you get the idea of Nina Davis is a hero?" one sputtered, setting the tone for the rest. "Her act of saving three of her seven illegitimate kids may be taken as a small token of repayment for all those tens of thousands of $$$$$$ society, the federal government and California taxpayers have put forward...."

"My husband and I," complained a woman from suburban Burlingame, "pay lots and lots and lots of taxes. I don't see this person has done anything.... That's the brutal reality of it. So there're a lot of us who feel this way. Sorry."

* * *

On it went. They had a field day with Davis on the radio talk shows and in the letters to the editor columns. How dare a woman on welfare have so many children? Never mind the fire. Never mind her grave injuries. Never mind her life story, which indicated Davis in fact had been working to escape welfare. None of that mattered to her critics. It was as though by receiving public assistance, the woman had forfeited her rights both to motherhood and basic human compassion.

Heavily sedated, Nina Davis never heard any of it, never learned she was so troublesome to those fine people who pay lots and lots and lots of taxes. At the service Saturday, Mayor Frank Jordan—apparently the rare politician whose moral compass is not always calibrated to opinion polls—spoke eloquently, compassionately, of what the woman in the casket had done for her children. He spoke of "the ultimate sacrifice" and of selfless love. And yes, he called Nina Davis a hero.

The children sat in the front row. The boys dressed in new, shiny blue suits, the girls in frilly white dresses. As the funeral ended, the littlest child refused to leave. She was carried away, sobbing for her mother. Then the casket was loaded up for the long ride to the cemetery, where Nina Davis would no longer burden this great, golden land of ours.

Writers' Workshop

Talking Points

1) King turns a barbed play on words in the third line of this story: "...where the fear and the stereotypes play." What song is the source of his inspiration? What is the effect of such a device? How does it affect the voice of the column? What does it reveal about the writer's attitudes?

2) King begins his retelling of the story of Nina King in the second section of the column with a simple declarative sentence: "The fire erupted on a Saturday afternoon." Study how he presents necessary background with drama and pathos. Notice how he varies the pace by alternating short sentences ("Flames were everywhere.") with long ones ("She shielded her children with her body—'like a mother in her den,' a doctor would say later, 'protecting her puppies.'") Discuss how this technique creates emotional impact in the story.

3) This column is fueled by the author's obvious anger and sorrow. Read the last paragraph aloud and then discuss your reaction to King's argument that "for a column, as opposed to a news story, or feature, or any of the other forms, emotion is good."

Assignment Desk

1) Even an opinion column demands solid reporting. This column draws on a variety of different sources. List as many of them as you can, and describe how you would go about tapping them if you were writing this column.

2) Stereotypes, what Don Murray calls "clichés of vision," abound in our lives. Peter King exploded the stereotype of Nina Davis's life with the simple act of visiting the project where she lived and died. Follow his lead and take yourself somewhere to challenge assumptions you have about a certain group of people. Visit an Elks Club, a retirement community, a biker bar, and write a passage that compares what you experienced with what you thought you knew.

One more Styrofoam parachute

MARCH 26, 1995

For 21 years he drove the same route, down the hill, across the city, from suburb to corporate tower—an hour-plus in either direction. Over the years he spent enough time car-bound to learn blues licks on a guitar, and once he listened to an entire novel on tape. Something about Van Gogh's sister. He got in assorted fender-benders and sat out too many SigAlerts to remember. Mainly, though, he just drove. Same road, same office. Twenty-one years.

He was what corporate headhunters once called a $60,000-a-year man, with a shared secretary, an office without windows and a deskful of the middling duties that make the business world go 'round. A decade ago there was much learned hand-wringing over whether L.A., with its inflated real estate and rough commutes, could attract enough of these white-collar workers. Then along came downsizing—later known, in the executioner's euphemism, as "right-sizing." After the elimination of thousands upon thousands of jobs, there were now more than enough corporate worker bees to go around.

Our friend—and his is a true tale, though he wants to remain anonymous—figured the hatchet would never find him. He worked hard and was loyal; he thought the company stood for something. He could make more money elsewhere, but he liked the security. "You have a job here," he'd been told when hired, "for as long as you want. You have security."

And he did, for 21 years.

* * *

The first signs were subtle. The top executives quit bothering to flash pretend smiles when they wandered through his department. He began to notice how new office clerks no longer were brought around for introductions. Before too long there were staff meetings and memos on a singular topic: "Belt-tightening."

Now the company was flush. In fact, its war chest of ready cash was a regular source of industry speculation. The best the worker bees could figure, the belt-tightening clamor was aimed at Wall Street. Investors like lean, and they adore mean. Corporate Darwinism, and all that. Or maybe the CEO simply didn't want to risk ridicule among his right-sizing buddies. Who knew? "In these deals," he said, "they never give you a why."

His supervisors went first, strapped to traditional golden parachutes. The new bosses promptly changed all locks. "Just for your security," he was assured. And then everyone in the department was summoned for an individual "chat" with an executive freshly arrived from New York. This one wore a gray suit, smiled wide with fine white teeth, and talked excitedly about how much fun it would be, bringing the department "into the 1990s."

Right away, our boy knew he was sunk: "Once he started talking about bringing us into the '90s, I quit listening and started to study his teeth. He lost all human form. All I could see was a big barracuda smiling at me. He had jaggedy, razor teeth, and they were worn down—like he had been using them a lot. And his eyes were in a feeding mood. I said to myself, 'Start swimming for shore.'"

In the end, it came down to this: He could volunteer to leave and receive a year's salary; or he could try to hang on in a hostile environment, risking, as he put it, "my Styrofoam parachute." He asked to think for a minute. "Not much choice," he said. The barracuda smiled. He remembered the long business trips, the working weekends. He remembered 21 years. He knew they meant nothing.

"Where," he sighed, "do I sign?"

* * *

In a few weeks, he'll be done. He'll surrender his pager, endure a boozy send-off full of lies, and hit the road home. Already he's watched the replacements move in, a brigade of $30,000-a-year eager beavers, all young and absolutely convinced of their security. The initial anger and hurt have faded. Worse than finally facing the barracuda is the dread of waiting for the encounter. He sees this fear in the few colleagues who declined the buyout. They huddle among themselves, whispering. Their eyes move too fast.

Such fear, of course, is almost everywhere these days. It is where the anger comes from, the anger that politicians misdirect toward easy villains like welfare mothers and illegal immigrants. This creates voter blocs while diverting attention from the true source of discontent—the steady elimination of good jobs in a recovered economy: one "business trend" no politician will touch.

And so our friend is on his own. Everyone tells him he looks happy. He's got resumes out and plenty of plans. Art projects. College courses. That vague new American frontier, called consulting. Shoot, he's only 50. He can do it. Of course, there's a lot of competition out there.

Writers' Workshop

Talking Points

1) "If you're going to write about one person," Peter King says, "the reader has to come away knowing that person." Study and discuss the various ways King reveals his subject, a victim of corporate downsizing, and how well he succeeds in familiarizing the reader with the character.

2) Anecdotes are stories in miniature with characters, conflict, and a climax. Charles Ferguson, a *Reader's Digest* editor and former minister, used to advise the magazine's contributors to tell their stories with anecdotes or parables "the way the Bible was written." A good example can be found in paragraph eight: "Once he started talking about bringing us into the '90s, I quit listening and started to study his teeth." What purpose does this anecdote serve?

3) King often favors a staccato style. "He's got résumés out and plenty of plans. Art projects. College courses." Look for examples in his other columns and discuss the pros and cons of using sentence fragments and their impact on pacing, economy, and style.

Assignment Desk

1) Look for anecdotes in your reading. Identify the characters, the conflict, the climax that make them seem like short stories. Report, write, and polish your own. As a starting point, ask yourself and others anecdote-producing questions, such as "What was the scariest experience in your life?" or "When did you know you had fallen in love with someone?"

2) King puts a human face on corporate downsizing, a social problem affecting millions of Americans. Identify a problem in your community—limited career opportunities for graduates, teenage suicide, Alzheimer's disease—and write a story through the prism of one person.

Required Unabomber reading

In order to get our message before the public with some chance of making a lasting impression, we've had to kill people...
  —From a manifesto attributed to the Unabomber.

The body is received in a white plastic body pouch which has on the zipper a Sacramento County Coroner's Office Tag....
  —Opening of an autopsy report filed in the death of Sacramento timber lobbyist Gilbert Murray, the last person to be killed by the serial bomber.

This is payoff time for the Unabomber. Gone are the days of ineffective little bombs that hurt nobody and barely made the papers. After 17 years in the trade, he at last has achieved full-blown notoriety, the target of the most intensive manhunt in the nation's history, a mystery figure with the power—the Power!—to shut down airports and disrupt mail delivery and make headlines coast to coast.

But that's not the best of it. In a conversion that must amaze even the Unabomber, he has begun to be treated as a man of serious thought and letters. The publisher of *Penthouse* wants to hire him as a monthly columnist. His 56-page manifesto—"Industrial Society and Its Future"—circulates through back channels among academicians and journalists. They pore over his every word, ostensibly for clues to his identity, but also as an intellectual pursuit. What does the Unabomber bring to the debate? they ask. What is his "point"?

"I really appreciated that he tried to educate me...," said a UC Berkeley professor to whom the Unabomber sent his treatise. "I would rather be having a dialogue [about] what concerns him and these issues in society."

The professor's relief upon receiving a kinder, gentler communiqué from the Unabomber was understandable, given the alternative. The alternative is what Murray, father of two, got one Monday morning in April.

The body is received partially clothed in the following garments, which are noted to be markedly disrupted by thermal and blast injury: There are remnants of a white button-down shirt on the upper torso. Present about the neck are remnants of a burgundy and blue necktie. Portions of gray plaid slacks are present about the lower extremities. There is a marked disruption of the waist and thigh areas of the pants, especially on the anterior surface....

The upper extremities reveal significant blast injury with the right hand and wrist absent. The right radius and ulna end with prominent fractures of the midshafts.

Multiple abrasions are present over the right biceps. The left hand has prominent laceration and blast injury of the left thumb and index finger. The second, third and fourth fingers of the left hand are relatively intact with multiple burns and abrasions present. Present on the third (or ring) finger of the left hand is a plain yellow-metal band. The ring is removed in the usual fashion.

Fascination with the case is strongest in the San Francisco Bay Area, which is thought to be the bomber's base of operation. In Southern California, he is known chiefly as the idiot who created temporary havoc at LAX. Up here, however, his status approaches that of cult figure. "One thing I've noticed among the intellectual elite at this place, where I do a lot of work," a defense lawyer told a *Chronicle* reporter at the courthouse, "is that this guy is actually kind of admired privately. They wouldn't necessarily say it in public, but 'cool' is even a word I hear used."

The skin of the face is markedly blackened and abraded secondary to blast trauma. The lips have large amounts of dry blood present. The tip of the tongue is clasped between the teeth....Multiple lacerations are present on the anterior chest wall. The ribs and sternum of the right lateral chest are visible through a large defect....The anterior abdominal wall, comprising the skin, subcutaneous fat, as well as the muscles of the anterior abdominal wall, is largely absent.....

It's not uncommon up here for people to confess, sheepishly, that they agree with at least some of what the Unabomber says. Yes, modern society is a mess. Yes, technology can make trouble. And so what? That, late in the game, the Unabomber has sought to sanitize his murders with a suggestion of political motive is irrelevant. He is what he is: a whack, a loon, a madman, and the time and ink spent in attempts to mine reason from his ramblings measure, not his lunacy, but that of the rest of us.

Want to read up on the Unabomber? Read Gil Murray's autopsy, which in the last pages describes, in cold coroner-ese, how they literally scraped what was left of the man off walls and ceilings. These specimens of skin and bone filled 11 large brown paper bags. Explain to me the societal implications of that.

Writers' Workshop

Talking Points

1) In this column, King demonstrates the power of using different types of documentation to convey emotion as well as information. Read aloud the sections from the autopsy report on the Unabomber's victim. King says the emotion that underscores this column "came not from knowing this man, but simply from reading the autopsy report." Consider what elements in the report are most powerful, and discuss the reasons why.

2) Journalism is guided by a litany of rules, some unspoken. "Never lead with a quotation." Discuss the risks King takes in this column: leading with quotations, devoting half of it to a document written by someone else.

3) The graphic nature of this column raises questions about ethics and privacy. If Gilbert Murray, the Unabomber's last victim, was a member of your family, how would you feel about reading his autopsy report in the newspaper? Debate the pros and cons of using a specific victim's autopsy report. Discuss how the column would have changed without the report details and whether the author had any alternatives besides quoting them verbatim.

Assignment Desk

1) Focus on an issue in your community—the debate over abortion, busing, drunken driving—and make a list of the different ways you could document the story: court documents, interviews, statistics, etc.

2) Collect as many different kinds of documentation as you can. Craft a story based on non-traditional use of documentation that King employs in this column.

3) Reporters, like coroners, must rely on their powers of deduction, their ability to draw conclusions based on evidence. Relying solely on details in the autopsy report, write a passage describing Gilbert Murray.

A long, strange trip, etc.

AUGUST 13, 1995

The Grateful Dead represents the end of the Sixties, basically.
>   —A 21-year-old college student, interviewed in the Haight after the death of Jerry Garcia.

Yes, they were saying it again last week. Jerry Garcia had died and so, it was proclaimed by many, had the Sixties. Again. By my rough count, this latest passing represented about the 25th time that the decade has died. It was said previously to have died in a kitchen of the Ambassador Hotel, and also in the stage pit at Altamont, and on a motel balcony in Memphis.

Or it died with Jim Morrison in Paris, or with Cesar Chavez in La Paz, or with Sharon Tate and the rest, in the house up on Cielo Drive. It died when the last chopper fluttered off the roof of the U.S. Embassy in Saigon. It died when John Travolta danced disco in *Saturday Night Fever.* It died when Marine One took Nixon away. And it died, oh, most definitely, when Jane Fonda showed up at the World Series, performing the Atlanta Braves tomahawk chop with Ted Turner.

A curious thing, this capacity to die and die again. It raises questions. Maybe some people have been overly eager to bury the Sixties. Maybe some other people have been afraid to let them go. In any case, the fixation on this long-gone decade—long gone, anyway, by the conventional calendar test—provides powerful evidence that they haven't made any like it since. Look at it this way: Has anyone out there ever wasted a single moment wondering just when, exactly, the Seventies died? Didn't think so.

* * *

On the night Jerry Garcia died, a memorial was under way in Golden Gate Park. The crowd, a couple hundred strong, huddled together at the center of the polo grounds. A breeze was up, bending the trees that encircle the vast bowl of green. News vans were parked on the perimeter, waiting to go live at 11 with the death of the Sixties.

While plenty of old hippies were present, most of the mourners seemed young enough to need Cliffs Notes to decipher Forrest Gump. They looked the part, though, with their tie-dye shirts and their soulful stares into the flickering light of candles stuffed into empty wine bottles and beer cans. The night smelled of pot and incense. Many people played music at the same time, but none played together. A wild man wandered the edges, screaming, "Sex, drugs and rock 'n' roll."

In short, everyone performed to type, acting precisely as one would expect at a keening for the man who was the soul of Sixties music, San Francisco-style. And it was precisely this that left me feeling unsettled, again. I'd experienced the same flash covering a farm workers march last summer...and watching protesters take over a UC regents meeting last month... and, back in my cub reporter days here, writing continually, it seemed, about the low-rent court trials or religious conversions of Sixties icons.

It is a gnawing sense that much of what transpires on the public stage anymore is but an acting job, a reprise of famous performances from The Decade. The right slogans are shouted, the proper songs sung. Even some of the old characters shuffle through in cameo roles. Still, it's all been said and sung before, by the original artists in real time: Ours is the age of the sequel.

* * *

All of which, no doubt, says as much about me as it does about the endless churning of decades. I was only 13 when the Sixties first died, back in 1968. I had read the operator's manual: *The Electric Kool-Aid Acid Test.* My bell-bottoms were decorated with flowers. I was ready. And then, boom, Bobby Kennedy, Charles Manson, the draft ends, the Beatles break up, leaving us with...Rod Stewart? No wonder I feel out of sorts in encounters with echoes of the Sixties: I was cheated.

No wonder, too, why so many people contrive to cling to that time. What has come after? Disco, Yuppies, New Puritans, computer nerds. Those who created the social and political revolutions of the 1960s had no script. They didn't know where it all was going. That was its beauty. Maybe if they did know— that Cleaver would turn to peddling codpiece trousers, that Hayden would wind up in the state Legislature, that Garcia would die trying to sober up in Serenity Knolls—maybe they would have canceled the whole deal.

They didn't, happily, and so they stocked the wine cellar with an irreplaceable vintage. What Garcia's death represents is the polishing off of one more bottle. There are others left, but not that many. So hang in, Dylan et al. When you go, a whole decade goes with you. Again.

Writers' Workshop

Talking Points

1) King devotes this column to discounting conventional wisdom, namely that yet another milestone—the death of Grateful Dead guitarist Jerry Garcia—marked the death of the Sixties. Examine how he marshals his arguments. Discuss whether he makes a convincing case.

2) Journalists need a command of history if they are to be adequate guides to news of today. But, as King points out, "Ours is the age of the sequel." How many of the historical references in this column do you recognize? How did you learn about them—from television, movies, books, newspapers, friends? Assess the extent of your historical knowledge about various periods in American history.

3) Good writers search for just the right word. Notice the word King selects in this sentence: "In short, everyone performed to type, acting precisely as one would expect at a *keening* for the man who was the soul of Sixties music... [italics added]." The word's origins are Irish for a "wailing lament for the dead." What other words could he have used to describe the event? Debate the merits of each.

Assignment Desk

1) In the first two paragraphs of "A Long, Strange Trip, Etc." King itemizes 10 separate incidents when the "Sixties died." Research and write a paragraph that explains each reference.

2) Tom Wolfe, author of *The Electric Kool-Aid Acid Test,* was a principal chronicler of the Sixties, and one of the most prominent of the so-called "New Journalists" who used the techniques of fiction writers to report the social upheaval of that time. To understand the time and the way writers approached it, read *The Literary Journalists,* edited by Norman Sims and Mark Kramer.

'Another little Vietnam'

SEPTEMBER 10, 1995

They were dispatched to engage an unknown enemy in a tidy little war of containment, but everything got complicated fast. During the course of the conflict, the soldiers would come to be regarded as demons by the nation that had sent them to fight in the first place. Naturally, they became demoralized. They learned to hunker down, do time, get the hell out—to survive.

Inevitably, infected by the craziness of it all, some weaker ones went around the bend. And thus America confronted its Calleys and Medinas. This proved to be a great convenience: Bearing down on the atrocities of renegades was a way to avoid nastier questions of national morality raised by the war itself. We sent them to do a job, Americans could tell themselves, but we never said anything about mutilated corpses or village massacres.

And that was Vietnam.

They were sent into the city, a small, fast army of police officers equipped with helicopters, battering rams and other tools of war. Their orders were clear. Be hard-nosed, "proactive." Do whatever it takes to keep the enemy pinned down, contained. Yes, another war of containment: The general idea—never overtly stated, for the obvious political reasons, but plain nonetheless to anyone paying attention—was to contain crime within certain neighborhoods. These happened to be neighborhoods the rest of the city would prefer to forget even existed.

This conflict, too, would turn out to be more complicated than first imagined. Again, weaker officers lost their way. The value of the Koons and Fuhrmans would be no different than that of the My Lai soldiers. Ripping righteously into rogue cops averted a more painful examination into why a city—not a police force, a city—would lay siege to a part of itself. We never imagined, citizens would exclaim, viewing the video, hearing the tapes. We wanted the cops to be tough, but nobody said anything about beating prone suspects, about spewing racist bile.

And that was Los Angeles.

* * *

One place to begin is 20 years back. In 1975, the last U.S. helicopter lifted off from the embassy in Saigon. A new L.A.-based cop show was introduced to the television watchers: Good old Joe Friday had been replaced by Lt. Hondo Harrison of *S.W.A.T.,* a drama that celebrated the employment of Vietnam-learned tactics on the domestic crime front. Also in 1975, Mark Fuhrman, home from the war, joined the Police Department, and a former LAPD detective named Joe Wambaugh published a bestseller.

It was called *The Choirboys,* and in a pivotal departure from most cop fiction it depicted the department in a way that, well, that Jack Webb would never have dared. Wambaugh's cops did not have all the answers. They sometimes made up the rules as they went along. They were not always polite; they talked dirty and invoked, yes, the N-word on seemingly every other page. These also were cops who worked under enormous emotional strain, isolated, embattled, and sometimes they broke.

Interestingly enough, the novel begins with a scene set in Vietnam, where two future LAPD officers huddle in a darkened cave, alone, scared. Wambaugh had seen the parallels: "These were men," he would say later of his characters, "who were going to be put into another crucible.... They were going to be put into another little Vietnam. And, like in Vietnam, there would be no heroes. No matter what they did they would be scorned, despised."

Two decades and many defeats later, the current attitude among many LAPD officers seems to be: hunker down, do time, get the hell out. "Now you have cops in huge numbers," Wambaugh said, "who are putting the hat down over their eyes, so to speak. Forget about 'proactive.' Just answer your radio calls. I think L.A. is on the verge of finally getting the Police Department it deserves, for not backing up the cops.... It's become a no-win situation for cops. Is it any wonder they go nuts in large numbers?"

Now understand. This is offered only to help explain, rather than excuse, the behavior of the Fuhrmans and Koons. What they get, they surely deserve. At the same time, though, is it fair for the city at large to be blaming the Police Department alone for these atrocious failures?

Culpability for the war in Vietnam belonged to all America, not just the soldiers sent to execute it. The attempt to throw a thin blue line around certain Los Angeles neighborhoods—and then, hopefully, forget about them—was the work of the whole city. Blame for its dismal outcome goes all around, too. The thrust of the public roar created by Fuhrman would indicate that this view has yet to take hold across Los Angeles. The prevailing attitude seems to be the city has a police problem.

If only it were that simple.

Writers' Workshop

Talking Points

1) King employs parallel construction in the first section of "Another Little Vietnam." Examine how he uses the nature of similarity and difference in word choice, sentence structure, and pacing. What is the effect of the structure on the reader? Discuss whether he had to devote so much space to make his point.

2) King says he sometimes takes steps to "inoculate against the obvious responses" readers might have to his columns, especially when the issue is controversial. Notice how, in the third-to-the-last paragraph beginning "Now understand...," he takes such pre-emptive action. Discuss what he was trying to accomplish with that passage, and whether it was successful.

3) King's goal for his "On California" columns is to "get people to think in a way that they hadn't thought before. It doesn't mean that they necessarily agree or disagree, but just understand there's a different way to look at it." Examine this and his other columns and discuss whether your thinking on the issues under consideration were changed. Consider which elements were the most persuasive and whether they were the product of observation, interviewing, or critical thinking by the writer.

Assignment Desk

1) King says he relies on a "Greek chorus of unofficial and never-attributed advisers" he uses as a sounding board for his column ideas and thinking on various issues. If you're working in a vacuum right now, where the only people who play the "Greek chorus" role are newsroom colleagues, try to identify a cadre of smart outsiders you can bounce ideas off and use to test the validity of your conclusions and information.

2) *The Choirboys,* a novel about Los Angeles police by former LAPD detective Joseph Wambaugh, plays a pivotal role in this column. Broaden your own reading to include fiction and search for parallels, inspiration, and understanding in a form other than journalism.

A conversation with

Peter King

CHRISTOPHER SCANLAN: What's your assignment for the *Los Angeles Times*?

PETER KING: At the time I wrote these columns, my column was entitled "On California." My assignment was to go around California and explain it to Californians with a certain emphasis on Southern California, where the main bulk of the readership resides.

They have, just in the last month or so, removed the "On California" designation, which is a little like getting your electronic bracelet removed.

I'm not quite sure what will happen now when I cross over into Nevada or elsewhere in the West, but it essentially remains the same. California is my city/state, as Breslin has New York and Molly Ivins has Texas.

What's your work schedule like?

Typically, I travel a day reporting, spend a day reporting and writing, gather myself, and then go out and do it again later in the week for the Sunday column. My column appears on Wednesdays and Sundays.

If I do good work on Wednesday and sort of look ahead, my weekends can be free. But it is always there. It's the beast on your shoulder, telling you to work a little harder, or get something lined up, or do an interview over the weekend, or rewrite on Saturday because you have the time to do so.

I try not to do that because it's a marathon; if you just run one or two good sprints, what are you going to do next Wednesday? So I try to keep a good pace.

Column writing is a marathon?

In spurts. As long as you're thinking of the next column, you're OK. When you start to think of the column five or six weeks down the road, this endless succession of turns at bat or runs up the hill, it could drive you crazy.

How long have you been doing this column?

This is my fifth year.

And how do you pick your subjects?

Mainly, I try to let news drive it, news being loosely defined as things that are going on that are on people's radar, or ought to be on their radar.

There are staples, wells that you can drink from from time to time. There's always a water war going on in California or the West. There's always the friction of growth. There's always the nostalgia versus the reality of what was as played against the future of what will be.

I don't have a lot of problem coming up with general topics. The hunt is usually for some moment, or place, or person that will define where I'm at, or where I think people ought to be at on the issue or the story line, if you will, at that moment.

Where does that hunt take you?

Everywhere from Humboldt to San Pedro. And now beyond. I do well going in after the news. I do well going into little towns that have seen the cavalcade come and go and are trying to make sense of what it was all about. I tend to have happy hunting for columns there.

I'm not obsessed with being first on a topic as much as getting in and getting my take on it, and often the best time to do that is sometimes during, sometimes before. That's a happy day, too. But sometimes after, in a traditional news sense, the story has come and gone.

What is the test for a column?

A column is an ongoing dialogue. You're going to have bland stretches. But for the good ones, it has to be something you care about. You just can't phone it in emotionally.

The key to emotional writing is leaving stuff out. You can't be shrill or hysterical about it. You have to be contained and measured.

**The column about Nina Davis seems to fit the cri-
teria you're talking about. Why did you decide to
go after it?**

A column has to meet a couple of tests. One, it has to
be a little more than a good story. It has to be a story
that I want to say something about.

And two, I think it has to be something that is of
interest to readers in Los Angeles, because they pay
the freight. There are a lot of things that go on in California or the West, or wherever, that are interesting,
but are not necessarily going to be interesting to a Los
Angeles reader.

There are also things that happen, say, in San Francisco where the same thing is happening in Los Angeles. I don't see the virtue in going and doing a story
in San Francisco that can be done out of your own
town.

Originally, the story of this poor woman who had
saved her children, while a terrific, tragic story, I
didn't think met the test as something that would be a
column for the Los Angeles readership.

And then they had a debacle over who should get
credit for catching the babies she hurled out the window to save. The meter started to flicker a little bit:
maybe there's something here.

Then listening to talk radio and reading the letters
to the editor and seeing some of the journalism up
here in San Francisco when she became a whipping
woman for these people who are opposed to welfare,
then my needle went crazy, because this is something
that strikes me as outrageous. It is universal, in terms
of a grain of hatred that's running through our public
discourse. It's in California. Everybody in Los Angeles can relate to it, and nothing that I know of that outrageous has happened down there. Therefore, it was
worth going for.

**You write, "And yet, somehow, standing beneath
the burned-out unit where Nina Davis lived, it all
didn't seem so swell. The cars were junkers, some
stripped, tires flat. The housing units were sagging,
dilapidated, the pastel paint chipped and scarred
with graffiti. Faded orange bedsheets hung in the**

windows, blocking out the sun and everything else." I take it you were there.

I went two places. I went to the projects where it happened, and then I went to the funeral on a Saturday morning.

Do you always hit the streets for your column?

Not always, but more often than not, by far.

Why?

Originally, I think it was the insecurity that anyone has when they begin to write a column. If you come to it as a newspaper reporter, you can always fall back on reporting. Reporting is what got you where you are, and it gets you out of any jam. You can always take that notebook and go somewhere that the readers can't go and bring back a story to tell.

As I've learned, and it's distressing to learn how to write a column because you do it in public, it's taken on a little bit trickier role. I feel that when I go out, a lot of things just sort of click for me out there. It would be one thing to sit in there and say, "What a bunch of yahoos, criticizing this poor woman who, all she did was save her children, simply because she was on welfare has therefore forfeited her right to basic human dignity."

It's another thing to go out there and see the lie of it all with your own eyes. When you see with your own eyes the reality of their dismal situation, then I think it not only informs the art, but it powers it.

The last line, "Then the casket was loaded up for the long ride to the cemetery, where Nina Davis would no longer burden this great, golden land of ours." You're tough.

I was feeling it right then. I think endings of columns are more important than beginnings, by far—when they work. And when they work, it's when everything just clicks. Everything that was said before, everything

that you saw out on the street, it all sort of funnels together, tributary by tributary, and then, boom. It nails
into one final point. It converges.

Those endings write one time, very fast, no notes.
They just happen. The God of Endings doesn't give it
to us every time. There are examples in the five columns that were submitted that I would say are examples of bad column endings. I didn't like the ending
to the '60s, to the Jerry Garcia column. I felt like I was
straining to find that inevitable last emotion I wanted
people to take away, and the best I could do was,
"Hang in there, Bob Dylan."

But that was one where I was feeling what I felt
when they pulled that little kid away from the casket,
and that was my vehicle for all this residual anger that
I suppose had been building up over some time over
nincompoops saying what a great thing it is to be poor
in America.

Why are endings more important than beginnings?

It's what the person walks away with. I know there are
a multitude of schools of thought. But my thought is,
what good is it if you have a tricky lead and you entice
them in, and then at the ending, you don't have any
goods to deliver.

**In the Unabomber story, you write, "These speci-
mens of skin and bone filled 11 large brown paper
bags. Explain to me the societal implications of that."
That strikes me as an ending that really works.**

My emotion came not from knowing this man, but
simply from reading the autopsy report and imagining
those clenched teeth, and the clothes blown apart, and
the remnants of the tie, and stuff like that. Juxtaposed
against all the blather going on about whether to publish the Unabomber's manifesto and what it really
meant, that created its own sort of anger.

I'm starting to sound like the last angry man here.

**If anger is the fuel for a column, does that guaran-
tee success in the writing?**

No. I think there are many emotions that don't guarantee success, but greatly enhance your chances. Anger is one of our purest and most easily tapped emotions. Ask any modern politician. Hope is a good one. Love is a good one.

For a column, as opposed to a news story or a feature or any other of the forms, emotion is good. You can't fake it.

An old editor who works at another newspaper, but who is sort of my closest adviser, says, "Every once in a while you're going to do your job, and when you feel your bowels in an uproar, go with it. Don't fight that. Those produce good columns."

If you did it twice a week, every Sunday and Wednesday for a year, people would just click you off.

How did you come upon the autopsy report? What was the genesis of that column?

It was sitting in a file in one of our reporter's desks in Sacramento, a reporter who had been covering the case.

Did you ask for it?

I begged for it.

What made you want it?

I knew that the public discourse over this seemed off-tilt. It just wasn't ringing true, the academic debate over the Unabomber's "point." I knew that going in. And then it was a question of, "Well, how do you show that?"

You can try to talk to the family. Or you could go try to talk to somebody who had lost a hand, like a couple of his early victims did, and get their story. But their stories have been told, and told well, and are, sad to say, somewhat predictable.

I thought a better 2-by-4 to wield would be a document like this, a police report or a coroner's report, because if you see enough of these, there is a wonderful clinical idiom—there is no language quite like those reports. Not that it's lyrical, but it makes its own haunting sort of music.

Did you worry about what effect the autopsy language might have on Gilbert Murray's family?

I always worry when we write about people who didn't ask to be in the news. There's a great Thomas McGuane line, you know. People just live their lives. They're not out there as cannon fodder for boys with newspapers.

My feeling was they buried the man. They knew what was in that report as well as anybody. And they were probably as offended—and I did not talk to them—but I have no doubt that they would be as offended as anybody about the Unabomber, in terms of the debate over his merits, or lack thereof. I did not see that as a problem.

Did you ever hear anything from the family?

No.

Was it difficult deciding how much of it to use? Who's writing the column, you or the coroner?

When you do two of these a week every week—and I know other columnists do more—there comes a point when you get sick of your own voice, and the reader, I am assuming by extension, gets sick of my voice. You look for ways to step out of the column and put another language in.

I've turned on tape recorders for people just to let them talk a column, as opposed to me writing a column. I don't do it often. But every once in a while, you feel a need to make that break.

It wasn't the bloody things described, but things like the tie, the white button-down shirt.

The banal entries. I couldn't say anything more powerful than that.

"Present on the third (or ring) finger of the left hand is a plain yellow-metal band."

Those were the passages that I went for. I think they were true to the structure of the report, but I tried to arrange them in increasing power. In the end, when they were talking about how they bagged and tagged and disposed of the evidence was where the description of the miscellaneous bags came in, which provided the ending.

When did you decide you were going to write a Unabomber story?

I have a Greek chorus of unofficial and never-attributed advisers that I feel comfortable saying, "Is something striking you strange about this whole Unabomber debate?"

He had shut down LAX the week before, and I had thought about going down there. But that wasn't a column, that was a story, people frustrated because this bozo had shut down the airport. And that wouldn't have the power to it.

Then when I learned I could get my hands on the coroner's report, again, come in behind the news, which to me was great because then everybody was learning about him. He wasn't front-page news the week I wrote, and that doesn't bother me a bit.

How long does it take you to write a column like this?

Work expands to time allowed. You divide between actually writing and when you pretend that you're actually writing. And the mornings are often spent pretending you are writing, and you think, "Humh. I got this knocked. I'll go get my cheeseburger and my fruit salad, and then I'll come back and finish it."

And then you get back at 1:00 and you go back up to the top again, and you say, "Ooh, boy. I'd better get moving." And then about 3:00, you get scared, and then you start to write.

I am of the "throw it on the wall and then ratchet it back down" school. I have met people who can write a sentence—the first sentence. And then they'll stroke their chin and walk around the room, and then they'll write the second sentence. I tend to vomit on the screen.

It's an outline, in a sense. It's just done on a computer screen that is eventually going to become the file.

And then I go back and, with that form in mind, I know where it began, and I know where it's going, and I think—and this is an important caveat—I think I know what it's going to say when I get to the end. Then I really start writing.

I've had situations, like in fires and stuff, where I've written a column in a couple of hours. You can do it.

At the same time, I think this whole process of thinking—one of the luxuries that I am afforded, because of what some of the more prolific columnists say is sort of a wimpy output, is thinking time. Beginning that morning is thinking. Sleeping on it the night before is thinking.

How do you rehearse these columns?

I often thought if there were a machine where they could put an electrode on your forehead, and what you're thinking in the shower and your brain would get printed out somewhere, these things could be written in a flash. You're constantly thinking the column that way, the phrases and images that you want running through your mind. You think they go away, but they don't. They go somewhere to be summoned up.

Do you jot notes to yourself?

One of my many crackpot theories is that the important stuff sticks. And that you're talking about a filtering process—what you're leaving out.

Typically, my first draft, my first run at a column will be twice as long as it should be. There's a column writing I am learning—and *learning*. It's a sort of unwriting.

What do you mean?

When I was able to do long features, I could aim for the lyrical phrase, the long-running vignette and do some capital "W" Writing. You've got to leave a lot of that stuff out. You remember Rudolf Flesch's *The Art of Readable Writing.* He began each chapter with an epigram from one of the Italian masters, all masters of writing. And one of these epigrams was going back after you had written and taking out all your favorite phrases.

This applies here. The pretty language gets in your way. The vignettes that ramble can get in your way. Long quotes. I use a lot of sentences that I would not have used in a story, but I may have used in a letter to one of my best friends.

Let the language be more of a tone rather than a poem, if that makes any sense.

It's like a chef who's been forced to serve a pot roast and he'll dump some cilantro on it, or a detective who goes to the door and no one answers and he sticks his calling card in there. Sometimes you'll want to throw a phrase in, or something, just to let them know you're on the case. But most of the time you end up rejecting all that stuff, and you go home thinking, "God, I had such beautiful things to say, but they just got in the way of the column."

But what you gain from it is this really strong evocative voice. "This is payoff time for the Unabomber." "Explain to me the societal implications of that." Do you have a reader in mind?

It varies from column to column. It is probably a collection of mentors and friends whose opinions I trust.

Tell us about this unofficial Greek chorus.

My theory on sources, even when I was a reporter, is that you don't need a lot, but you need the right ones.

Are they ever editors?

That's a different thing. I've been blessed with some very good editors, from day one in the 20-odd—very odd—years I've been doing journalism. And I keep in touch with about three or four of them, beyond the good editors I have at the *L.A. Times.*

You develop a relationship with an editor, when it's right, where you speak in shorthand. And there's no baloney; you can get business done real fast, and while everyone's ego needs massaging, that becomes a side issue that you can, with trust, put away and you can say, "Hey, now, I feel like I'm in a rut. These columns aren't working." And this person can say, "You're looking pretty good to me. You've got to get out on the street more. You gotta put your heart into it more."

They tend to boost you as much as guide you. I have built that relationship with my editor at the *Times,* Carol Stodsgill.

How does she edit you?

What she might say, and what I've heard her say publicly, is that twice a week on deadline, or a few minutes thereafter, Pete will file his column and I'll read it, and take a bump out of a sentence here, and a bump out of a sentence there, and Pete writes his own headlines, and so I don't have to worry about that, and I move it.

What I would say is that her editing begins a day or two in advance and is crucial. It begins with a casual conversation about the Unabomber, where I'm saying, "I think this public debate over how smart a guy he is is a bunch of junk. This guy is a killer, and I would like to take people right into the mayhem in some form and let them understand that, and get a sense of that—to make the death real as opposed to the debate, which is unreal."

And she might say—in fact, she did say, "I've been noticing the same thing, and that's a terrific idea," or "That's a good idea and you ought to go for it." And then we might talk about how.

That is the best editing that a columnist can get, is on that front end, where sometimes it won't even be detected that she's editing.

She's a smart woman, and I assume she gets it most of the time, but it can be very casual conversation, but you're trying out a line, or you're trying out a scene, and you're hungry for some response. And once you get it, and it's sort of validated, then you have a sense of purpose, then you have a mission.

I think good journalism comes out of insecurity. Supremely confident people, while they have value on a newspaper staff, I think insecurity is also a useful tool. Mine hasn't gone away from me, and I've been a reporter in some form or another since I was 18 years old. I've learned to live with it. There's a great introduction to one of Joan Didion's collections where she's wishing she had a dollar—she puts it more elegantly—for every time she sat on the edge of a bed in the Best Western motel and tried to summon up the courage to call the assistant district attorney.

I've been through towns seemingly aimlessly, just knowing that I was going to have to knock on some stranger's door and get them to deliver. You know, the good news is, I think they sense that.

I think they respect that a lot more than backing up the satellite truck and saying, "We're going to have to rewire your house to get some voltage, and when did you last see your little girl?"

I used to think it made me less of a reporter, because I was shy or insecure about knocking on that door for the first time. I've come to believe that it could be turned to my advantage; you know, shy people hear a lot.

What's the most important lesson you learned, or relearned, doing the work that won you this prize this year?

The lesson would be—and I think this applies not just to column writing—find things to write about that interest you, that you care about. I'm not talking about being an advocate. I'm talking about being interested and active. If you're bored with the subject, why shouldn't the reader be.

The other lesson is get out there and fill up the notebook, as an old city editor told me. Get input. Nourish what you know going in with new stuff that you didn't know, or might surprise you.

This is Journalism 101 to most people, but I find it true in every column I write. I've learned again the value of knocking on a door, of making the extra phone call, of going out at midnight and watching them perform their 60-ish wake for Jerry Garcia.

Every time I do one of those things, I say, "Whew. Good thing you did that. If you hadn't done it, you'd just be sitting here sucking on your thumb, writing in ignorance." Which, you know, on a rainy day will get you by, but you don't want to make a habit of it.

Do you write your own headlines?

Usually first. Which is backwards to what they teach in headline writing school, but it's a trick that Jim Willse, an editor who's now at the *Newark Star-Ledger,* taught me when I was a baby reporter at the *San Francisco Examiner,* and was all muddled up on a series of stories about Mexico. He said, "What do you want the headline to say?" That gets right to the meat of it.

So now, I ask myself that same question, and I get to answer it before I write the column. And I'll change it sometimes, after, but if I can get it down to six words—"The Story of the Season"—I know what the column is about.

It's that first and most important cut. We were talking about what you're leaving out. The headline leaves out a whole lot. You've committed yourself to the path, and if you've thought it through, it helps a lot.

How did you get into journalism?

I once wanted somebody who's going for his master's degree to do a thesis on how many journalists begin because they wash out in high school football or baseball, and writing for the sports pages of the high school newspaper was my way to be a part of it.

I was probably the worst high school sportswriter that ever walked the planet, but that's how I got into it.

Had you ever written columns before "On California"?

No. I had wanted to. I had been a student of the form. I've read all the Breslin and Bob Greene anthologies that I could find, and the Russell Bakers. You know, I had always loved to read Breslin—every word. I loved what he could do with the form, could do with reporting, and then writing with that little extra dagger in it.

What did you have to learn to make the transition to be a columnist?

I don't think I *have* learned. I think I am learning—and I think the distinction is crucial. If I thought I had learned, I would probably want to move on.

The biggest thing that I am learning—and have learned—is the difference between feature writing and news writing and column writing. A good feature writer will take the readers to a place they can't go and show them things they can't see, and do it in an evocative, lyrical way, and it's a wonderful thing.

I think a columnist has an extra obligation. A columnist has to take the readers to places where they can't go, but they've got to tell them—not *what* to think, but what they might want to think about it when they get there. And it has to have a point. It has to have a certain edge. And that edge has to come from you. You have to perform a bit.

How do I apply this to my writing? How do I know what to leave out? How can I look at my copy and know, "That can go," or "I can say that more efficiently"?

What was the Faulkner line—"Write on whiskey, edit on coffee"? I think you have to be your own worst critic and best editor. I think you write it, you'll love it, you would marry it if it were possible in this realm. It's your writing and it's beautiful. And if you have the time, you get up the next morning. Or if you don't have the time, you take a walk around the office and sit right back down on it.

And you say, "All right. What's really interesting here, and what is just pretty?" You almost develop a different set of eyes and a different standard. You know, "I'm going to hate this thing. Show me what I really like."

You'd be surprised what you find. Call up a friend and say, "Hey, I just wrote this lead. You want to hear it?" And you say, "Tell me what you think," but what you're really saying is, "Tell me that you love it." And halfway through the reading, again, you're saying, "Blah, blah, blah. God, I do go on." And you hang up the phone embarrassed and start chopping the heck out of it.

I think anybody can go back to anything they've written, and cut. You go back six months after you've written it, and then read it. Then that piece of writing can teach you.

But it's a humbling experience.

What do you read for inspiration?

It's real hard to know what to read, because you can't help but be influenced by it, and it washes across you. If I'm reading too much John Cheever as I'm writing columns, I can hear a little bit of an unfamiliar voice creeping in.

When I read Joan Didion, I pay attention. She writes wonderful sentences that no one can match, but I don't want to match them, anyway. I'm going to have to write my own sentences. But what she has is this other radar system that sees little details and hears little pieces of idiom or phrases that I would not bother normally to put into the notebook. And she makes great hay with those.

And so that teaches me, as I go out to report a column: Keep those ears open. Those throwaway lines can be useful. They're the most substantive part of some interviews.

Jimmy Breslin will catch the light coming in through the courthouse windows that plays off the ring of the Mafioso defendant or something. Keep your eyes open for things that are happening naturally.

It's like watching a football game. Don't just watch the ball. Watch the receiver they don't throw the pass to, because sooner or later he's going to come open and it's going to be important.

I read Mark Twain. Just how feisty can you be? How outrageous can you be without going over the top? The envelope has been pushed in a number of ways by many people who are great, and we are humble to fly in our limited way in their same air space. We can learn what the airship can do by studying them.

Is the column your favorite form?

This is the best job I've ever had in newspapers. There comes a time in most reporters' careers when they get frustrated with the notion of objectivity, which can be demonstrated to be shaky at best. They get frustrated at having to call up people that they might know, or suspect, are lying to them just to get the other side. They get frustrated listening to people who they know aren't half as smart as they think they are. They get frustrated with editors.

It's a young person's profession, and oftentimes they either become editors, or they leave the business. People leave newspapers in frustration many times. This is a way for me to transcend a lot of those built-in frustrations. I feel a lot more in control of what I do. I pick what I want to write.

Who or what made you a writer?

I guess the person who did the most first was somebody who broke into our house when I was in about the third or fourth grade and took our TV when we were on vacation. We didn't replace it for a few years. I got on my bicycle every day and went to the Sunnyside Branch of the Fresno County Library, and became a reader in earnest. The first thing to writing, of course, is to read and so that shaped me. I think the writing bug is a symptom that follows the reading bug.

In "One More Styrofoam Parachute" you have this wonderful passage: "Right away, our boy knew he was sunk. 'Once he started talking about bringing us into the '90s, I quit listening and started to study his teeth. He lost all human form. All I could see was a big barracuda smiling at me. He had jaggedy, razor teeth, and they were worn down—like he had been using them a lot. And his eyes were in a feeding mood. I said to myself, "Start swimming for shore." ' "

How do you get a quote like that, and how do you decide how and when to use it in your story?

You get a quote like that by interviewing intrinsically quotable people. He's an Oklahoma product that has that sort of Oklahoma kind of dryness to him.

It's listening. It seems to be a hard lesson for some people sometimes to grasp, but if you sit there and let people talk, they eventually get to where you want them to be.

How do you get it down?

Just scribble, scribble, scribble.

So you're there with a notebook?

I just scribble as fast as I can. Because you want to keep pace with the conversation. When I'm interviewing somebody, I'm just trying to get them to tell their story. You want to start scribbling fast and early and filling up your notebook because if you don't they'll start into something unexpected that's real good, and if you're not calibrated to keep up with them, you lose them.

Are you a good note taker?

No. I kick myself for not going to shorthand school. But writing a column takes care of that a little bit, because you don't have that much space for longwinded quotes anyway. And, what is important, you remember the quotes that you really need to remember.

How do you decide, "OK. I've got the quote. I've listened. I've written it down. It's a great quote." How do you decide to use it?

The first standard, which is true in any kind of journalism writing, still applies. If they say it better than you can say it, you use their words.

In "Another Little Vietnam," in the last passage you write: "Now, understand. This is offered only to help explain, rather than excuse, the behavior of the Furmans and Koons." You seemed a little uncomfortable there, that people might misunderstand you on that one.

In the part of column writing that is persuasive, or argumentative, it helps to inoculate against the obvious responses. You want the reader to come along with you.

You don't want to give them a door where they can jump out. You want them to get all the way down the hallway.

And every time that you say, "Ah, I don't need that door. I'm just going to let it hang," you get letters saying, "You son of a gun. How could you defend these people for beating Rodney King?"

I put a deadbolt over that door with that phrase. This isn't about whether or not it was right to beat Rodney King. This is about whether it's right to put all the blame for beating Rodney King or the stuff of Mark Furman just on the cops.

What are you trying to accomplish with your column?

Get people to think. So much of our media society is not based on thinking, but reacting. We're a society, putting our thumbs up and our thumbs down and not thinking about the middle ground of that. There are other places on the spectrum.

A column for me works if it makes people think about a thing in a new way. It doesn't mean that they necessarily agree or disagree, but they just understand there's a different way to look at it.

What is the most surprising thing you've learned writing this column for five years?

That people will read it. Beyond my mother.

Writing is nothing if it isn't read, and when you get feedback that people are reading it, and not only reading it, but they're thinking about it, and they write you an intelligent letter, and you've made that connection —that is the most gratifying.

Every time someone calls up and says, "You know, I read your column all the time," I'm floored. I say, "You do? Great."

What starts a column, then—a line, an image?

You don't know until you get there what will grab you. But it's like they say about basketball: The shot you don't take, you never make.

Do you go to find a focus? Do you go out and report?

Think of it like a team in the horse and buggy days. You have two reins in your hand. One is a story. There's got to be a story. It's got to be a little bit more than just a story. It's got to be something you care about.

It sounds a little lonely. You don't have a photographer with you, no companionship.

I have a telephone. I talk to the kids and my wife at night. I think loneliness, in a weird way, is important, because if you want to fill up and not think about anything, I mean, writing is supposed to be lonely, right?

Sooner or later, you have to do that. You have that period where it's just you. That it isn't home and no one cares. You're feeling all sorry for yourself, and the coffee isn't any good—all that stuff.

That's where you begin. And then it takes some sort of shape, and you begin to have a faint glimmer of hope that it's actually going to be printable, and then your pace quickens, and as it comes down to the end, you say, "Well, it ain't my best, but I survived another one." That's a glorious day. You can get back on the road and go home.

Paul Greenberg

Finalist, Commentary

Paul Greenberg is the editorial page editor of the *Arkansas Democrat Gazette,* which he joined in 1992 after presiding over the editorial page of the *Pine Bluff Commercial* for 30 years. Among his many honors, Greenberg was awarded a Pulitzer Prize for editorial writing in 1969, and in 1981 he was one of the first winners of the ASNE editorial writing award. He is the author of three books and has been syndicated by the *Los Angeles Times* Syndicate since 1971. He has a bachelor's degree in journalism and a master's degree in history from the University of Missouri.

In "Confessions of a Fan," Greenberg brings his trademark wit and historian's sensibilities to this dual tribute to the music and magic of Patsy Cline and Mozart. His skills as a writer and commentator will leave you wanting to head for the record store to browse the country & western and classical music sections.

Confessions of a fan

SEPTEMBER 6, 1995

What do you call somebody who would never think of hitting the road without his tapes of Mozart and Patsy Cline—eclectic? weird? bipolar? nuts? Or still another Patsy Cline fan who doesn't fit the profile? There must be jillions. You don't have to be into country music to bond with that *voice*. Any more than you've got to keep your car radio tuned to KLRE all 24 hours of the day to grow into Mozart.

It's possible to belong to both cults, I explain to people who give me strange looks when the subject comes up, as it did at intermission last week at the Arkansas Rep in Little Rock. The Rep was previewing its road-company production of *Always...Patsy Cline* before starting the season with *Amadeus* on the 21st of this month. Double-header heaven. Cliff Baker—the Rep's artistic director, founding father and residing genius—strikes again. Twice.

And, yes, cult is the right word for devotees of Patsy Cline, not fan club. The difference is that each member of a cult is sure that he and only he truly understands the reasons for his idol's appeal and, worse, would be happy to explain it at great length. Many an eye glazed over while I started to go into all this at intermission to people who kept sidling away.

You needn't be wild about the general run of chantoosies for something mysterious to happen inside when you hear Piaf. Any more than you have to like English journalists in general, thank goodness, to admire Rebecca West, or to pick up an essay by George Orwell and gasp at the lucid light shining through, as if his prose were the clearest window pane.

The sublime W.A. Mozart and the earthy P. Cline do have some things in common. Both are an elegant mix of light and dark, sunshine and shade, although one drips with sex appeal and nostalgia, while the other seems utterly free of all earthly passions as each note drops into its preordained place, like the heavenly choir singing when the world was first created. Which may explain why the most credible explanation for Mozart's music is that he was not an 18th-century European composer at all, but an angel. To consider him in tandem with Patsy Cline may be the best illustration of the difference between honky-tonk angels and the usual kind.

Someone whom Kitty Wells, Hank Williams, Willie Nelson and all the rest leave cold can swoon over Patsy Cline, and souls immune to the whole classical repertoire have been known to sprout wings and take flight after awakening to Mozart.

Karl Barth, who as a theologian explored many a mystery, explained the sensations Mozart's music inspires in his *Letter of Thanks to Mozart:* "What I thank you for is simply this: Whenever I listen to you, I am transported to the threshold of a world which in sunlight or storm, by day and by night, is a good and ordered world. Then, as a human being of the twentieth century, I always find myself blessed with courage (not arrogance), with tempo (not an exaggerated tempo), with purity (not a wearisome purity), with peace (not a slothful peace)."

Yes, an ordered Creation (but not a dull one). On the contrary, a world of perfect, crystalline beauty. The world not only as it should be but surely really is. It was Kierkegaard who thanked Mozart for living because otherwise he would never have known what it was like to be in love. As for the author of *Church Dogmatics,* Karl Barth confessed that "if I ever get to heaven, I would first of all seek out Mozart and only then inquire after Augustine, St. Thomas, Luther, Calvin..." Dr. Barth would listen to Mozart every morning, as if watching the dawn.

The music of Mozart would be the last place to seek a sense of nostalgia—another proof of its timelessness —while Patsy Cline's is redolent of a whole past, a whole subculture that ain't so sub- in these latitudes, but comes alive again with the opening chord of the Rep's production. It's a world of gas stations and truck stops and cafes, of bacon-and-eggs and ghastly bourbon drinks, of lost loves and you-done-me-wrong songs, of Longneck Buds and Black Jack and Blue Sock, of drive-ins and D-I-V-O-R-C-E, of pink-and-black Pontiacs and all-night trips halfway 'cross Texas aboard a Con-ti-nen-tal Trail-ways bus.

One of the more authentic aspects of Candyce Hinkle's hammy performance as Patsy's fan/friend is the occasional lapse into over-enunciated speech, as in solemn lines like "She seemed much re-lieved," or "Sub-*con*-scious-ly..." Call it Redneck Formal.

Patsy Cline was at the Rep last week in the personage of Jessica Welch, a singer who has her down to a throat-catching T, and comes by it honest, being a Pine Bluff girl. It would be impossible to keep such a talent from throwing in just a little Jessica Welch from time to almost unnoticeable time, but the Pure Patsy numbers come through like sparkling dew: the crowd-pleasers so intimate they seem to be sung just to you or for you, like "Crazy" and "I Fall to Pieces" and "Walkin' After Midnight" and "Sweet Dreams" and...

Well, it's enough to say that in her time Pasty Cline may have been responsible for more *au*-to-mo-bile *ac*-ci-dents than fast driving in these parts. When that *voice* poured out of the car radio, she blotted out concentration like an opiate. This little ol' gal would have made the sirens' song sound like a tuneless Johnny Cash number.

Not that Patsy Cline was above borrowing a trill or two from Kay Starr or Patti Page, but she had a way of improving on it. Her early songs, with their authentic bad-country-band twang, remain the most moving, with their combination of delight and cynicism. Listen to "I Love You Honey" and smile. ("I love you honey...I love your money...most of all I love your *au*-to-mo-bile.") It's flapperism flipped to the Fifties. Even the Patsy Cline songs that cross the always thin line into parody can shine, like "Three Cigarettes in an Ashtray." Mozart's isn't the only music that transports. Patsy's just transports you in a different direction. To a place in time instead of out of it.

Or as an anonymous fan once said, she was "the first woman who could make me feel like crying out of one eye and winking out of the other!" Nobody ever said that about Piaf. And imagine the theology Dr. Barth might have written if he'd started every morning with "Back in Baby's Arms."

Lessons Learned

BY PAUL GREENBERG

Let's call this "Seven Lessons *Re*learned."

1. Break the rules. If it isn't the first rule of column-writing, it should be near the top of the list: Never write about yourself. Or about your family, dog, hobbies, likes, and dislikes—even if those are the subjects you know best. Columns should be personal but not *just* personal. The personal will come through in a well-written column about impersonal subjects. Leave it at that. As fascinating as we may find ourselves, the subject is likely to bore others. It's a sound policy, after finishing a column, to go through it and see how many words like "I" or "me" or "my" one can strike out.

And yet this column, "Confessions of a Fan," is almost solely about personal taste. And must have been one of the widest read I've ever written, to judge by the volume of mail from Patsy Cline fans. (Mozart fans must be less given to correspondence.) When a personal taste is shared by so many others, the rule can be bent. Which leads to:

2. If it feels right, go with it. Ordinarily it's a good idea, when writing about oneself, to check out the result with the paper's Good Taste maven (every newsroom ought to have one), but in this case it didn't seem necessary. The result just felt right. Most of us have a feeling about a column, an editorial, or any piece of commentary by the time we've punched in that last punctuation mark. Sometimes we want to applaud, sometimes boo, sometimes wipe the whole thing off the screen and start all over again. Trust that feeling. But always remember:

3. It's OK to take the subject seriously, but not yourself. If you do write about yourself or your own tastes, remember to do so lightly, conversationally, with due self-deprecation: "Many an eye glazed over while I started to go into all this at intermission to people who kept sidling away." Which may be just what you, Dear Reader, would like to do at this moment on plowing through "Lessons Relearned." But it always helps to review.

4. Take notes. Don't hesitate to review a show, a ballgame, a stump speech, a traffic accident, a sunset. A columnist never knows where his next subject will come from. Carry a pen and take notes, or at least mental ones. You never know what you'll get a column out of. A writer, said

Henry James, is someone who never wastes an experience. His observation still stands as both goad and warning. (Some of us think Mr. James would have done better to waste more.)

Notes let us avoid generalities—the kind of songs Patsy Cline sang—and be specific: "Crazy," "I Fall to Pieces," "Walkin' After Midnight," "Sweet Dreams." With notes, we can get the culture right, sharp, exact—not 1950ish Redneck but the specific artifacts: "It's a world of gas stations and truck stops and cafés, of bacon-and-eggs and ghastly bourbon drinks, of lost loves and you-done-me-wrong songs, of Longneck Buds and Black Jack and Blue Sock, of drive-ins and D-I-V-O-R-C-E, of pink-and-black Pontiacs and all-night trips halfway 'cross Texas aboard a Con-ti-nen-tal Trail-ways bus."

5. Go with your instincts. If you feel the words you've just written are right, especially after looking at them again in the morning, print 'em. You can hardly go wrong when your enthusiasms happen to be Mozart and Patsy Cline. Or as a publisher (a publisher!) once told me: "If you know you're right, forget caution."

6. Don't be afraid of the unconventional. Some of the best chords are composed of the most unlikely notes. Again, see Mozart, W.A., and Cline, P. You can put the most unlikely elements together in American, and especially in "Southron," in a way you might not be able to do in other, more rigid languages.

7. (And my favorite rule of all:) Go to the second level. Anybody who attends a Patsy Cline show might be able to just describe it, or self-indulge in a little personal nostalgia. But a columnist ought to go to a second level: talk about the universal element in the particular subject. Or find another particular (Mozart) to compare and contrast with the first (Cline). The reader doesn't need us to echo his own immediate reaction. He needs and enjoys a reviewer who will challenge or validate, broaden or articulate, his own responses. One of the delights of reading Maureen Dowd is that she brings a drama critic's visual eye to the passing scene. All the world's a stage.

Robert Lipsyte

Finalist, Commentary

Robert Lipsyte is a sports columnist for *The New York Times* where he also writes the weekly "Coping" column for the paper's *City Weekly* section. He is on his second career at the *Times* where he spent 14 years as a sports reporter and columnist. During a 20-year absence from the paper, Lipsyte was a network news correspondent for six years—four at *CBS Sunday Morning with Charles Kuralt,* and two at NBC, where his reports appeared on the nightly and weekend news progams. In 1990 he won an Emmy as the host of *The Eleventh Hour,* a nightly public affairs program. He returned to the *Times* in 1991, and in 1992 was a Pulitzer finalist for commentary. A prolific writer who is equally at home in the broadcast studio, he has published 18 books, including sports biographies and young adult novels, and written screenplays. He graduated from Columbia College and the Columbia Graduate School of Journalism.

In his "Coping" column, Lipsyte discovers the small town in the big city. With sensitivity and a craftsman's skill, he sketches a graceful portrait of a caregiver spouse, revealing to a city of strangers how their neighbors contend with life's daily dramas.

Life as a caretaker

MARCH 26, 1995

Beverly Kidd gets out of bed at 4 a.m. after Maxwell the cat stands on her chest and licks her awake. She goes into the kitchen and drinks coffee until 6, talking back at talk radio, reading books on alternative therapies and plowing through stacks of medical bills and insurance forms. It is the best part of her day.

At 6, Robert Kidd wakes up.

She unhooks his catheter, showers and shaves him and helps him dress. This takes at least two hours because she makes him do whatever he can: struggle into a shirt, for example, although he can't button it; pull on his shoes, although he can't tie the laces. Sometimes she sounds like a master sergeant, she says, but if he stops being engaged, what is left of his life will wither away.

"Robert was the best thing that ever happened to me," said Mrs. Kidd the other day, remembering when they first met seven years ago. She was divorced, an Upper East Side real estate agent reluctant to be fixed up with an actor. But rockets went off. "It was hectic, wow, it was dynamite. He was fascinating. He was even more hyped up than I was. He got me into Shakespeare. I couldn't get a word in edgewise. He never stopped talking."

Until one morning in 1989 when he didn't answer when she asked what he wanted for breakfast. She was running late, so she brought him back coffee and an egg sandwich from the deli, left it by his bed and went off to work. When he didn't answer the phone, she came back home to find him still in bed, and silent. At the hospital, they said he had suffered a stroke.

* * *

The Kidds were placed on the medical-industrial conveyor belt. She has lost count of how many doctors and therapists have worked on their piece of Mr. Kidd, how many tests have been administered, how much money has moved around the system under his name. She is only sure that hardly anyone has treated him as

a whole person, and that too many routinely pre-
scribed drugs have taken his balance, his mobility, his
speech, his independence.

As she talks, an intense 50-year-old who seems always about to laugh or cry, Mr. Kidd sits in a lounge
chair and seems to listen. He is a slim 70-year-old,
wide-eyed behind his glasses. Sometimes he raises a
hand or smiles or actually says, "I knew..." or "That's
right." With his deep voice and matinee idol mustache, it is easy to match him with the 8-by-10 glossies
in the album on the table. Once, proclaim the neatly
mounted reviews, Mr. Kidd had given a "thoughtful
portrayal" of Edward II at the Theatre de Lys, once
Mr. Kidd was "the impressive longshoreman" in *The
Time of Your Life.*

"I was never the caretaker type," said Mrs. Kidd,
carefully blowing smoke from her cigarette out one of
their tiny walk-up's two windows overlooking East
22nd Street. "Whoever thinks you wind up doing this?
It's life as you live it, and that's that. You marry a man,
he gets sick, you take care of him. But sometimes I
think I'm going nuts."

Neither of them have family in the city, and help is
a constant problem. Mrs. Kidd says she has run
through 30 or more home health aides in the past five
years. The best took off to other jobs, often suddenly,
and many of the others, she said, arrived late, were untrained, filled with attitude, unable to understand English. Medicare pays for four hours a day, up to 20
hours a week, which is not enough for Mrs. Kidd to
take a full-time job. Once a week, Mrs. Kidd attends
computer classes at nearby Baruch College. Working
out of her home may be her only chance to make
money again. Mr. Kidd's veteran's pension and gifts
from Mrs. Kidd's parents are their main sources of income. The rent-controlled apartment is only $187 a
month, but paper diapers alone are $200 a month out
of pocket.

But working at home wouldn't solve the problem of
isolation. She belonged to a stroke support group until
the leader died of a stroke. She talks regularly only
with Maxwell, the plump 10-year-old orange tabby
who was born in the Public Theater and helps connect
her to that brief, glorious time when Robert never

stopped talking, and with Al Weaver, a doorman down the block, during Mr. Kidd's daily outings.

* * *

"I've got to get out, snow, rain, doesn't matter, only ice keeps us in," she said. "Robert can't get into a taxi, but city buses are great if I can't get Access-a-Ride. He seems to love Chinatown; he smiles, doesn't drag up his feet there. We go to the library twice a week; he's reading biographies of Harlow and Marilyn Monroe now.

"And the Stein Senior Center on 29th Street is wonderful. He's taking art classes. He's going to have a show."

Mr. Kidd's oil pastels are mostly of faces in the middle of tunnels and cocoons.

"Look at the art," said Mrs. Kidd. "Robert still has a lot to offer. Some mornings I want to scream, 'Robert, get better.' And then I whisper, 'I'm sorry, Robert, I'm just exhausted.'"

Lessons Learned

BY ROBERT LIPSYTE

Beverly Kidd is among the most important of my many journalism teachers, the people I live with and write about in this sudden, thrilling turn in my career, writing a small-town weekly column for an all-world daily.

For the first time, I live inside my beat. After so many years covering big-time pro sports (I still do that, too) where I've always felt the outsider (an anthropologist on my best days, otherwise a buzzing green fly, according to the jocks) covering real people living real lives required an epiphany: People are the only true experts of their lives, not the officials we quote, the academics who study them, not the journalists parachuting in. I check in on Beverly several times a month (this has led to follow-up columns about her, and tips on others). My first and most unforgettable teacher, however, was a bum I called Bill.

I actually started writing the city column called "Coping" before it existed, before the *Times* even began publishing the Sunday *City Weekly,* which is circulated only through four of New York's five boroughs. I had recently moved into the downtown Manhattan neighborhood, and strolled past a big broad-shouldered bum in his forties who dominated one corner of my block, mooching off smaller, older bums who sat against a whitewashed brick wall. They read paperbacks while Bill smoked and paced and harangued them.

"Reality," he would shout through the prematurely white beard that covered his lips, "what do you know about reality? You're bums."

He yelled at me for strolling through his sidewalk seminar. I didn't catch the words, but the tone was pure outrage at my rude invasion of his space. I couldn't let him intimidate me or I'd be crossing three streets instead of one just to get my paper. I glared at him and growled like a dog. He wearily shook his head and rolled his bright blue eyes and waved me through.

It was the first step toward staking a claim to my own block, and the first step toward thinking seriously about my immediate surroundings. One thing we tend to do in New York is shut down, avoid eye contact, mind our own business, except to be aware of who or what is coming too close. Of course, you miss a lot that way. But I watched my bum deteriorate; first, he began begging while limping on a right foot sloppily wrapped in dirty bandages. He was an aggressive toll collector, shoving his crumpled paper coffee container in my face. I wouldn't give him a dime. "Outta my face, Bill," I snarled. There was a short period during which I would actually cross to his corner just to challenge him.

Meanwhile, he was drinking more and more, leaning against the brick wall, his blue eyes filming over. Week by week, he escalated his props, a soft shoe over the bandages, a cane, crutches. He began whining, then just begging with his eyes. My resentment became intense dislike. Why should you be here, Bill, fouling the quality of my life? If my mood was dark enough, I might say it out loud. He disappeared for a very long time. And then he re-appeared in a wheelchair, without his right leg.

Let's waste no sympathy on how bad I felt. Urban guilt is for those who just want to say they're sorry. I decided that Bill was my bum now, a dollar a day when I saw him, a fiver on holidays and my personal celebrations. One day, after I paid my Bill, a bum hawk began to circle him and I said, "Don't even think about it," and he said, "The guy's almost dead, I'm hungry" and I growled, "You'll be dead, too" and he sidled away. I might have been feeling tougher because my son, an Alphabet City rocker, was covering my back.

We were halfway down the block toward home when the bum hawk doubled back and struck. I took off screaming, how could you rob a bum, you bum, but I was lucky and he escaped. When I got back, Bill was nodding out and my son said, "You're as crazy as they are." I thanked him for that and stuffed another dollar in Bill's pocket.

That experience enabled me to begin thinking of myself as *of* the block, not just *on* it, and of Bill as some kind of secret sharer helping me find my street legs.

Just about then the *City Weekly* appeared and I wrote the first column. Executive editor Max Frankel had named it "Coping," which I at first thought clunky, but came to realize was exactly what the column should be about—New Yorkers, urban survivalists, coping with a tough, noisy, demanding environment that was also extraordinarily accessible and supportive when you learned how to break it down into neighborhoods and blocks. The word "cope" became my litmus test; I tried not to use it in the column, but I always thought, "Is this about coping?"

Nobody was more about coping than Beverly Kidd, and by the time I found her (actually, there was this friend of mine who had a doorman who...well, that's exactly how it works), I was learning how to cope with this new column, too. Just keep hanging out and talking to people, asking them how they're doing, which is another way of asking how they are coping. In return, I get to learn something new every day.

Including Bill's real name. Mike. He told me a few days before he died on the street.

Daniel Henninger
Editorial Writing

Daniel Henninger's work has graced these pages several times, as an ASNE finalist in editorial writing in 1985, 1986, and 1994. He is deputy editor of the *The Wall Street Journal*'s editorial page. A native of Cleveland, he graduated from Georgetown University in 1968 with a bachelor's degree from the School of Foreign Service. After graduation, he worked for *New Republic* magazine until 1971 when he joined Dow Jones as a staff writer for *The National Observer.* Henninger joined *The Wall Street Journal* in 1977 as an editorial page writer. In the years since, he has served as the paper's arts editor, editorial features editor, assistant editor of the editorial page and chief editorial writer, and senior assistant editor with daily responsibility for the "Review and Outlook" columns. He was a finalist for the Pulitzer Prize in editorial writing in 1987 and 1996, and he won the Gerald Loeb award for commentary in 1985.

The editorial page of *The Wall Street Journal* is required reading on Wall Street, in Washington, and beyond, in no small part because of the provocative writing of Daniel Henninger. With verve, wit, and style, his editorials plumb the social and political significance of the day's stories from the Waco disaster and the O.J. Simpson verdict to the downfall of an international bank.

The nationalized pastime

FEBRUARY 9, 1995

The trouble with baseball is it ain't a railroad.

Back in the good old days—when men were men, the Oval Office had a spittoon and Babe Ruth thought the President was just a fella who made less money than he did—the person who sits where Bill Clinton sits would have known how to deal with a bunch of oligopolists and their strikers.

He would've ordered those railroad magnates into his office, whomped them across their gold watch chains with a copy of the Railway Labor Act of 1926, locked them in a room with a referee from the National Mediation Board, and dadgummit if that didn't work, he'd order the Army out to get the railroads running again.

Golly, but the times have changed. Today the President calls the oligopolists of baseball into his office and "sets a deadline" for the two sides to settle their strike. That deadline passes—strike one! Then the President sets another deadline, and it passes—strike two! But Bill Clinton's not about to strike out completely with a third deadline, so he tells Congress to go in and bat for him.

It figures. We'll bet Bill Clinton managed to never actually strike out in a childhood baseball game. Oops, gettin' late; gotta get home for dinner; too dark; looks like rain; got something in my eye; I think that plane's gonna crash!

But seriously, we sympathize with the President on this one. Look what he's dealing with. Here's one of the President's player negotiators quoted in yesterday's *Washington Post:* "This is not a dispute about money. This is not about getting $10 million a year or $6 million a year. I'd be willing to play this game for $3 million." If memory serves, Cornelius Vanderbilt once said exactly that about the New York Central (with appropriate inflation adjustments).

Now, when Mr. Clinton this week tried to send Congress into the game, Tris "Speaker" Gingrich refused to leave the bench: "I'm not sure Congress is the right place to try to organize the national pastime."

Organize the national pastime. What an intriguing phrase. When you consider that radical Republicans now run the country, that communism's been overrun by McDonald's and that Hillary's health care plan is dead, chances are we'll never see another bona fide state-run industry in our lifetimes. In a way that's sad, because viewed from a certain perspective, state-run industries are kind of fun: They're extravagant, showing up for work isn't that important, the bosses are toothless tyrants, they support the local economy into eternity.

Why not? Let's nationalize the national pastime. Seriously. Who cares whether baseball is run by Bud Selig or Ira Magaziner? That's right; we think the structure of the United States Baseball Agency (USBA) is perfectly suited to Mr. Magaziner's arcane skills. Admittedly, the distances between the bases and home might go metric under Mr. Magaziner, not to mention the probable pooling of salaries and a cap on hotdog prices. Also, all the games—well, some of them—would be broadcast on public television. Also the Dole-Gingrich Baseball Reorganization Act of 1995 makes Little Rock one of the new USBA franchises in 1996, and Secretary of Baseball Magaziner gets to appoint Bill Clinton as its general manager. Oh yes, the first Latin American franchise goes to Havana, provided Fidel steps down from his present job to run the club.

So what's the problem? Tell George Steinbrenner and Marge Schott to get lost and tell Ricky Henderson and the rest of them to show up for their Civil Service exams this Monday at 8 a.m., Department of Labor, Building C, 10th floor, Section C-3, the Reich Auditorium.

Writers' Workshop

Talking Points

1) *The Wall Street Journal* makes no secret of its dissatisfaction with President Bill Clinton as a president and as an individual. Study paragraph five, beginning "It figures." Discuss the meaning of this imaginary litany of excuses and whether you think it's fair.

2) Henninger displays both wit and invective in this editorial about the baseball strike. Consider how he uses a commentary on a baseball strike to weigh in against Ira Magaziner, one of the architects of the failed Clinton health reform plan. Does Henninger enjoy an advantage because of the sophistication of his audience? Discuss how familiar a reader would have to be with health reform to appreciate this comparison and the risks an editorial writer faces when assuming the scope of readers' knowledge.

3) Irony is the key to the success of this editorial, the notion that *The Wall Street Journal* editorial page would, on the surface at least, come out for turning baseball into a state industry. What is the value of irony, when the writer intends a different meaning from the normal association?

4) This editorial certainly falls afoul of grammarians as well as guardians of political correctness. Consider the opening paragraphs: "The trouble with baseball is it ain't a railroad." In the second paragraph, Henninger writes "Back in the good old days—when men were men, the Oval Office had a spittoon and Babe Ruth thought the President was just a fella who made less money than he did—the person who sits where Bill Clinton sits would have known how to deal with a bunch of oligopolists and their strikers." What would you say to someone who expressed outrage at this statement? Explore Henninger's intent and whether he was effective.

Assignment Desk

1) Write alternative headlines for this editorial, trying to echo the word play of Henninger's title.

2) An economics term, "oligopoly," plays a major role in this editorial. Look up the word in a dictionary. Research its origins and the role journalists played in combating the evils of this system. See if you can come up with another contemporary version of oligopoly, besides Major League Baseball. Research and write an editorial attacking the problem, employing Henninger's wryly ironic tone.

Leeson loses Barings

FEBRUARY 28, 1995

As 233-year-old Barings PLC went up in a puff of
electrons, a market watcher of our acquaintance wondered what Nicholas William Leeson's mother must
think. We figure it one of two ways: Either the 27-
year-old lad who brought down Barings at a keystroke
had a strict mum and saw his job as liberation from
constraint; or alternatively, young Nicky is simply the
youthful product of our unconstrained age. Either way,
what we know now is that Nick needed watching.

As of this writing, we assume that the unaccounted
for Mr. Leeson is somewhere calculating whether to
turn himself over to Singaporean justice or to the
Queen's back home. This, too, will no doubt tax his
skills at risk-assessment; the Queen herself is a Barings client, but on the other hand 950 million whacks
with a bamboo cane is no small matter.

At this early juncture in so fantastic a tale, we'll
leave open the possibility that Mr. Leeson, like the
Great British Train Robbers, in fact knew what he was
doing. Setting that aside, though, we assume the largest lesson here has to do with risk management.

Decentralization is a key tenet of much modern management theory. One hires good people and lets them
perform without a lot of intrusive and bureaucratic reporting upward. It's a good theory, and as Wall Street's
annual year-end bonus stories attest, vast fortunes are
now made by individuals trading for their firm's account. The firms we have spoken with in recent years
assert vehemently that they have the traders' operations
supervised every which way from Sunday, and the in-
centives would hardly suggest otherwise; after all it's
their profit shares riding on these positions.

Still, something went awry with Joseph Jett at Kid-
der, Salomon Brothers' management took the fall for
Paul Mozer's activities and Bankers Trust's executives
must now walk the earth trying to explain why the over-
sight responsibility was Procter & Gamble's. Ultimately, someone in authority has to take responsibility.

So far, the derivatives business has been given a wide berth to assert that responsibility. When Washington held hearings awhile back into Bankers Trust's troubles with its clients' derivatives trades, most of the regulators testifying were remarkably supportive of both the idea of derivatives and the market's ability to supervise them. So far that judgment is holding up. While further tangles may yet emerge here, the Barings meltdown so far doesn't appear to have created system risk.

If indeed Barings' demise holds a lesson for our time, it may lie in the behavior of the Bank of England. When Barings bid to go belly up in Argentina back in 1890, the BOE bailed it out. Not this time. Tradition, old boys and all, Barings was allowed to go down, and we're attracted to the suggestion in yesterday's *Journal* coverage that the British authorities did so to make an object lesson of the venerable bank (losing the people who financed the Louisiana Purchase does give one pause).

Barings PLC is hardly going to be the last big name to run aground in the uncharted waters of the global economy. One could have read in these pages in recent months, for instance, of huge Western oil ventures going sour amid Russia's disorganization, of eminent investment banks getting stiffed by China, of Mexico's old political pressures flattening its new economy, of global hedge funds run by financial geniuses who bet badly and lost big for their clients.

These blowouts, however, are the exception. As sophisticated securities instruments, such as derivatives and options, supply liquidity and appropriate hedges, the system will seek the most promising investment opportunities worldwide and supply them with capital. That may mean software designers in India, garment assemblers in Malaysia, optical instrument makers in Germany or pharmaceutical researchers in New Jersey. These successes are more commonplace than the burning of a 233-year-old financial cathedral.

The system's continued success, though, will depend crucially on integrating the requirements of the modern age with the values that formerly sustained a Barings. That means market participants who support such modern business values as information transparency and internal financial controls, while preserving the bedrock of honesty and credibility.

Somehow or other, Barings PLC let a kid go off to Singapore and get lost amid the paper millions. Now Barings is gone, somebody else has their money and Nicholas William Leeson is on the lam. It's an amazing story. It could happen to anyone.

Writers' Workshop

Talking Points

1) The notion of taking responsibility for one's actions is a key element of this editorial. It also features prominently in Henninger's editorial about the Waco case. Compare the two editorials and discuss the differences and similarities in the treatment of that theme.

2) A firm grasp of history as well as current events informs Henninger's editorials. List the news stories and historical events in this and his other pieces. Study and discuss how the writer weaves a sense of news and history through his prose.

3) Despite the serious subjects his editorials address, Henninger often injects a sense of play in his writing. "Either the 27-year-old lad who brought down Barings at a keystroke had a strict mum..." and "...on the other hand 950 million whacks with a bamboo cane is no small matter." What do these allusions indicate about the sophistication of *The Wall Street Journal*'s readers?

Assignment Desk

1) Puns and other word play feature prominently in the headlines Henninger writes for his editorials. "Leeson Loses Barings," "The Nationalized Pastime." Try to come up with alternatives for Henninger's headlines that are just as playful. Write headlines that echo this spirit for your own stories.

2) The reference to "950 million whacks with a bamboo cane" alludes to another celebrated case involving Singapore authorities. What was it? Research the story and write an editorial that owes a debt to Henninger's style and wit.

Waco

JULY 31, 1995

Attorney General Janet Reno appears today before the congressional committee looking into the events at Waco. Ms. Reno, a formidable and stolid presence, will come before this panel of hectoring solons as a kind of contemporary Lear—a power well-intended and adrift.

Ms. Reno first arrived at Justice only to find her authority usurped by Webster Hubbell, a Clinton crony whispering about Waco to the President unbeknownst to the department's nominal first officer. In short order, a local neighborhood problem outside Waco so escalated that only the Attorney General of the United States could issue the authority to commence the fateful assault on the compound with CS gas. The burning building ran forever on America's home TVs.

Some two years later, we get Waco's death rattle—a congressional hearing broadcast to a suspicious nation. This hearing was unavoidable and indeed overdue; it was compelled into life by pressure from a wide range of citizens and a few journalists dissatisfied with the government's account.

We're not fully happy with how this is playing out. As catharsis, the hearing works. Notwithstanding the harping about right-wing weirdos in the woods, enough people in all walks of American life have had bad experiences with the federal government's many enforcement agencies, not all of them armed, that it should have come as no surprise that a Waco could drive this disaffection to critical mass. In short, Uncle Sam dug himself a deep credibility problem.

But what comes after catharsis? What follows the hearing? Given history, many wrong things, we'd predict.

Begin with Janet Reno. Today she'll say: Based on the information at the time, based on her concern for the Davidian children, she made what seemed the right decision then, that in retrospect it could be seen as a miscalculation and certainly, the whole thing was a great tragedy.

But don't expect an apology. Don't expect any high public official in our time to simply say, we screwed up and we owe the American people an apology. It doesn't work that way in the nation's capital. There are reasons why the strongest words heard in Washington from those who've made a big mistake are, "I regret."

We have created a formula in this country for deterring prudence and judgment in our public officials. Whether a Love Canal, an Ivan Boesky or a $400 toilet seat, the sanction for erring—public vilification and even ruin—is so great that none can go before a forum like the Waco committee and flatly admit wrong. So no one does. Thus the past week, every FBI official appearing about Waco has insisted they were right. This almost mindless certitude persists despite the work of skeptical journalists such as Dean M. Kelly in the religion journal *First Things* and *The Ashes of Waco* by Dick J. Reavis (Simon & Schuster), who calmly investigated the event to produce first-rate accounts of its misunderstandings and mistakes. But for our public managers, survival demands denial.

That can't be healthy.

Deputy FBI Director Larry Potts and perhaps others deserved to be meaningfully disciplined for Waco and the Ruby Ridge shootout. It would be a large mistake, though, if we somehow believe that the bonfire of these Waco hearings settles much, that it is going to leave us with better governance by our enforcement agencies. More likely, every FBI field agent in any sort of vague situation is now going to buck the onsite decision upward, with no one doing much of anything until the highest reachable authority signs off. That is, more denial.

Remember the thalidomide tragedy? When it came out in the early 1960s that a drug called thalidomide had caused some badly malformed infants, the ensuing cauldron of horrible photographs and congressional melodrama meant that various Food and Drug officials got their heads handed to them. To avoid future public floggings, the FDA turned itself into an agency of fanatical caution.

Ours has become a dynamic, complex and often disruptive modern society. Governing it well will mean hiring, or electing, the most skilled public managers available and accepting that they'll need flexibility to deal sensibly with unimaginable nightmares like Waco or imaginary threats like someone's back yard "wetlands" violation.

As for the politicians and the media, the past week's hearings into who did what and why at Waco have been revealing and helpful. Getting the facts out is always helpful. Next time, let's try to do it sooner.

No doubt our assessment of the Waco aftermath will disappoint those more in the market for prescriptive fixes. But we're far past believing that the traditional response—loading up our already titanic bureaucracies with more deck chairs—will solve anything.

Writers' Workshop

Talking Points

1) A firm sense of civic, literary, and linguistic history infuses Henninger's editorials. Notice how he describes a congressional committee as "this panel of hectoring *solons*," [italics added] a word derived from the name of an seventh-century Athenian statesman and poet who instituted legal reforms. The word is also a headline writer's cliché that most style books would advise avoiding. Discuss whether Henninger's usage was appropriate or hackneyed.

2) Henninger has a gift for the phrase that hits the bulls-eye of his subjects. "Some two years later, we get Waco's death rattle—a congressional hearing broadcast to a suspicious nation." What is the impact of the word choice and structure of this sentence? Assess the power of the sentence without the phrase "Waco's death rattle."

3) Henninger seems ever-mindful of *The Wall Street Journal's* place on the conservative right of the political dialogue. Notice how, in the fourth paragraph, Henninger writes, "Notwithstanding the harping about right-wing weirdos in the woods, enough people in all walks of American life have had bad experiences with the federal government's many enforcement agencies...." Effective writers try to think pre-emptively by anticipating reader response. Discuss what Henninger might be trying to do with the opening phrase, and what effect it might have on readers who embrace a different ideological stripe.

Assignment Desk

1) Henninger credits two "first-rate" journalistic accounts of the events at Waco that reflect what he calls his eclectic reading habits: a trade press book, *The Ashes of Waco,* and a religion journal with a limited subscription list. Review your own reading list. Are you relying on the mainstream press or do you look to more obscure, but often useful outlets, such as newsletters and journals, in print and online?

2) The history of government intervention, or the lack of it, is marked by milestones of death and injury. This editorial

harkens back to the thalidomide tragedy of the early 1960s and what Henninger describes as a bureaucratic response that led to "fanatical caution" on the part of federal Food and Drug officials. Research the thalidomide case or study the writings of Upton Sinclair, Ida Tarbell, and other muckraking journalists of the early 20th century with an eye for historical parallels. Write an editorial that relates a contemporary issue or event to one from the nation's past.

The jury's right

OCTOBER 4, 1995

There is a school of thought which holds that juries, like democratic electorates, are always right. Not necessarily correct or appropriate, but *right*. What this means is that a jury's decision, like an electorate's, is a complex rendering of *opinion* about some public matter—a person on trial for a capital crime, a corporation on trial for personal injuries, or a politician presenting himself for the public's judgment of his policies or his character. We, individually, often don't care for the outcome of elections, and we often don't like the outcome of jury verdicts—but we would be fools not to see that the Simpson jury is trying to tell this country something important.

We would be fools for showing ourselves incapable of responding to the clearest signals that some part of our system is in trouble. It has come to be our view that the broad system of justice and law enforcement in the United States is damaged.

We can't know whether Mark Fuhrman's racist tapes tipped the case against the prosecution. But it's clear that the 12 women and men of the Simpson jury clearly do not trust the law enforcement institutions of Los Angeles. That may be galling to those who believe that any disinterested assessment of the prosecution's case against O.J. Simpson was overwhelming. But all who are maddened by this verdict would do well to make their own disinterested assessment of the credibility of our legal system.

The Simpson trial itself was widely viewed as almost anything but a serious criminal trial—a circus, a soap opera, a rich man's exercise. Similar sentiments emerged around the televised Menendez brothers trial in which two confessed murderers won a hung jury after the defense accused their dead father of molestation. In the Rodney King police-abuse case, LAPD officer Stacey Koon is tried and acquitted, south-central Los Angeles riots, so Koon is tried a second time near that neighborhood—and convicted. Television, though, only makes these the most obvious symptoms. There's much more.

Yesterday morning before the Simpson verdict was read, newspapers carried stories that some conservative members of Congress, supported by Democrats, were pulling back from their support of the anti-terrorism bill passed in the wake of the Oklahoma City bombing. After congressional hearings into the Branch Davidian siege at Waco and the shootout with the Weaver family at Ruby Ridge, these legislators wish to think some about increasing the police powers of the FBI and other federal law enforcement agencies.

In the days preceding the Simpson verdict, stories appeared in which residents of black city neighborhoods generally expressed the view that their relations with the police are poor. That is, the most criminally besieged among us mistrust the people whose job is to protect them from the criminals. Why?

Last Friday on this page, we published a piece by our Dorothy Rabinowitz about the picture-postcard town of Wenatchee, Wash., where local prosecutors, abetted by child-care workers, have arrested numerous citizens on accusations of the most lurid sexual abuse of children, have imprisoned the accused and taken their children from them. People who speak out are arrested and themselves charged. No higher state or federal legal authority seems inclined or able to intervene. Similarly wild prosecutions based on extreme child-abuse theories have resurrected the Salem witch trials in a surprising number of American communities. The accused are helpless.

In Congress there is legislation to finally address the abuses of this country's tort liability system, which even its defenders admit is riven with abuses such as junk science and hired-gun witnesses. Corporate executives regard the discovery process as a mockery of justice. Academics and reporters who write skeptically of tort cases get hit with broad, financially crippling subpoenas by plaintiffs' lawyers abusing their officer-of-the-court powers. On the political right, critics argue that federal agencies given the authority to undertake criminal prosecutions of environmental statutes have greatly abused that authority.

Whether one is of the political right or left, what must be admitted is that what we have here in total is an astounding level of public cynicism about the law and law enforcement. For many different reasons, people at all levels of American society—on the streets, on the farms, in the boardrooms—now think the legal system is rigged against them. Its credibility with the various publics it is supposed to serve is eroding. No one doubts that much honest, hard work gets done every day by officers of the court, but there is also obviously a broad problem that is damaging respect for the system. It is this problem that deserves our collective attention, much more so than any "race issue" from the Simpson verdict.

It is no doubt going to be impossible to avoid discussion in the days ahead of the role race played in the Simpson verdict. It's a stillborn subject. Our sense is that many people, black and white, are becoming exhausted by the constant raising of the "race issue," which for all the effort, seems to go nowhere. Can anyone seriously take pleasure in watching the Simpson verdict make it worse?

For all their notoriety, the men and women of that Los Angeles jury are just a small corner of the American criminal justice system. But on Tuesday their verdict offered us a large message about that system. They don't trust it. Neither do a lot of other people. We better find out why.

Writers' Workshop

Talking Points

1) Writing the day of the verdict in the O.J. Simpson murder trial, Daniel Henninger uses the case as a prism through which to view the "broad system of justice and law enforcement in the United States." What is his central conclusion? What examples does he use to buttress his opinion? Discuss whether you find his argument persuasive.

2) This editorial challenges the reader—and all of America—to pay attention to what the Simpson jury was saying about the criminal justice system: "They don't trust it. Neither do a lot of other people. We better find out why." Discuss how editorial writers could take up this challenge. Consider possible subjects and ways you would report editorials that would have the best chance to produce thought-provoking answers.

Assignment Desk

1) Henninger cites several other headline-making incidents in this editorial: Waco, the Oklahoma City bombing, the Rodney King case. Select one and research and write an editorial that explores the deeper ramifications of the event.

2) As deputy editor of *The Wall Street Journal*'s editorial page, Henninger says he looks for editorial writers with reporting experience and instincts. In paragraph six, Henninger describes news stories "in which residents of black city neighborhoods generally expressed the view that their relations with the police are poor. That is, the most criminally besieged among us mistrust the people whose job is to protect them from the criminals. Why?" Visit one such neighborhood to ask residents that question. Write an editorial based on your reporting.

A conversation with
Daniel Henninger

CHRISTOPHER SCANLAN: Could you sketch the landscape in terms of _The Wall Street Journal_ page and your place in the landscape?

DANIEL HENNINGER: It's unique. Our page generates its material, both its editorials and many of its signed features, from a variety of geographical locations. Not all of our editorial writers are based here in New York City.

We also use editorials that are produced by the editorial pages of _The Wall Street Journal Europe_ based in Brussels and _The Asian Wall Street Journal_ based in Hong Kong. We feel that having those people closer to their sources and the news there produces a higher quality product than we could, purporting to be the fount of all wisdom in New York City. And we share our editorials with them for publication over there.

It all ultimately flows through my computer, this torrent of editorials.

Tell me about the demands on your time today.

I edit all of the editorials. I write two or three a week, but all of them pass through my hands for editing of varying degrees. If there's one reality that keeps pressing itself into my world, it is the constraints of time. No one today seems to have as much time as they want, but I think the reason for that is because of the technology—fax machines, e-mail, and, of course, telephones. It's now possible for so many additional people to get our attention, that at newspapers like mine the claim on your time has risen, which, in effect, means that somehow one feels that the time left over to write editorials and think about them has become more pressed than ever.

One keeps fighting to create time to do what presumably you're mainly in business to do, which is to produce editorials. But it takes a much greater degree of concentration on organization and focus.

How many editorials do you edit a week?

Ten—two a day, five days a week.

Where do you work?

I have a fairly large office with seven or eight chairs in it. I call my office "the village green," because it's not very formal. We have something you could call a meeting most mornings in my office, but what seems to be just people sitting and talking about all sorts of things. It could be described as a group of people expressing their opinions about what's in the news, what they think is going on. Occasionally, people will talk about subjects that aren't in the news at all, that they think we ought to think about.

At some point, it's my responsibility to raise the subject of what we're going to put into the paper that night. Sometimes I may already have material ready to go. Or to try to discern among this random conversation that someone has raised an issue or subject that we ought to editorialize about, and then I or (*Journal* editor) Bob Bartley will say, "Yeah, that would make a good editorial." And once it's been identified as a subject for an editorial, the conversation about it might change a little bit. People will stop bringing up random subjects and we'll focus on this one for a while, until we get a sense in which direction we would like the opinion to go. And the person who brought it up probably is the one who's going to write about it, though not necessarily.

But once we get focused on an editorial subject, everyone pays pretty close attention because it's possible that one of the other writers is going to end up having to write about it. Having done that, the herd will move on to another subject. It's very much kind of contact thinking.

There are editorial pages that have writers assigned to specific subjects who are expected to bring to the table something to write about on any given day, maybe every day, and that subject then gets discussed by the editorial board. The process here is really substantially more informal than that. I would venture to say we have one of the most informal editorial page processes in the business.

What do you mean by "contact thinking"?

Random, people bouncing ideas off one another. One idea generates someone's thinking on something else, which then may trigger another train of thought. I think probably it could make a lot of writers uncomfortable because it seems unstructured, but I think that that would be a misimpression. I sometimes compare what we do in the editorials day to day to what a columnist would do two or three times a week. I think that on balance over a year what we do day-in and day-out, the quality of our work is higher than what any individual columnist can maintain. I think that simply because we have a larger-capacity computer dedicated to our material. It's striking sometimes. You will raise an issue or a subject that's in the news, and it seems difficult at first, what the heck are we going to say about this. If I had to go off in my room by myself and produce something, I could, but it would be really hard if it wasn't clear what I wanted to say. As a result of these kinds of meetings we have in which people don't feel constrained about contributing to whatever's on the table, ultimately we end up with a much stronger piece of work than you would doing it by yourself.

This process breaks up every day around noon. You go off and write till maybe 4 o'clock. I would like to see something by 4:00 or 4:30, 5:00 at the latest, because our drop-dead hour is 7 p.m.

What does your editing involve?

Rewriting to a greater or lesser extent. Sometimes a lot, sometimes not at all. The editing is necessitated by the fact that most of the time people are writing under deadline. If I write something under that kind of time constraint, I sure would like someone else to look at it and help it and fix it, if it needs it.

The other thing I do in my editing is try to serve as the page's historical memory. To keep our editorial position, the fundamentals of the editorial position, consistent over time. Certainly, it can change, but we probably would want to talk about that some before making a large change, so I try to maintain that consistency.

Do you consult with the writer if you're going to be doing some rewriting?

I might ask for some additional information, but as far as what gets rewritten we probably won't talk about that too much. If there's time, I always let the writers see the editorial. Once it's in the computer system they have access, and I tell them, "Take a look at it." If there's time for them to read it before I send it to the copy editor, I'll do that. If we're really on deadline, I will send it to the copy editor and say, "Read it over his shoulder," so to speak, on the screen. "And come talk to me if you've got a problem." It works fine.

Who edits you?

Bob Bartley or sometimes I'll have Melanie Kirkpatrick, the assistant editor, look at it. Sometimes I will ask Paul Gigot to look at something I've written, or John Fund to check whether the political facts are accurate.

How important is the lead of an editorial?

Everyone wants good leads, but I think it's more important than ever. Readers of newspapers have become absolutely brutal in their choices whether to read something or not.

I tell a story based on experience in seeing this brutality, so to speak, in practice. I commute on a train from New Jersey into New York every day. It's a 45-minute train ride in the morning and every seat is taken and everyone's sitting there quietly reading one newspaper or another; and because it's this region, a fair number of people are reading *The Wall Street Journal* in the morning. So I'll be sitting on the aisle, and there'll be somebody sitting next to me or a few seats in front, and they're reading the first section of the *Journal,* paging through it.

The editorials appear inside the last two pages, and the editorials are on the left-hand page. I'll watch a person going through the paper. They'll get toward the end of the first section and they come to the international pages and they'll kind of look at that and read something. Then they'll turn the page to the leisure and arts page, and they may look at that material. Now, the next page is going to be mine, right? And they'll turn it and their eyes will cast up to the lead and they'll hover there for, say, three seconds, they'll drop to the second editorial for about two seconds, and then they'll turn to the features and maybe even turn the page. You practically want to jump out of your seat and yell, "Wait a minute! I worked on that for eight hours! Give me a break!" It drives me nuts.

On the other hand, if I see them start reading a lead editorial and stick with it, then I figure I've succeeded. Obviously, the first thing they read is the lead. Every day I make sure that that first sentence or two is going to give us a fighting chance with those kinds of readers.

What makes a good lead?

Strong writing, freshness, something out of the ordinary. I'm constantly looking for ways to give the reader a jolt. Because editorials in a newspaper, a daily newspaper, are not freestanding essays. They're not articles in a magazine that have a life of their own. An editorial is just 700 words among thousands or tens of thousands that a reader is trying to absorb in a big daily newspaper.

Once they encounter my editorial, I've got to break through the kind of dazed sensibility or fractured sensibility that the readers bring to the newspaper reading experience, and I've got to grab them somehow. Writers talk all the time about grabbing the reader. I don't think of it as grabbing the reader. I think about it as jolting the reader.

In "The Jury's Right," the opening paragraph on the Simpson verdict will seem to have taken the declarative position that the jury's verdict was "right," in quotation marks, which I think on that given morning would clearly have been a jolt to most readers who thought the verdict was, in some sense, wrong. Having jolted them that way, I was pretty certain I was going to hold them for a while.

The only reason for doing that is to try to stake a claim to three minutes of that reader's extremely valuable time. I see myself in a relentless daily struggle for the reader's time.

I hate to call all this stuff "tricks of the trade," but I think at the end of the day that's unavoidably what we're talking about. We're in the business of using words to convey ideas and feelings and sentiments, and writing at its best involves all sorts of manipulations of words and sounds and syllables to create an intended effect.

"As 233-year-old Barings PLC went up in a puff of electrons, a market watcher of our acquaintance wondered what Nicholas William Leeson's mother must think." That's a surprise.

It's a surprise and it's kind of funny. It's not hilarious, but it's just enough to maybe make a reader chuckle a little bit.

"The trouble with baseball is it ain't a railroad."

You know what those leads guarantee? That they'll read the next sentence. That's all I'm asking for, is to get past that first sentence or maybe the first two sentences. Because then you've built some momentum. You have to give people an incentive to keep reading. I liken it to being a stand-up comedian. Obviously, editorials are not comedy, but being a stand-up comedian out there on the stage is really a tough business. People either laugh or they don't.

I remember reading an interview with Joan Rivers. She said she figures that a novice has about five minutes to capture an audience and that a pro like herself has about 10 minutes, and if people aren't laughing by then you will never get them. They're gone. And I feel the same way about the first paragraph of an editorial.

Who are you writing for?

Most of the time, I think we're writing for the average *Wall Street Journal* reader, and I have to say that I think most of us here at the editorial page feel extraordinarily fortunate to have the readers that we do. It's obviously a very high-quality readership, they're very well-informed, you don't have to write down for them. In no sense do you ever have to dumb down copy for the *Journal*'s readership. You can write it pretty much as sophisticated as you want.

In terms of the writing craft, it sounds like you may have those train mates on your commute in mind?

The men and women on the train would be a perfect stand-in for the typical *Wall Street Journal* reader. You're trying to hold their attention, you're trying to provoke them into reacting to what you're writing about. I sometimes think that collectively *The Wall Street Journal*'s readership knows everything. If we make a mistake, a factual mistake about some arcane matter on our page, invariably one of our readers will let us know. One of them, somewhere, knows this fact, and they will find their way to a fax machine or a word processor and send in a correction.

How does the awareness of such an informed readership drive the reporting, the fact-checking, the writing?

It is a real form of discipline. I don't think anyone in our business consciously sets out to fool readers. But I think most people who reach a certain level of skill in the writing business do understand that it's possible to use rhetoric and prose in a way that has a certain kind of expectable effect on an audience, that it's possible to lead an audience in certain directions by using very emotional phrasings and techniques. With our audience, you have to be conscious that they're pretty sophisticated, pretty skeptical, and that most of the time you have to play it straight with them.

An editorial by its nature is a piece of political rhetoric. But that's not quite the same thing as being able to take readers in places they don't want to go. If you're going to try to take our readers into new areas —an example would be school choice, giving parents vouchers to choose the school that they'd like their children to attend—you're going to have to give them a pretty deep basis of facts and examples to convince them. You can't simply give them a piece of opinion, saying that school choice is good or that term limits is good.

What is the role of the editorial page and the role of the people who create it every day?

One of its primary roles is to reflect the editorial principles and philosophy of the newspaper, which is generally taken to be free markets for free people, to comment on the news and the events in that context. Secondarily, we are in the business of trying to affect political and social outcomes. We are trying to change things. It's a pro-active editorial page. In that sense, it's radical, if radical means change.

The Wall Street Journal's editorial page is regarded as a conservative editorial page, which automatically seems to suggest that we are in favor of defending certain kinds of status quo or that we're opposed to the kind of change that's normally associated with liberalism. Our answer to that would be that American liberalism has been affecting the nation's laws at the federal and local or state level for a long time, and that we have been trying to alter that course. So the status quo, until recently, has existed in many places as something we've been trying to change rather than defend.

The third purpose is to provoke thinking in our readers, which I think is probably an assignment that any editorial page tries to take on, to get people to think about things in a newer, different way. To react. Without trying to get too highflown about it, that's pretty much the point of having a First Amendment. We get to say whatever we want and, hopefully, people out there who read us get to think whatever they want, and out of that process the political system benefits.

What do you want readers to do as a result of reading your editorials?

I hope they'll agree with us. We're trying ultimately to make the most coherent, persuasive case that we can for a point of view on these subjects. You hope, over time, that enough people will agree that it results in a change, whether in a piece of legislation or in the political coloration of the country.

Who writes the headlines?

The writers put their own headlines on a lot of them. I'll do some of them. Not infrequently, the headline will come out of the meeting and the headline will drive the entire editorial.

"The Nationalized Pastime," "Leeson Loses Barings." You guys like wordplay and puns, don't you?

I try to write the headline before I write the lead. It helps crystallize the point, much the same way a lead does. I know there are writers who say, "The heck with it, put it aside, I'll deal with it later." I cannot do that. I've got to get the lead down, and 90 percent of the time I will try to get the headline written before I start, as well.

The headline is a sales tool, a focusing device, your first shot at that brutal commuter who just glances up there and if the headline doesn't pull him in, he may not even look at the lead sentence. "The Nationalized Pastime" is a clever pun. Baseball's the national pastime.

On July 31, 1995, I thought that there was only one word needed: "Waco," and everyone would read it. That subject was hotter than a pistol at that point. And all we're announcing is we have something to say about Waco, and I assumed everyone was going to read it. We'll frequently do that.

There are other times when I'll say to writers, "I don't care what your headline is, I just want the following word in it, this one word has got to be in the headline," because that means the readership is almost guaranteed, the rest of it doesn't matter.

"Leeson Loses Barings" combines both the *Journal*'s propensity for puns and the news. That was obviously written about Nick Leeson and Barings going bankrupt, and the only words I really needed in the headline were "Leeson" and "Barings." I got both in there and managed to make a pun out of it, as well. That was kind of a hat trick.

"The Jury's Right."

That was the morning-after Simpson editorial. That headline is also a pun, but that's not just a pun for the fun of it. It's an intentional pun. The full phrase there is, "The jury's right to tell us something about the case they've just decided." The editorial was a fairly subtle editorial, very hard to write. I've reached a point now where it's not hard for me to write editorials any more. There's a degree of professionalism involved in that. This one, however, was hard.

Why?

It was hard to hold its integrity together from start to finish, because it was discussing several different phenomena going on in American society right now, and trying to sustain a theme. The child abuse trial in Wenatchee, the tort liability system, Waco and Oklahoma City, and the Simpson trial. This is what remains the difference between our business and all this punditry and the like that goes on on television.

If I had been on television the night of the Simpson verdict and this thought about the jury had suddenly occurred to me, and I tried to defend it, I or almost anyone would have had trouble pulling it off and most people listening to it would have said, "Aw, that's a stretch. Come on." With television, you make up your mind about what's said as quickly as the people say it.

But given the opportunity to sit down for four hours and write 600 or 700 words, as carefully as I could, I think there's a much greater opportunity for reflection, reading editorials of this sort, than there is getting your opinions off the television. Which is to say there's still a place for newspaper editorials. I hope.

Let's talk about your writing process. You said that "The Jury's Right" editorial was hard and that you really needed that four hours. How did you write that?

This one was actually written under a tremendous amount of pressure. I probably started around 2:00. I have this office I go off to write in. I don't write in the village green office any more because there's just too many interruptions. I couldn't sustain any thought. I go off into an office in another part of the floor and sit and start staring at that screen and thinking and hoping something organizes itself in my mind. With three or three and a half hours to get it done, there's not much alternative. I don't start scribbling on a pad or anything for something like this. You pretty much just have to consult the muse and hope it shows up.

My expectation by now, at this point in my career, is, "The muse will show up." I mean, I am not allowed to fail.

How did the writing begin?

The first thing I came up with was the idea in the first paragraph, which is that juries, like electorates, are always in some sense right. A handful of us had talked about it a little bit before in my office. I had suggested that it was striking that the justice system was coming in for criticism in a lot of different areas of American life. Bob Bartley thought that made sense and maybe that was the line of argument that I should pursue. The question then was how to get into that point of view. And the first paragraph is the way I found my way into it.

Having written the first couple of paragraphs or so, I open another computer window and just start jotting down lines. Not sentences, but words or phrases: tort liability system, Waco, the DEA, militias, Dorothy Rabinowitz's Wenatchee child care stories, and make a few notes underneath them not in any particular order. And then I just look at it and think about it. There was a point, years ago, where I'd go at something like this in a much more structured way and might even make an outline. It's very important that you try to make these editorials as well organized and logical in your argumentation as you can.

Do you make outlines?

I've gotten to the point where I don't have to do outlines. I can organize it in my mind and then pretty much see what belongs where, and then move back to the other screen and decide that this is the point where I'm going to start writing. At some point you have to just let go of the notes, because time is short and space is short, and move on to the next subject.

Fortunately, we're able to get a length count as we go along, and I do that a lot because you just develop an instinctive feel for how much space you have left, how much you want to say, and how you want to say it. And when I got down to the point where I was about two-thirds of the way through, it was time to stop talking about these examples and get back to what it all means, and press on through what looks to me like the final three paragraphs.

The third to last paragraph summarizes my feelings about the problems with the criminal justice system, and the last two paragraphs return to the Simpson verdict, because I understood that, even though I thought I was making a pretty good case for the fact that the Simpson verdict reflected larger problems, the verdict's impact was simply so overwhelming and was clearly causing some divisions in the country, that I had to get back and somehow deal with that.

I'm trying to write a serious editorial that covers a lot of ground and I'm addressing people whose minds were probably made up. Having said what I wanted to, I had to get back and deal with that emotionalism at the end.

How important are endings?

The lead is more important because you will never get to the end if you don't have a good lead. But one of the things about an editorial is it is imperative at the end that you wrap it up and get out of the editorial in a very clean and neat and energetic way. I choose "energetic" consciously. You don't want readers to drop off. You want to pump them up a little bit at the end.

What are you looking for from the reader?

I want a reaction. I want the process to continue in their minds after they stop reading the editorial. I want the wheels to keep turning. I've finished turning the crank, and rather than have it stop right there, I would like to see the wheels in their mind keep turning. Because I think some good will come of it.

How does a writer improve?

A person has to write a lot. It's sort of like becoming a professional tennis player. Nobody walks out on the court and starts playing well the first time. They go out and they practice their serve about 50,000 times; that's why they're so good at it and it looks so effortless. And I think most writers have got to write a lot, but maybe don't do as much as they should.

What influences were important to your development as a writer?

At the outset—and I recall it pretty distinctly—it just required a tremendous amount of effort to make it good and to make it as perfect as it could be and to make it better the next time. I used to think a lot about the technique of my writing and look at it and study it, and I used to read good writers all the time, trying to discern why their writing was working as well as it did and what techniques they were using.

There was a book out in the late '70s or early '80s called, *Smiling Through the Apocalypse*. It was a collection that Harold Hayes made of the best writing in *Esquire* magazine while he was editor. All sorts of people were in there: Gay Talese, Tom Wolfe, Norman Mailer, Garry Wills, and so forth. And it was really a golden age for *Esquire*. I don't know whether it was my favorite magazine, but this was one of my favorite collections of writing.

Maybe it was a good thing for me to have come through that period, when journalists were being given the freedom to incorporate novelistic techniques in their writing and be very stylized.

There is a danger of writers in our business who are good writers or strong stylists of letting that style get in the way of their argument or their point. It can overwhelm it.

I've found myself in recent years pulling back frequently and taking things out and just writing it straight.

What do you look for in an editorial writer?

Strong daily newspaper instincts, a strong news sense, an ability to recognize significance inside breaking news, an instinct to want to chase news, to get on the phone and call sources, and get more information about something that's going on in the news.

More often than not, people applying for editorial jobs, at least here at the *Journal,* tend to see themselves as political essayists in a kind of traditional British style, and not so much as reporters. And frequently, they don't have much reporting experience. By and large, we try to hire people who've had some reporting or newspaper experience, but also have shown a propensity for writing philosophically or editorially.

How do you see your role as editorial writer?

To make a political or philosophical or ideological argument as strongly and as effectively and persuasively as I can. I am trying to win my readers over to my point of view. That's my primary goal.

Failing that, at least to produce a piece of editorial writing in a way that shakes up their own thinking on a subject and elicits a response from them that gets them to think about the subject and make some judgment of their own about it.

Thirdly, it's to identify subjects in our political life that deserve attention. Some that are in the news are obvious, some that are out of the news are not so obvious, and part of our job here is to raise the level of visibility on subjects like that.

What advice would you give to someone who aspires to be an editorial writer?

My first advice would be to get some reporting experience so they feel comfortable with a world in which you have to accumulate a lot of information quickly and transform that pile of information into a piece of writing. That seems to be one of the hardest things for anyone in our business to do, whether they're starting out as a reporter or as an editorial writer. But for an editorial writer, it would help them a lot to be conscious of the fact that something more is required than mere opinion. I don't know that you can sustain a career any more at a big newspaper just writing mere opinion. You have to get over your fear of picking up a telephone and blind calling sources to help you understand a subject.

Secondly, it would help, I think, if they could find a job writing editorials where they feel that a paper's editorial policies and positions are congenial with their own. That is the best thing you can do if you want to do this for a living, find a place that will let you write a lot, because by and large, writing is like any other learned skill. You get better at it by doing it over and over and over, and thinking hard about what you've been doing and how you can make it better. Most of us in this business would agree that, yes, we brought a certain reservoir of innate talent to the job, but it was only after doing the job over and over for a period of time that we became as good at it as we have become and feel comfortable with doing it.

Where did you learn to write?

I learned to write journalistically in an odd way, a way that I think is very, very hard to do any more because of computers. I worked as a copy editor at the *New Republic* magazine after I got out of college. The managing editor at the time was a fellow named Alex Campbell, who had worked at *Time* magazine before that for years. He was a very skillful prose editor. We had a lot of important people writing for the magazine, or at least famous name writers. And Alex Campbell would take their manuscripts and go over them with a blue pencil and take material out and simplify them. He would use two words where they might have used five or six. There would be the line through their five or six words and his two words above it, just jumping right over all of that material.

I would read over all of that stuff. It would be a pile of articles and manuscripts every week. In the process of doing that, I learned how to write tightly and clearly and effectively. It was invaluable.

I'm convinced that computer screen reading is allowing more copyreading and editing errors to get into newspapers, because I think you simply catch more on a printout on your desk than you do on a screen.

What do you do to get yourself writing?

I fuss and fidget a lot. I try to clear the decks of all the details that I had set for myself to do that day. It's kind of like someone going on a trip and deciding they have to turn the heat down and make sure the water's turned off and pay two or three more bills and leave a note for the kids. I get that junk out of the way because I don't want it hanging over my head.

That, of course, chews up a half-hour or 45 minutes and I know full well I'm depriving myself of valuable deadline time by doing that. But having done it, I just sit myself down in front of the screen and set up a file and maybe try to get a headline to galvanize the thought or the theme, and get through that first paragraph. I pretty much strap myself into the chair and stay there till it's done.

But if it's coming slowly and it's early in the afternoon, I'll go upstairs and get a sandwich and bring it down and take a little break. I believe that your mind keeps turning this stuff over even subconsciously if you've gone away for a little bit. But I'll get right back to it and, one way or another, I will produce the thing by mid- or late afternoon. It's do-or-die in our business. And you're never allowed to die.

Are you still learning about writing?

I read an interview recently with a concert pianist. This pianist was told by the interviewer that another pianist had said that he had mastered his instrument and, as a result, it was no longer so interesting to play. And the musician being interviewed said that was an appalling thought because he didn't think one could ever master an instrument completely, that the instruments were simply too large for that. I feel exactly the same way about writing. Really good writing, and God knows, even great writing, is just so large and so powerful that nobody can fully master everything that goes into it.

One of the things that keeps me going is the process and delight of discovering new ways to use words. I have to say, at this point in an editorial writer's career—I've been at it a fair number of years now—you do have to discover aspects of the business to keep your approach fresh. And part of that, even for a conservative editorial writer—which might surprise some people—is to keep yourself fully open to new ideas, new ways of accomplishing public policy goals. But in my case, it is trying to discover new ways of writing about all of it.

The Seattle Times

Lance Dickie

Finalist, Editorial Writing

Lance Dickie is an editorial writer for *The Seattle Times*. Before joining the newspaper in 1988, Dickie had been a reporter, editorial writer, and editorial page editor at the *Statesman-Journal* in Salem, Ore. He was born and raised in Portland, Ore. He received a bachelor's degree in political science from the University of Oregon and a master's degree in journalism from the University of Missouri. Dickie is a past winner of the Scripps-Howard Walker Stone Award for editorial writing excellence. He has been a Congressional Fellow of the American Political Science Association, a John J. McCloy Fellow of the American Council on Germany, and in 1994 he was a Jefferson Fellow of the East-West Center in Hawaii. He has reported from Central America, Cuba, Germany, and Asia.

On many editorial pages, humor is in short supply. From the opening word play of "Peggy Sue, a Noble Lass" to the final, familiar compliment, Lance Dickie provides a delightful change of pace to the genre's more ponderous ruminations. With detail and wit, his editorial is an ode to Scotland as much as to the winning breed.

Peggy Sue, a noble lass

FEBRUARY 18, 1995

An unblended Scottie, a fine single-malt of a terrier, brought more than a wee dram of fame to Woodinville.

Champion Gaelforce Postscript won highest honors Tuesday at the nation's top dog show, the Westminster Kennel Club in New York City. The winner, who answers to a thriftier name, Peggy Sue, is owned by Vandra and Mike Huber.

Peggy Sue earned her title of Best in Show with a coat that is as black as a lump of Caledonia coal and ears as sharp as a Glasgow shopkeeper's pencil. But what wins is attitude; champions demand attention, they hate to yield the spotlight. She was all that, and more.

Missing from the list of her attributes was one word: restraint. Amidst all those other hounds, her regal bearing prevailed. Scotties of our acquaintance are a rowdy crew, with a permanent glint of tartan red in their eyes. They are eager to tangle with anything as long as it's bigger: German shepherds, mail trucks and 18-wheelers.

Peggy Sue behaved herself, and won. Good dog.

Lessons Learned

BY LANCE W. DICKIE

The inspiration for "Peggy Sue, a Noble Lass" was four inches of vacant white space on a Saturday editorial page.

From such practical motivations spring little editorials that attract the damnedest attention.

My ASNE entry was five pieces that covered such weighty topics as putting Miss America contestants in sweat suits, musings about the auctioning of Nelson Mandela's clothing and eyeglasses, and, of course, reaction to the verdict in last year's big trial in Los Angeles, the Three Stooges bankruptcy proceedings.

Day to day, editorials necessarily deal with important, complex subjects, but one of the delights of editorial writing is the opportunity to roam far afield.

So why write about a dog? Peggy Sue is essentially a local editorial: a couple in a nearby suburb raising a champion. More importantly they won a dog show that is no longer an obscure event. Chances are our readers had heard of the annual show, if not that a local dog had her day.

Add in the fact my in-laws used to own a beloved terrier that was as feisty as a U.S. senator in heat. I felt I knew the breed.

The editorial—a tiny editorial on a Saturday morning—got noticed in part because the world is populated by dog lovers. Even cat people and grumpy newsroom types responded to the playful language. But the real reason the editorial worked was because it was unexpected. Breezing through the opinion pages everyone has a sense of what they will find. They stumbled across something different.

The lesson is a reminder about taking the occasional risk, whether the subject is serious or silly. I still have a vivid memory of a 1978 editorial in a North Carolina paper that lamented the closing of a favorite café, and described the hot biscuits and pitchers of gravy that were gone forever.

Those bits of commentary at the bottom of *The New York Times* editorial page provide some of the best snapshots of life in the Big Apple, and the loveliest writing.

When I worked on a much smaller editorial staff, we used to joke that we did not have time to write short. Crafting a tiny editorial is not exactly like building a Fabergé egg, but there is a challenge in providing readers with a clear point and maybe a dash of humor in a few dozen words, not hundreds.

What really counts is getting an offbeat editorial published, and that requires an editor who is willing to take a chance on unexpected offerings. Peggy Sue was let off the leash to the apparent surprise and delight of readers.

Michael Gartner

Finalist, Editorial Writing

Michael Gartner is making his third consecutive appearance in *Best Newspaper Writing*. In 1994, he became the first past president of the American Society of Newspaper Editors to receive its Distinguished Writing Award for editorial writing. He was a finalist in the category in 1995. Gartner is co-owner and one-person editorial staff of *The Daily Tribune,* a 10,000 circulation newspaper 38 miles from his hometown of Des Moines. The son and grandson of Iowa newspapermen, Gartner has been in the news business for four decades. He is a former page one editor of *The Wall Street Journal,* former editor and president of *The Des Moines Register,* former editor of the *Courier-Journal* of Louisville, former general news executive of Gannett Co. and *USA Today,* and, most recently, former president of NBC News. Gartner began his newspaper career at age 15 when he took a job answering phones and taking dictation in the sports department of *The Des Moines Register.* He writes a column that appears regularly in *USA Today,* and for the last 15 years he has written a syndicated column on language.

Gartner says he likes to use facts in editorials to persuade as well as to inform. In the following piece, his opening salvo in a series attacking property tax inequities, including the break given his own newspaper, Gartner manages to do both with equal power.

Property tax exemptions: Legal but terribly unfair

AUGUST 2, 1995

Have you ever driven by that terrific piece of wooded land on Mortensen Road near Elwood? It's a great plot —about three acres—and city assessor Richard Horn values it at $196,900. Dr. Massoud Shahidi owns it, and at the new Ames tax rate for residential land it should be taxed at $4,228.

Should be, but isn't.

Dr. Shahidi pays not a penny on that land.

Have you ever stopped in to visit the folks at the Iowa Poultry Association's headquarters? It's that nice-looking little building at 535 East Lincoln Way. Assessor Horn puts its value at $128,400, which could make its tax bill, as a business, $4,085.

Could make, but doesn't.

The Iowa Poultry Association pays not a penny on its building.

Have you ever stopped in the Elks Club? It's on Douglas, across from the library, and Assessor Horn says the building is worth $317,000. The property tax on that, at the business rate that other restaurants pay, would be $10,087.

Would be, but isn't.

The Elks pay not a penny on their club.

Dr. Shahidi, the poultry people and the Elks own just three of 116 buildings or sites in Ames that have applied for total exemptions from the property tax—and gotten them. Owners of another 114 homes or buildings— including *The Daily Tribune*—have received partial exemptions. All told, these 230 exemptions have taken off the tax rolls property valued at $52,974,895. The annual taxes that would produce—at the business rate for businesses and the reduced residential rate for homes— would be $1,676,936.

Would.

It's all perfectly legal—and terribly unfair. What's more, this $53 million of untaxed property is just a small fraction of the total tax-free property in Ames, but it's the only amount you can put a precise figure

on. These 230 homes and businesses had to apply for
their exemptions, so they were first assessed. But other
property is tax-exempt by statute, so assessors never
even bother to value it. This includes the Iowa State
University campus, the state-owned headquarters of
the Department of Transportation, the city-owned
Mary Greeley Medical Center, the federally owned
Animal Disease Lab and all other land and buildings
owned by the city or county or area or state or federal
governments. The total is easily in the hundreds of
millions of dollars—and would produce tens of millions of dollars in taxes.

Would.

What this means is that the 8,846 homeowners and
the 1,250 business owners and the 32 factory owners
pay extra to provide the police and fire and roads and
parks and other city services for the people who live
and work in these tax-free spots.

It is, as we said, terribly unfair.

So why doesn't Assessor Horn make those people
pony up so taxes can be cut for those who pay the
full amount? He can't. He must grant exemptions
to some people who seek them. Those include
churches and the church-owned homes of ministers
(that takes $20,771,650 off the tax rolls), religious
schools ($80,300 for the Grand Avenue Baptist
Church school), fraternal organizations ($633,900),
agricultural societies ($3,427,900), nonprofit retire-
ment homes ($7,017,900, which is the assessed value
of Northcrest up on 20th Street), and other charitable
and benevolent societies ($2,090,350).

And he must not tax—not a penny—the so-called
forest reserve land in the city, which can be any plot of
two or more acres on which the owner has no house
and on which he plants some trees and bushes. The
land remains private—only the owner can enjoy it.
That's the exemption that frees Dr. Shahidi from taxes
on Mortensen Road.

There's more. If you own undeveloped but unfor-
ested land in the city, you can plant a crop on it and
have it valued as agricultural land, which is taxed at
less than half the tax on residential land and which, by
a quirk, is taxed even less than agricultural land outside the city. There's more than 1,700 acres of this so-

called agricultural land within Ames, and probably half of it is really land being held for the bulldozer rather than the plow, land valued—and taxed—far below its worth. An example: the land on Airport Road where Sam's Club will be built was taxed at $1,000 an acre; it sold for $45,000 an acre.

Finally, you can have your taxes rolled back if you are in an urban revitalization district and improve your home or building. You can petition to have the taxes on those improvements forgiven for three years or reduced for five to 10 years. It's this exemption that allowed *The Daily Tribune* to escape paying taxes— about $3,100 a year—on $100,000 of improvements for three years.

All of this is, as we've said three times now, terribly unfair. It's also, as we said, absolutely legal. "There's nothing in the law that says it has to be fair," Assessor Horn notes. And he's right.

But there's also nothing that says the law couldn't change. And it should.

Why shouldn't the Iowa State Memorial Union—in effect a restaurant and hotel—pay the same rate as the Holiday Inn/Gateway Center?

Why shouldn't the Elks Club pay the same rate as Aunt Maude's?

Why shouldn't Rev. Scott Grotewold of Collegiate United Methodist Church pay the same rate for his $138,000 house as Ted Tedesco pays for his home?

Why shouldn't *The Daily Tribune* pay the same rate for its new facility as the Red Lobster, which is not in an urban revitalization district, pays for its?

The answer is, they—and we—should.

It may be legal that some people don't pay taxes.

But—for the fourth time—it's terribly unfair.

Lessons Learned

BY MICHAEL GARTNER

The property-tax editorials were complicated.

The law was confusing. The records were scattered. The experts were scarce.

And there were a zillion numbers.

But no one challenged a single fact in the series.

Maybe it's because no one read it. But I think it's really because I showed the editorials to several people before the pieces ran. "I don't care what you think about my opinions," I said, "but please go over every fact with me." I spent several hours going over the editorials line by line with the county auditor and her deputy. I spent about the same amount of time with the city and county assessors. I faxed portions of it to a state finance official. I read and re-read and re-read portions to several school-finance experts. I sent a series of proofs to a county supervisor.

Everyone I showed the series to found little mistakes— and one school guy found a big one. I had a couple of numbers transposed. I didn't quite understand one piece of a statute. I had wrong assessments on a couple of pieces of property. One of my sets of numbers didn't add up. And I greatly misinterpreted the school-finance law.

But by the time the series ran, as I said, there wasn't a mistake in it.

It's because I did what every editor I have ever had told me never to do, what many journalism professors warn their students never to do, what most reporters swear they would never ever do: I showed the pieces to people in advance.

"I wouldn't show my own grandmother what's in the paper tomorrow," a wonderful old editor told me 35 years ago.

Well, I wouldn't, either, unless the story were about my grandmother. And over the past several years, I've concluded that I probably wouldn't run the story on my grandmother *unless* I showed it to her in advance. So that's what I've been doing for a few years: showing people editorials or reading the pieces to them in advance. Invariably, they find mistakes of fact—a wrong age, an outdated title. Usually, it's something little. But more than once it's been a fact that I premised an entire editorial on—wrongly.

I started doing this after I was in the news a lot myself when I was president of NBC News. Virtually every story written about me had something incorrect. My age would be wrong. Or my address. Or the years I worked in Des Moines. Or my education. It was usually small, but it was always something. I thought it damaged the credibility of the reporters who wrote the pieces, of the newspapers that ran them. So I began to rethink my own reporting and to rethink that one inviolable "rule" I had always been taught.

And I couldn't come up with any reason not to show stuff to people in advance.

It goes a long way to eliminating mistakes, as I said.

But it's also a matter of courtesy. I write a lot of editorials that are less than glowing about a person. Almost always, now, I call that person the day before it runs, tell him or her what's coming, and, as often as not, read it to the person. Some will argue about my interpretations and opinions, but I always say that's not on the table. I explain I'm calling to double-check facts and just to make sure the person isn't surprised when he opens the paper the next day.

I'm often corrected.

I'm usually thanked.

I'm always glad.

And no one has yet come up with a good reason not to do what I do—except to say, "That's the one thing you should never do. That's awful. No one does that."

Well, I do.

And I'm never sorry.

Mitch Albom
Sports Writing

Mitch Albom is the nationally syndicated sports columnist for the *Detroit Free Press* and a familiar voice and
face on ESPN and sports talk radio. A native of Philadelphia, he graduated from Brandeis University and
earned master's degrees in journalism and business administration from Columbia University. He has worked
for the Fort Lauderdale, Fla., *Sun-Sentinel,* is the author
of six books, and has appeared in *Sports Illustrated,
GQ,* and numerous other national publications. Before
working as a journalist, he was an amateur boxer,
worked as a nightclub singer and pianist, and is a songwriter and lyricist.

There's a good reason why America's sports editors
named him the number one sportswriter in the nation
for nine straight years. Albom is a champion at the
keyboard whether the subject is a superstar or a local
hero you've never heard of. Writing about the promising young race car driver killed by a drunken driver,
a high school girl whose dreams of success are threat-

ened by illness, or a community divided by a rape case, Albom's empathy and skill guarantee that you'll never forget their stories.

Small town split as football star faces rape sentence

JANUARY 13, 1995

The boy was wearing his varsity letter jacket when the jury announced its verdict.

"Guilty," the man said. Guilty? It was Wednesday afternoon. Late September. Back at Saline High School, the football team was getting ready for practice, awaiting his return. He had told them not to worry. He was confident. He would be there.

Guilty?

"How am I gonna graduate?" he remembers thinking. They took his jacket and wallet.

"What about college?"

They took his keys.

"What about Dad?"

His father stood helpless, a few feet away. All he could say was, "Call me. As soon as you can, call me."

The courtroom crowd mumbled in disbelief. The boy was put in a cell. They took his tie and shoelaces.

"What about my future?"

Guilty?

A few miles away, the girl was feeling nauseated. She had spoken on the stand, told them what happened that night, the guys, the sex, the crack about "let's use a bottle on her," all of it. Several times the lawyers had to stop because she was crying so hard. At one point she went into a restroom and vomited.

She didn't stay for the verdict, and neither did her family. But soon enough, they knew the town's reaction. A car full of students drove past the mother's store, spotted the girl, and yelled: "You bitch! You whore! We're gonna get you!"

Five high school boys, one high school girl. And when this story is told, you might not feel sorry for any of them. In the pre-sunrise hours of one cold Saturday morning, they had group sex in the basement of a condo. The boys took turns doing things with the girl. And the girl, depending on whom you believe, either encouraged the whole thing or cried her way through it, frozen with fear.

Two days later, the boys were finishing school, and some were heading home.

"Did you hear?" one said.

"What?"

"----'s going to the police."

"The police? For what?"

"She's saying we raped her."

"Raped her?"

"The police?"

This is a story of a small town taking sides, as if some invisible line were drawn in the snow. You can stop anywhere today in Saline, by the red brick storefronts, or the Taco Bell, the Ford plant, the apartments in town, the custom homes out on the wide dirt roads, anywhere, doesn't matter, just ask the question: Whom do you believe? The football player? The girl? Fewer than 7,000 people live in this normally quiet town, and this morning, it might feel like all of them are squeezed inside Washtenaw County's Circuit Court No. 5, awaiting the word of Judge Melinda Morris.

Today, 18-year-old Bobby Shier Jr., the only one arrested, the only one tried and the only one found guilty that night of first-degree criminal sexual conduct—rape—learns his fate.

It could be a new trial.

It could be 20 years in prison.

He insists he's innocent. And much of the town agrees with him.

Meanwhile, the girl has switched schools, undergone counseling and, according to her family, is too afraid even to take a shower when she's alone in the house.

"She struggles with this every day," said her mother, fighting tears in speaking to the press for the first time. "This has been a year from hell. I know Bobby is in prison. But my daughter's in a prison, too."

How did this happen? How can families that used to be friends not have spoken for more than a year? How can kids who used to trust each other now walk through hallways tensing up, glaring, yelling insults, clenching fists. Teenage boys with schoolbooks under their arms say, "She wanted it. She was a slut." And teenage girls with their hair in ponytails say, "They gang-banged her"—until it sounds like something out of a bad soap opera.

She says they did.

They say they didn't.

How, in one night, can the world change so fast?

From Bobby Shier's police interview:

Police: Did you get the impression that she didn't want to have sex?

Bobby: Sort of, yeah, I did.

Police: What made you think that?

Bobby: Just the way she was acting.... If you have sex with them before, you can tell they're different the next time....

Police: You continued on?

Bobby: Yeah.

Police: Figuring, well, she'll be a little more responsive?

Bobby: Yeah.

Police: But that didn't happen?

Bobby: No, and I quit then.

A GANGLY YOUTH

When the jail door opens, and he first steps out, your immediate impression is "teenage." He is kind of thin for a football player, with a gangly walk, dark hair that falls onto his forehead, a thick neck, crooked teeth, a few pimples. This is not Michael Douglas or some dashing character out of a made-for-TV movie about sexual harassment. Bobby Shier, a solid loaf of a kid, has surrendered his No. 70 Saline football jersey for a green cotton shirt that reads "Washtenaw County Jail."

On the day they brought him in, Sept. 28, 1994, the first inmate he met was a guy nearly twice his age.

"You're so young, what are you in here for?"

"Breaking and entering," Bobby lied.

The next day the guy had a local newspaper.

"What'd you say your name was again?"

"Bobby."

"Bobby what?"

"Uh...Shier."

The guy held out the paper with Bobby's picture on the front page. *Jury convicts Saline student of rape.* Bobby swallowed. The guy ripped out the story, crumpled it up.

"Flush this down the toilet before anyone sees it."

It is hard to believe that two days earlier, Bobby had been at football practice at Saline High, going through tackling drills and knocking back blockers from his defensive lineman position. There was a big game that Friday night, the team was undefeated, and Bobby, who actually went to trial in the morning and practice in the afternoon, planned on being there.

The son of a Ford plant material handler, he had no previous record, and although he admits to drinking beer and smoking pot, he maintained a "B" average in school. "I always liked him," said Saline football coach Jack Crabtree. "You asked him a question, he was honest."

At one point, Bobby and the victim—whom we will call Linda, which is not her real name—were a couple, at least as much as high schoolers can be a couple. They went to movies, parties, even went skiing once. They had sex numerous times. After a few months, they broke up, he said, because she slept with someone else. No big deal. Bobby admits to having had three sexual partners himself. This might not sound like high school to you. But maybe it has been awhile since you have been in high school.

Linda is a smallish, blond-haired girl, the oldest of five children. Her father drives a truck and her mother owns a shop. Linda has a learning disability and was held back a grade. Because of this, her mother said, she is often compared to her next-younger sister, who is now in the same grade, but is a star student and a star athlete, whereas Linda is not. Linda was always being told, "You're so pretty, you're so pretty." Maybe, after a while, that became her identity.

"I know about her promiscuity," her mother said.

At Saline High, it seems to be a favorite subject. But understand this is the only high school in town, so stories here are shared like a drinking fountain.

They met in science class, Bobby and Linda. They had sex a few times. That should have been the whole story—if not for that night.

"I wish I had just stayed home," Bobby said, leaning over the prison table. "People can say anything they want to, they can say you raped them when you didn't even touch them.

"It's them against you. It really is."

GOOD PLACE FOR A PARTY

She wasn't at the condo five minutes before one of them unbuttoned her pants, someone hit the lights, and they all said good-bye to childhood, right there on the beige carpet.

That much they agree on. What happened that night is told at least six different ways by the six people involved. None of it is pleasant. Most of it is shocking. About the only part not in dispute is that Linda, then 17, did go willingly to the home of schoolmate Paul Castellucci at around 4 a.m. Saturday, Nov. 20, 1993. She had snuck out of her house, along with her sister, looking for a party, and now it was late. They never found the party, her sister was sleepy, but Linda still wanted to have fun.

Fun, she will tell you, not trauma.

She considered the five guys "my friends."

Until that night.

Bobby was one of the guys. He was staying at Castellucci's house, along with his football teammate Jeff Rathiewicz, then 17, and buddies Todd Mills, then 17, Chris Calhoun, then 16, Ryan Fox, then 18, and Castellucci, then 16. They had been drinking earlier in the evening, and how drunk they were is still in question. They had tickets to the Michigan-Ohio State football game later that day, which is why they were all sleeping over.

Some were half-asleep when Linda called.

"We shoulda just hung up," Bobby said.

Instead, he, Todd, and Chris got in Todd's blue minivan and picked up Linda from her girlfriend's house. She wore a flannel shirt and baggy blue jeans. They offered her a beer on the ride over, and they entered the condo on Woodcreek Court through the back entrance and the sliding glass doors. It was a typical teenager's lower-level quarters—two bedrooms, a center den area, couch, table, couple of posters on the walls, a TV. Good place for a sleep-over. Good place for a party. Paul's mother and younger brother were asleep upstairs, which neither surprised nor worried any of the teens. Most, including Linda, had been there many times before.

"Me and her began to wrestle, playing around," Bobby said. "She was teasing me about football and I was teasing her about soccer, because she played soccer. It was frisky playing, you know? Then I got up off her, and she sat on Jeff's lap."

After numerous interviews with the subjects, the rest—which, we should point out, is not for the puritanical—must be told in separate voices, because the versions are different, and the difference is what this whole thing is about.

THE BOYS' VERSION:

Jeff began to unbutton Linda's baggy blue jeans. Todd pulled them down from the bottom cuffs. Linda said: "If you keep doing that, they're going to come off," but she didn't seem to mind. Once her pants were off, Todd—who later said, "I couldn't believe she let us do that"—offered them back to her but she waved them away.

Someone turned off the lights, and Todd, Jeff and Chris helped her down to the floor, out of her clothes, and along with Ryan took places around her. She was now naked and laughing, and feeling around her, saying, "Who's this? Who's this?" Bobby, who had gone into Paul's bedroom, re-entered the room and joined them. Paul stayed in his room.

In the minutes that followed, she performed oral sex on one of the boys, while engaging in intercourse with another. The boys fondled her, moving around to different positions. They maintain she did everything with no coercion, and that she laughed and joked during the process.

Todd: "Her arms were free and her legs were free and if she wanted to get up and walk away at any time, she could have."

Jeff: "I remember her giggling; she unzipped Chris' pants....He made a remark about (her skills) and she said, "Oh, yeah, where did you hear that?"

Bobby: "She wasn't saying no to anybody."

Eventually—maybe a half hour after this began— Bobby took Linda's hand and went to a back bedroom, which contained two bunk beds. The two of them had had sex in this bedroom a few weeks earlier. Now, Bobby said, "I asked for oral sex and she said no, she didn't want to do that. And I was like, well, you wanna have sex then? And she was like, yeah, I don't care."

He put on a condom and there, on the bedroom floor, began to have sex with her. He noticed she was not acting "as into it" as he recalled and he asked why. She said she was tired. He continued, maybe for 10 minutes, until several of the other boys banged on the door. He then left the room. He admits she might have been crying at this point.

Ryan entered, with whom she had oral sex.

Todd followed, carrying a bottle the others had given him. They made jokes about "using a bottle on her." But he told her he would never do something like that. He asked if she wanted her clothes. She did.

She came out dressed, and sat and talked for a minute. She said she had to get home before her mother woke up and realized she was out. Todd drove her home.

Todd: "It was close to 6 a.m. We were laughing and joking the whole way to the van.

"On the way home...I remember asking her, 'Why do you let guys use you like that?' She was like, 'Guys don't use me, I use them to get my pleasure.'...

"A few minutes later, I dropped her off and she ran up to her house."

That was the last time any of the five boys talked to her.

That is their story.

THE GIRL'S VERSION:

What Linda told the police was significantly different.

Yes, she had gone there willingly, and yes, she had wrestled with Bobby. But when Jeff began to unbutton her pants and Todd was pulling them off, she told him to stop. The lights were then shut off, and the boys began leaning over her, undressing her, holding her down. She admits saying, "Who is this?" and "Who is by me?" but in a confused and frightened way, not a playful one. She said whenever she expressed concern, the boys told her to shut up and not worry. She also said one of them joked, "This is like an orgy," to which she replied, "No, more like a gang bang."

She said she was forced into oral sex with the boys, that her arms and legs were held down, and that she was confused and scared and worried that if she didn't go along, they might become violent.

When Bobby led her to the back room, she says she was crying. Although she never yelled for help—"I thought they were my friends"—she says she told Bobby she wanted to stop and he didn't.

During the trial, she said, "My whole body was numb. It happened so fast. The situation was out of control. I couldn't handle it."

She also denied that Bobby, her ex-boyfriend, asked her if she wanted to have sex. "If he had asked I would have told him no."

She also told police the boys were drunk and, in addition to the talk about the bottle, made jokes about taking pictures.

When she got home, she was sore and confused. She worked that day at a nursing home, and the next morning, told her sister what had happened.

"They raped me," she said, crying.

Her sister later told police: "At first I was upset that she would let them do that to her. But then I asked for details and decided it was not her fault."

That night, Paul called her house, asked how she was doing. "I told him I was sore and he said, 'Well, all's good in fun,' and he said the guys were worried about something getting out.'

It would get out.

And they were right to be worried.

'NOTHING TO HIDE'

Sgt. Bob Dietrich, whose straw-colored hair matches his mustache, has been with the Saline police department 18 years. He said he knew from the start "this case would be a pain in the butt." Linda had left school Monday after telling her story to the school counselor and had gone to a hospital emergency room, explaining that she had been raped. Under law, this requires a police report.

After taking her statement—"she was pretty shook up"—Dietrich sent officers out to pick up the five boys for questioning.

Four were not home.

Bobby Shier was the fifth.

He was in his father's apartment, and his father had just left. When the knock came, he thought about not answering the door. He answered it anyhow. He was not obligated to go with the officers, but he did, he said, because one of them barked, "Do you know what the word *arrest* means?"

At the station, he told them his version of what happened, all the graphic details, without a lawyer present, because, he said, "I didn't have anything to hide."

Had he not done this, even Dietrich admitted, "he might never have been charged."

But Bobby Shier was not the type to hold much back. He was cocky, vocal—his football teammates say, "You always knew where he was on the field"—and he knew some of the police because, after all, this is a small town, and so, on tape, he told the story of that night in his typical fashion, which some call "flippant" and others call "Bobby." There was no regret for what happened. He felt he had done nothing wrong.

"It was consensual," he said. "She never said 'no' or 'quit.'"

A few weeks later, he was picked up again to take a polygraph test. During that conversation with Dietrich —which once again, Bobby agreed to without a lawyer —he made the most damaging statement of all.

Dietrich: "Why don't we back up to the beginning of the night. Who was talking about what?"

Bobby: "Me, Chris, Todd, we planned on gang-banging her, all of us."

Dietrich: "Was that the exact word used, 'gang-bang'?"

Bobby: "Ahhh...I wasn't saying that we could all do her, it was Chris and Todd saying how we could all mess around with her and see how many guys she could do."

Dietrich: "What made them think that?"

Bobby: "She has a reputation of sleeping with a lot of guys...."

Dietrich: "What words did you use? It's OK. You're not going to tell me anything I haven't heard before."

Bobby: "OK, words like, maybe we can double-team her or triple-team, something like that. I already knew what she was like..."

When he was done talking, they didn't even administer a polygraph because, the police chief now says, "He wasn't denying anything. What would we polygraph him on?"

This is one of the points being challenged today.

Meanwhile, Jeff and Todd hadn't even made police statements, and the others had done so only with lawyers. None of them was charged.

But Bobby? Well. This was too much to ignore. Two full statements, in his own brazen words. The reports went to the Washtenaw County prosecutor's office, and prosecutor Brian Mackie, who had been elected on a tough stance on sexual assault crimes, saw plenty to go on.

"To the untrained eye, he appeared to be the ringleader," Mackie said. "You bet we were gonna use those statements."

Bobby Shier, who said he had "nothing to hide," had just taken his first step toward jail.

WHAT THE JURY HEARD

In the small, lower-level apartment where he and Bobby used to live, Robert Shier, Bobby's father, a beefy autoworker with a straightforward manner, sits with numerous friends, including the Mills family, whose son Todd was part of this whole mess. Todd admits to sexual encounters that night with Linda, but, like the others, has not been charged and probably never will be. Without a statement like Bobby's, it's too much "he said, she said." Too hard to prove.

Such an odd assembly, one family luckier than the other. They sip coffee together and do what the whole town has been doing for months. Talk about the case. There are some of Bobby's sports trophies on the shelves, and some photos of him on the table. Although he phones frequently from jail, the last time they all saw him free was at the trial.

"We didn't meet our lawyer until 15 minutes before it began," Robert Shier recalled. "That's my fault. I didn't know how it all worked. I said, 'Aren't the other boys gonna testify?' He said they weren't.

"Hindsight is 20/20. Bobby shouldn't have talked to the police without a lawyer. And then, at the trial, I couldn't afford private, so I had to go with the public defender. Our guy (Lorne Brown) did a good job, but (Linda) got up there and started crying..."

Bobby never testified. The prosecution simply played the tapes of his two statements, and a police officer later admitted, "You could see it in the jury's eyes. When he said, 'We planned to gang-bang her'...I knew it was over."

Brown, the defense attorney, argued that lewd circumstances don't mean rape. Nine women and three men were on the jury. The trial lasted two days. The deliberation lasted 2½ hours. During that time, Bobby read the sports section of the local paper, looking for news of his football team.

Then the jury came back.

And that was the end of football.

"It was rape," Mackie says now.

"The jury said it was rape, and it was."

"I'm not surprised Bobby denies it," said Eric Gutenberg, the assistant prosecutor who argued the case. "He feels if he didn't tie her ankles to the table, he didn't rape her. He wasn't looking for the signs."

"He showed no remorse," said Phil King, the probation officer who, after a two-hour conversation with Bobby, labeled him "a threat to the community," recommended extensive psychotherapy and suggested a sentence of five to 20 years in jail. "He still denies doing anything wrong."

What if he believes he's innocent?

"Well, then, there's something wrong with him."

Here, in the Shier apartment—and elsewhere in Saline—they disagree. They talk about the preliminary hearing, where Judge John Collins asked the prosecution: "Are you sure you really want to try this case?" They question the way Bobby was interrogated, claiming he was led to say certain things.

And, as you might expect, they talk about Linda. How she had consensual sex with Bobby just a few weeks before that night, and did the same with Jeff the weekend prior. She admitted this in court.

Besides, they say, she hardly behaves like a victim. They claim she was out with a boy two days after the incident—the boy confirms this, although it was "just as friends"—and, after Bobby's conviction, she was seen at a party hoisting a beer and yelling: "I put that son of a bitch behind bars."

They argue that the rape charge was something Linda made up to stay out of trouble with her mother. They claim Linda is starved for attention and cite countless boys she has supposedly slept with. (Some, when contacted for this article, admitted sexual relations. Others denied it.)

Finally, they point to another party, just a few weeks after the incident. There, three witnesses confirm, Linda danced and flirted and got drunk on beer. She hung on different boys, kissed them, and at one point, a guest said, "was on the floor, laughing, letting boys flick their cigarette ashes on her head."

Photos substantiate this.

Robert Shier has the photos in front of him.

"How can somebody who was just raped be out there acting like that?" he asked, holding a picture. "Does that seem like someone who's traumatized?"

REPUTATION ON TRIAL

The rape shield law, which Michigan adopted 20 years ago, forbids bringing an alleged rape victim's sexual history into a case. It was designed, partly, to reduce a victim's possible humiliation at trial. But it does nothing about small-town humiliation once the trial is over.

So it does not stop the passing shouts of "whore" or "slut" that have gone on for a year, nor does it stop certain football players from vowing revenge, because Bobby's arrest disrupted their perfect season. It does not stop people from driving up to the fast-food window where Linda now works, buying food and dropping the money on the pavement.

A few miles away from the Shiers' apartment, on a snowy weekday afternoon, Linda's mother sits inside the small country store she owns on one of Saline's main streets. Her daughter—who, when asked to be interviewed for this article, said, "Thank you for asking me. You're the first person who's wanted to hear my side of the story"—was later advised by her lawyer to wait.

But her mother, for the first time, has agreed to talk.

She is in tears.

This is the other side of the story.

"We have heard all the rumors, believe me, we have," she said. "And I know all about my daughter. I know what she does. But none of those people were with me in that emergency room.... None of them saw the blood on her underwear.... None of them saw the swelling which was so bad, she couldn't even urinate....

"Those people weren't with us when my daughter couldn't sleep, the nights she had to be sedated. These were her friends! *Her friends did this to her!* My daughter checks the locks every night, she's afraid all the time.... She started to cry a few weeks ago and said, 'Mom, I'll never, ever have a normal life.'...

"She's had to switch schools.... She's lost her senior year, her chance to graduate with her sister....

"I've heard the people say she's making all this up. But they don't know my daughter. *I* know my daughter. She was so ashamed. She took great lengths not to tell me. There is no doubt in my mind she was raped. She doesn't have the stamina to maintain a lie for this long."

She stops talking, wipes her eyes, then says: "Why would she?"

Contrary to some of the popular theories, it was Linda's mother, not Linda, who pushed to file criminal charges. Linda reportedly begged her mother to keep quiet. She said she couldn't go through with it.

"I have to live with that," the mother says now. "I made her go to court. And I would never, ever, put a child of mine through something like this again...."

She said she sees the accused boys and their families all the time. They look down. They walk the other way. She cries again at the mention of Cindy Calhoun, Chris's mother, who before the incident was a good friend. Their kids played soccer together. They used to meet at a Big Boy restaurant for breakfast.

They have not spoken since that night.

"It was crushing," she said. "We're shut out from so many families we used to know. Every school event, every open house, the minute we're in the same room, the tension is so horrible...."

Linda's mother said she is aware of her daughter's promiscuity. She knows of the assorted parties, even after the incident. She said Linda went through intense emotional swings, first shutting herself in, then pushing herself out.

"If you talk to rape counselors, that is not unusual," she said. "And to be honest, I don't care what she does if it helps her get through this."

Nothing, she said, will change what happened on the lower level of the Woodcreek Court condo that Saturday morning.

"She was raped. She was...raped."

She begins to cry again.

NO AGE OF INNOCENCE

What is really on trial in this case is what is on trial in most cases of acquaintance rape—the believability of the people involved. One side will argue the victim's reputation should not be under attack, that even prostitutes can be raped. The other side will argue that making an accusation does not make it true, that people accuse for all kinds of reasons—witness the recent Derrick Coleman case—and besides, what does a girl think she's doing joining two former sex partners and three of their friends at 4 a.m. at their place?

So when the sun rises on this winter Friday, the questions will float like paperweight snowflakes all the way down to Circuit Courtroom No. 5. If Linda truly felt violated, why didn't she yell for help—from Paul in the other room, or his family upstairs? Then again, if Bobby admits she was crying, why didn't he take that as a sign to stop?

Is it true that Sgt. Dietrich made a statement: "Bobby's a stupid kid. We can get him to say anything," as some of the parents claim? (He denies this.) And if this crime were so apparent, why weren't the other boys charged?

Do you believe a friend named Georgie Carlton, who said Linda has never been the same since that night? Or do you believe a former friend named Alison Cotellesse, who says: "It's all this big act."

Five high school boys, not one of whom remembers her saying no.

One high school girl, who can't understand how they don't.

Rape? A ruse? Maybe the only real answer is that they're all too young to be doing what they're doing. How do you lasso a speeding generation? As Nancy Mills, Todd's mother, says: "We never taught our children that sex was a spectator sport."

Or as Linda's mother says, between sobs, "Can you

imagine the *rage* when you hear someone say they're going to 'gang-bang' your daughter?"

It's a case for our times, an athlete, a girl, sex, outrage, anger, accusations, all of it before they graduate.

And, this morning, Saline draws its daily line in the snow. Whom do you trust? Why did they do it? How, in one night, could the world change so fast? One kid's in jail. One's in a nightmare. You wonder if anyone is ever young anymore.

Writers' Workshop

Talking Points

1) Mitch Albom tackles a controversial topic—acquaintance rape—that has divided a small town. Study and discuss how he presents each side. Do you think he takes sides? If not, how did he avoid it? Be specific.

2) "Five high school boys, one high school girl," Albom writes. "And when this story is told you might not feel sorry for any of them." By the time you've finished reading, does Albom's prediction come true? Discuss where your sympathies lay, and identify passages that influenced your reactions.

3) Effective stories anticipate readers' questions and provide timely answers. Notice how Albom presents the questions that lay at the heart of this story: "How did this happen? How can families that used to be friends not have spoken for more than a year? How can kids who used to trust each other now walk through hallways tensing up, glaring, yelling insults, clenching fists?" Does the writer deliver on the implicit promise to answer those questions? How does he do it?

Assignment Desk

1) In your stories, identify and itemize the readers' likely questions and the answers your reporting provides. Use them to create a structure for your story.

2) Too often, humanity is represented in news stories by an age, a title, and a street address. A person can be sketched quickly and with powerful effect with a few brushstrokes, as Albom does with his portrait of football player and convicted rapist Bobby Shier: "He is kind of thin for a football player, with a gangly walk, dark hair that falls onto his forehead, a thick neck, crooked teeth, a few pimples." Study Albom's stories for other word portraits. Collect examples from your reading. Write descriptions of several people: a teacher, a police officer, your best friend, yourself.

3) Similies heighten understanding by drawing comparisons. They are bridges between ideas. Albom uses them

often: "...stories here are shared like a drinking fountain,"
"...the questions will float like paperweight snowflakes all
the way down to Circuit Courtroom No. 5." Look for similies in your reading and decide which ones are most effective and why. Try using them in your stories.

Why do we focus on body over mind in high school?

APRIL 11, 1995

The little chocolate doughnuts were in a box, next to the coffee urn. Normally, high schools don't provide food for their assemblies, but today was special, all these TV crews, radio people, sports writers. A table was arranged near the front of the room, and a reporter set down a microphone, alongside a dozen others. "Testing 1-2......testing 1-2," he said.

Suddenly, the whole room seemed to shift. The guest of honor had arrived. He didn't enter first. He was preceded by an entourage of friends, coaches, his grandmother, his aunt, his baby brother, more friends, more coaches and his girlfriend, whom he identified later as "my girlfriend." She wore a black dress and jewelry and had her hair pinned up, as if going to the prom, even though it was midafternoon and math classes were in progress upstairs.

Her boyfriend took his seat. He wore a stud earring and a colorful jacket. Only 18 years old, he was the largest person in the room, 6-feet-9, 300 pounds. It was for his body—and what he could do with it—that these people had come.

"Good afternoon," Robert Traylor began, reading from a sheet of paper. His voice was deep as a businessman's, but his words were those of a nervous teen. "I'd like to welcome everyone.... My dream is to play in the NBA one day....

"I've chosen the college that can best help me achieve my dream...."

The crowd held its breath. For three years, a parade of grown men, employed by major universities, had been coming to Detroit to watch Robert Traylor play. They called him at home, they called his friends, they called his relatives. They showed him videos, promised him stardom. They wooed him like a golden child.

Now, the payoff.

"The school I will be attending," Traylor said, "will be the University of Michigan...."

The room erupted in applause.

U-M GOT TWO BLUE-CHIPPERS

Down the hall, sitting alone by a computer, was another high school senior named Kevin Jones. Like Traylor, Jones is black, lives in Detroit, and is being raised with no father in the house. His mother supports the family by working as a janitor.

Like Traylor, Jones will also be attending Michigan next fall—on a full scholarship.

But unlike Traylor, Jones, a thin kid with a disarming smile, got his scholarship for studying three hours a day, getting the highest grades, keeping his attendance over 95 percent, and never violating school conduct rules.

Kevin Jones is the most important currency in the city of Detroit, a kid with a brain. He did not announce his college decision at a press conference; he had to wait for Michigan to accept *him*. A letter finally arrived at the house his family shares with another family in northwest Detroit. He peeked through the envelope and saw the word "Congratulations." He smiled. His grandmother hugged him and said, "I'm so proud of you! I'm so proud of you...."

Back at the press conference, reporters were yelling questions:

"Robert, when did you decide on Michigan?"

"Robert, do you think you'll start?"

"Robert, what did the Michigan coaches say?"

Traylor smiled at the last one. "I don't know. I haven't told them yet."

Not that it mattered. At that moment, it was being announced all over the radio.

HE'LL STAY THE COURSE

This is crazy. A press conference for a high school ballplayer? What message are we sending the other students at Murray-Wright High School, who were peeking through the doors, wondering what the fuss was about?

Don't misunderstand. Robert Traylor is a bright young man with a special talent. But a press conference about where he will dribble and shoot? Isn't there enough spotlight on these kids already? Besides, encouraging inner-city teams to shoot for the NBA is like encouraging them to win the lottery. Most will be disappointed.

Several years ago, a high school star named Chris Webber had one of these press conferences—and two years later, he held another to say he was leaving school for the pros. Someone asked Traylor about that Monday.

"I hope (I can) leave college in two years," he said excitedly.

Later he tried to correct this, but everyone knew what he meant. In his dreams of swimming in NBA waters, college is the diving board.

It is more than a diving board to Kevin Jones. He has no plans of leaving early. "I want to study business and open my own one day," he said. He showed a resume he had done himself. It noted his awards in the Navy ROTC, and his computer literacy in IBM and Macintosh systems.

This is no nerd. This is a good-looking kid who hears bullets in his neighborhood and remembers what his grandmother said, "When there's trouble, just keep walking." He works hard, because he was taught to work hard, and he doesn't read off a sheet when he says, "One day, after I get my business going, I'm gonna come back to this school and teach math."

Which is more important than coming back to sign autographs.

The doughnuts were mostly gone now. Traylor's aunt was being interviewed, so were his friends, who mugged for the cameras. Traylor himself posed, wearing a maize and blue Michigan cap.

Down the hall, the computer flipped on, and a young man began a new application for room and board money. He started with his name, "Kevin Jones."

No offense, but if there had to be a press conference Monday, it should have been his.

Writers' Workshop

Talking Points

1) "Where do I line up?" is a key starting point for Albom as he begins writing. In this story, he says he trained his sights on the apparatus of the press conference, specifically the little doughnuts set out for the media. Consider what other vantage points exist in this story that could also have served as effective starting points.

2) Albom is a student and big fan of *Chicago Tribune* columnist Mike Rokyo. He says he admires the way Rokyo leaves the message of his columns until the end. Study Albom's stories and see how he has modeled his style after Rokyo's punchline endings.

3) Albom begins this story deliberately intending to lure readers into thinking they are going to read about a familiar subject—a press conference starring a famous athlete—only to find the event is for a high school basketball player. What's the effect? Consider other ways he could have opened this story.

Assignment Desk

1) In *The Complete Book of Feature Writing,* edited by Leonard Witt (Writer's Digest Books), David Finkel, a staff writer for *The Washington Post Magazine,* says he tries to "look at any site that will be the focus of a narrative passage as if I were a photographer. I not only stand near something. I move away for a long view, I crouch down, I move left and right. I try to view it from every angle possible to see what might be revealed." Use this technique when you are reporting your stories and use what you see to help you decide where to line up.

2) Albom has a rare gift for writing unforgettable stories about unsung heroes. Find a story that is about an invisible star. Profile the high school musician instead of the star quarterback, the anesthesiologist instead of the surgeon, the evidence technician instead of the detective. Look, as Albom does, for inequities in the media's treatment of different occupations.

Mackenzie football star another gunplay victim

DECEMBER 22, 1995

"A person like me needs all the support he can get, because of all the things that happen to me."
—From a 10th-grade English paper by Dewon Jones

The first gun in his life was a gift from a relative, a rifle that had been snapped in half. "Let the kid have it," his step-grandfather said. So Dewon Jones took it and fixed the trigger and the barrel, and soon he had a weapon instead of a toy. One day, he was playing with his best friend James. Dewon put the gun in his pocket and danced like a cowboy. The gun went off.

"I'm shot!" he yelled. "I'm shot!"

At the hospital, doctors used tweezers to remove the bullet. Dewon and James made up a lie to police. They said they were on the porch when someone drove past and fired four random shots, and one hit Dewon's leg. The police wrote this down. It was not so unlikely, not where these kids live. No one was arrested. No one was charged.

Dewon Jones went home the next day, wearing the unofficial tattoo of his city: a bullet hole.

He was 10 years old.

* * *

The second gun came two years later. It was a starter's pistol, which belonged to an older kid named Cisco. Dewon, by this point, had been kicked out of several schools, his father was not around, so he looked up to older kids. When Cisco said, "We got something going down, you want in?" Dewon said yeah. He didn't even ask about his share.

A few days later, on a warm autumn night, Cisco brought a girl to a Coney Island near Eight Mile and Fleming. His crew—which included Dewon and James—jumped out and demanded the girl's money and car keys. One kid waved the pistol. Cisco acted frightened, which was part of the plan. Dewon, the youngest, was the lookout. He checked both ways, then jumped into the stolen car with the others.

A week later, when the police figured it out—Cisco wasn't too bright; he parked the car in front of his house—the helicopters flew overhead, beaming down spotlights. It was like something out of a movie. Dewon was scared. He hid in the attic. When the police left, he packed a small brown suitcase, planning to run away.

"Where you gonna run?" his uncle said.

"I dunno," Dewon said.

He went to a friend's house. An hour later, the police picked them all up. Armed robbery. Dewon and James—who pretty much went along for the ride—were considered accessories. They were fingerprinted. Put in a holding cell.

James got probation. Dewon was not as lucky. He was sent away to Starr Commonwealth, a residential treatment program for juvenile delinquent males—in Albion, 100 miles from home.

Dewon calls it "getting locked up."

He was 12 years old.

* * *

The third gun—we can only hope the last—came when Dewon returned from that treatment program three years later. He had calmed down. He had learned a lot. Out of the city, in a place where you can see trees and lakes and men without weapons, he had become a young adult, a certified lifeguard and a promising athlete, playing flag football and lifting weights. In group therapy, he spoke about his problems—no father, working mother, no money, no discipline—and he was even looked up to as a leader. One time, a kid named Darnell ran away. The whole class went looking for him, but it was Dewon who found him, hiding in a barn, sitting on a tractor behind bales of hay. Instead of turning him in, Dewon told the kid he should come back on his own.

"Where you gonna run?" he said, the way his uncle had once said it to him. "Where you gonna run?"

That night, when everyone was asleep, Darnell crawled back into his bed. Later he thanked Dewon for "saving him." Dewon felt good.

But good only lasts so long. When Dewon came back to the city, things were just the way he left them. Drugs.

Guns. He had been home less than three months when, on a Saturday afternoon, he walked over to James' house to get a pair of pants. The same James who had been with him for the biggest trouble in his life.

"I got a heater," James said, greeting him at the door.

"Whose is it?"

"Ray's."

"You better give it back."

"You wanna see it?"

They went to James' room. They checked out the gun. It was a .22-caliber pistol that Ray, their friend, had gotten for protection.

"You should give it back to Ray."

"Nuh-uh."

"I'm telling you."

"Watch this."

James started twirling it, spinning it on his thumb. "I'm Robocop," he said.

Pow! The gun went off, a small blast followed by a ping. The two teens instinctively covered their faces. But Dewon felt something weird beneath his fingers. Warm. Then sticky. He couldn't open his left eye.

"I'm shot!" he yelled, for the second time in his life. James grabbed a towel to stop the blood. His mother screamed. Someone called an ambulance, and the police came, too. As he ran downstairs, Dewon glanced in a mirror. His face was already swollen and bruised. Everything he saw was red.

"Where else are you hit?" the ambulance people yelled. They were ripping off his clothes, searching for wounds.

"What are you doing?" Dewon asked, stunned. "Why are you ripping my clothes?"

"Where else are you hit?"

He was in a hospital for 10 days. They took X-rays, gave him IVs. The shot had ricocheted off a wall and entered just above his left eye. It had cut through several arteries and nerves and was lodged somewhere near the nasal cavity. They couldn't remove it without risking blindness in *both* eyes. The doctors shrugged. He would have to live with it.

Dewon went home with a bullet in his head.

It is still there today.

He is 16 years old.

GUNS, GUNS, GUNS

Everyone should have a gun. That's what some people say, right? Protect yourself. It's in the Constitution. Dewon Jones, sitting now in his football coach's office at Mackenzie High, shakes his head and says those people "are fools. What you need a gun for? You ain't the police."

The kid sitting next to him agrees. That kid is James Montgomery, the one who shot Dewon in the eye. Maybe in another environment, you shoot somebody, you are no longer his friend. Not so in northwest Detroit.

"I knew he didn't mean to do it," Dewon says. "That's why I told the police I didn't want to press charges.

"To be honest, I blame myself for asking to see the gun. I should have known better."

Dewon Jones is a big, bruising kid, 6-feet-1, 250 pounds, with a broad neck and shoulders thick from lifting weights. He has an impish smile, a rolling laugh, and if not for the way his left eye droops, you would hardly be surprised that he plays football at Mackenzie, a middle guard on the defensive line. It was a guidance counselor's idea, the football. She thought it would give him direction. She was right. Dewon was depressed after the shooting. He had to wear a patch for six months and apply medication several times a day. His face was bruised and swollen, the left side partially paralyzed.

But football gave him focus. He loves it now. Dreams about it. Wants to be the first in his family to go to college and play ball.

If he has to take the bullet with him, so be it.

A HIT ON THE FIELD

"What do you see right now?" he is asked.

"I see you," he says.

"What do you see if you close your good eye?"

"I see a lot of red, and some black. You're kind of a blur."

"Doesn't that make it hard when you play football?"

He laughs. "I know where the quarterback is. And that's who I gotta find."

In the first game of this season, against Detroit Western, Dewon, a junior, sacked the passer on the opening play. He had three sacks against Detroit Henry Ford. He finished the season as the team sack leader and was named honorable mention All-Detroit by the *Free Press*. You have no idea what that means to a kid like Dewon, who has rarely heard a compliment from any voice of authority. Bob Dozier, his coach at Mackenzie, says Dewon's strength and quickness give him a good chance at a college scholarship. Dewon lights up when he hears that.

"I'm gonna make it out," he says. "I have no doubt."

James Montgomery, who shot him, looks at Dewon and nods in agreement. James, 18, is smaller, with a sad, round face. He also attends Mackenzie, when he feels like going. The two young men have known each other for as long as they can remember. They've been in church together and in a cell together. One summer, they were swimming in the high school pool when James tried a fancy dive off the board and tore cartilage in his knee. He panicked.

"I came up swallowing water and yelling for the lifeguard. He didn't hear me. But Dewon saw me and jumped in and came up under me so I could breathe. He pushed me to the side and got me out....

"The fact is, Dewon saved my life."

Four years later, James shot him in the eye.

CITY CAN'T BE IGNORED

If this doesn't sound like normal friendship, well, this must not be your neighborhood. The bullet life goes on every day in Detroit, right under our suburban noses, and so many of us act as if it doesn't matter, as if the city is just some place we pass on the Lodge Freeway, hit the gas, get it behind you.

But you can't get it behind you, because we are all in this together, geographically, economically and emotionally. Dewon Jones might have been shaped by his encounters with guns, but he is also a precious resource, a kid who has learned from the horror and wants to graduate and make a better life. He is doing well in school. He is serving as a mentor to some other students. He swears he wants nothing to do with guns, hasn't touched one since that day, "never want to see one again." He is adamant about this.

He is also a statistic, one of thousands of black youths to be shot before his 16th birthday. Bullet in his head. A permanent souvenir.

"How big a shock was it," he is asked, "when you told your friends you'd been shot?"

"Not so big. I know people been shot all over their body and they're still living."

"And James, how many guns had you fired before you accidentally shot Dewon that day?"

"Seven," he says.

Seven? No big deal. Guns are toys, guns are status, guns are everywhere here. Finding them is not the problem; avoiding them is.

"I don't want a gun," Dewon says. "I'm sick of guns. You got a gun, stay away from me."

He blinks hard. Sometimes, he says, his vision goes red, as if gazing through a veil of blood. You wonder if it's his eye or his perspective.

THE WRITE WAY

The bell sounds. School is out for the day. Students race through the halls, some screaming, others laughing. A few wave to Dewon through the open door. He nods.

He has taken to the staff at Mackenzie, especially Dozier, his football coach, and an English teacher named Ellen Harcourt. She encourages him to write, and one day, to her surprise, he gave her a composition called "Reflection on My Life."

"My life is moving on and there is nothing I can do about the problem that most changed me around. Guns are not toys, but I had to learn the hard way. That's the big reflection on my life. Or should I say, my unforgotten picture?"

It is a touching phrase, "my unforgotten picture." How can he forget? The world he sees every day is not the one shared by many of us. It is bloodshot, literally, but in that way it is much closer to what our city's children see every day, every night, everywhere. And it has to stop.

You look at these two high schoolers, you hear them talk about police and holdups, and you realize what a war it is for kids today. When Dewon was shot, a female officer told James, "If your friend dies, we're gonna charge you with some kind of murder."

"What were you thinking?" James was asked.

"I thought, 'I'm little, and I'm going to jail.'"

I'm little, I'm going to jail.

I'm little, I've been shot.

Who's little anymore?

Dewon Jones and James Montgomery pull on their coats and leave the school building out through the metal detectors and into the winter snow. One has a bullet on his conscience, the other wears that bullet in his head. They are high school kids who have fired on and been fired at and they swear they want nothing to do with guns anymore. "Guns are nothing but trouble," they say.

They came to this conclusion the hard way.

What's our excuse?

Writers' Workshop

Talking Points

1) In this story, Albom uses the device of three gunshot wounds suffered by Dewon Jones. Does it take too long to learn what this story is about? Consider other ways to begin this story. Make an argument for and against Albom's approach.

2) This is an anti-gun piece without polemics. Or is it? Where, if at all, does Albom's attitude about kids and guns surface? What is it? Discuss how the National Rifle Association and Sarah Brady of Handgun Control would react to the story.

3) A columnist is "still a reporter," Albom says. He likens it to getting "another stripe in the military...You don't throw out the other ones that you got on your patch...you're still obligated to report, and you're still obligated to give people enough of the story that if they choose to disagree with you, there's the detail and the evidence in your column to allow them to disagree with you." Are those details and that evidence present in this story to allow a reader to disagree with Albom?

Assignment Desk

1) This story is drawn from a series called "Dreams Deferred" that focuses on "heartbreaks and hopes of unsung Detroit area athletes." Look for subjects for a "deferred dreams" series of your own, whether your beat is sports, education, or police.

2) Albom quotes from a school composition written by Dewon Jones. Vary the documentation and voices in your stories: the coroner's report, the profile subject's diary.

3) Albom skillfully shifts the length of his sentences to shift the rhythm and pace of his stories. Count the words in each sentence. What is the shortest? The longest? The average? Now go through your own stories and compare sentence length. Model the pacing in your stories after Albom's work.

Christmas mourning

DECEMBER 24, 1995

You could hear him coming from miles away, the roar of his engine spitting down the gravel road. Noise meant speed, and to a supercharged, grease-under-the-fingernails racer like Chad Schlueter, speed was what life was all about. His family would listen from the kitchen and they'd hear his truck and its eight-cylinder thunder—*rrrrrrRRRRRRMMM!*—and they'd grin and say, "Chad's home." Some nights his sister Nicole, who adored him the way only a younger sister can, would lie awake until she heard his rumble. "Then I knew he was safe," she says, "and I could sleep."

A year ago today, the morning before Christmas, Nicole was waiting again, this time in the living room of the house in Howell, with her mother, Paulette, and her father, Dennis. Chad hadn't come home yet. That was unusual. Paulette asked her husband about the night before. He and Chad had been at a party. It broke up around 10:30.

"You want me to follow you home?" Dennis had asked.

"Nah, I'm fine," Chad said.

"You sure? Your truck doesn't sound too good."

The old red Bronco was coughing badly, blowing smoke. Chad pulled away, then backed up, smiled at his father and said, "See ya." Chad was like that. Why worry? What could happen? He could fix a car in his sleep. What could happen?

"Maybe he's at his girlfriend's," Dennis said now.

Suddenly, Nicole heard something. An engine, but it was too quiet, not Chad's style. She stepped to the window, looked out and froze. A state trooper was pulling up the driveway. Here, in the lonesome, rolling hillsides between Detroit and Lansing, that can only mean one thing.

"Ma'am, I need to talk to your husband," the officer said when Paulette opened the door.

"Is Chad all right?" she gasped. "Is anyone else hurt?"

"I need to talk to your husband."

"Anything you tell him, you can tell me. Tell me!"

Dennis appeared at the door. The officer looked at him.

"Sir, I have some bad news..."

A drink. A drive.

One less soul alive.

* * *

This is a story about two men whose only contact came when one's body smashed through the other's windshield and was flung into a ditch along the highway. When police found Chad Schlueter the next morning, his bones were broken and his face looked as if it had been ravaged by an animal. His light brown hair was soaked with blood, and his sweatshirt was pushed up around his chest, leaving his muscled back naked in the cold dirt. This is what you look like when someone plows into you at high speed. It is not pretty. It is hard to understand.

Chad had been walking along M-14 and U.S. 23 for nearly six miles. His coughing Bronco had broken down, and he was most likely heading for a phone. It was a mild winter night, and he carried three things. Two of those things would land inside the car that killed him, and, amazingly, stay on the front seat, framed by shattered glass, even as the driver sped away; one was a racing magazine, with a story about Chad, the other was a videotape of a TV interview Chad had done.

Had the driver looked at either item—instead of continuing home, going to bed, letting the alcohol disappear from his system, ensuring he could never be proven drunk—he might have known the soul he'd just snuffed out: a loving son, a rising star, a broad-shouldered, good-looking, 22-year-old driver with a disarming grin and a knack for the spotlight. *Chad Schlueter. Rampage Racing. Two-time World Champion of the Short Course Off-Road Drivers Association.* He drove racing 4X4s, souped up trucks with big wheels and no windshields that thunder around grass and dirt courses like fuel-injected buffalo.

Chad had talent. Chad had guts. In his very first race, in 1992, he barely made the starting line, forgot his sponsor's stickers and lined up in the worst possible position—yet he bolted from the gun and was in second place by the first turn.

Anyone watching could see something special. Chad Schlueter was born for the road.

He didn't know he'd die there.

AN EMPTY ROOM

The house on Gentry Court is large and tidy, with a wood-grained kitchen and a bay window that looks out on the back yard. Dennis, Paulette, Nicole, three of Chad's friends, all of whom were part of his race team, sit around the table and try to forget, even as you ask them to remember. They pass around his old helmet. It is red, white and blue. "A Christmas present," Paulette says, and they all nod quietly.

You can feel Chad Schlueter's absence here almost as much as you once felt his presence. He was the family's brightest light, always teasing and laughing. He had the best stories, the best jokes, he had a line for everything, even for the dog. "He was sarcastic," his friends say, "and hysterical." And loyal—he only drove Fords, because Dennis works for Ford—and protective. He watched his kid sister like a small-town Sir Galahad, checking her boyfriends, giving his approval. When the doorbell rang, Nicole would race for it, because if Chad got there first, the guy might turn and run.

"I actually didn't mind," she says now, smiling. "If they couldn't stand up to Chad, I'm not sure I wanted to date them anyhow."

Upstairs, in Chad's bedroom, the walls still are covered with his posters, and his trademark racing motto, "Stand On It." There are trophies he's won. Plaques he's received. Photos that chronicle his love affair with speed, the bicycle motorcross when he was 7, the minibike when he was 9, the Mustang he fixed up as a junior high schooler, working every night in the shed behind the house, the first ride he took in an off-road race truck. It was California, in the desert, on a warm summer night. He was 15. The driver floored it. They zoomed around, bouncing like a turbulent jet, and that was it, the kid was addicted. "He made that truck dance, Dad!" Chad later said.

He'd been chasing that sensation ever since.

Now in his bedroom, on the desk, between the trophies, is one more item, a small charcoal container, which holds the ashes of Chad's once-strong body. He was cremated. That was his wish. And one year from that tragic night, his family still cannot understand why their boy, who survived such a dangerous life behind the wheel, had to die as a pedestrian.

Because someone lost control.

"When I think of the man who did this," Dennis says, his voice flat as steel, "I hate him. I feel rage. I want to reach out and kill him."

A drink. A drive.

A FATAL MEETING

The man who hit Chad Schlueter is a 41-year-old salesman named Daniel Moskal. He works for Melody Farms, the dairy business. He has a wife, two kids and, until last year, a clean reputation. He had gone from his Livonia office that day to the Derby Bar, where many of his coworkers were gathered. As often happens on the last day before a holiday, work stopped early. And the drinking began.

Moskal opened with a vodka. In the next eight hours, by his own admission, he had at least six to eight beers. When he left the place, according to several witnesses interviewed by police and lawyers, he seemed noticeably affected by the alcohol. But so were others. In one of many ironies too sad to believe, someone actually offered him a ride, but Moskal felt the guy was too drunk. "He's gonna drive *me*?" Moskal said to himself. "Come on."

So he got in his 1993 Grand Prix, and started the long trip back to his home in Hartland. And this is the moment that this whole sad story is about, the moment you say, "What the heck? I can make it."

It is never about what you *can* do; it is always about what you cannot.

Moskal could not handle his condition. Sometime around 1 a.m., in the cold and dark near Joy Road and U.S. 23, his car plowed into an innocent man, and one life was ended and a dozen more were changed forever.

A drink. A drive.

"I fell asleep at the wheel," Moskal says now. "I woke up when my windshield blew out. I was going underneath a bridge, and all I could think of was that someone threw something off. I was scared for my life. I cried for three or four hours. I was hysterical. I thought someone was trying to kill me...

"The next morning, I looked in the car, saw the videotape and the magazine and some hair and some blood, and there was a feeling I can't explain. I woke up my wife, and asked her to take me to the state police."

Were you intoxicated that night, he is asked?

"Not as intoxicated as the family thinks."

Of course, the Schlueters see it differently. They see a man who was too drunk to even spot their son in his headlights. They see a man who was too cowardly to face up to what he'd done once he'd done it. They see police photos of a windshield with a hole the size of a suitcase. "How could he not know?" Dennis Schlueter asks. "With Chad's tape and magazine on the seat? He drove all the way home, 30 or 40 miles, and his wife was waiting for him, and they both went to sleep, knowing what he'd done. I can never forgive that."

This much is certain. By leaving the scene, the alcohol question could never be answered. It is a tragic loophole in the current law, one that almost encourages drunken drivers to flee an accident. With no Breathalyzer proof—Moskal went to the police around 9 the next morning, and by then he tested clean—the Washtenaw County prosecutors did not press for a drunken driving homicide felony. That, under a new statute, carries a maximum 15-year prison sentence.

"We felt we could show he had been drinking," says chief assistant prosecutor Joseph Burke, whose colleague, Julia Owdziej, actually handled, the case, "but we didn't think we could prove he was above the legal limit. It's very difficult, using toxicologists and witnesses."

Instead, despite the Schlueters' pleas, the prosecutors went for negligent homicide and leaving the scene of an accident. Lesser charges. No mention of alcohol. And because this was Moskal's first offense, even a conviction on those charges would have not brought much prison time. "Maybe 60 days," Dennis says they told him.

"All these prosecutors want is high percentage wins. They want convictions. That's their report card. ...Sixty days? For killing our son? Sixty days?"

In the end, it wasn't even that much. A plea bargain was arranged. Moskal got five years' probation and two weekends in the Washtenaw County Jail.

Two weekends.

For a gruesome, senseless death.

Is that fair, Moskal is asked?

"Nobody wants to go to prison," he says.

Is that fair, Burke is asked?

"Sometimes people get away with things they shouldn't," he says.

Is that fair, the Schlueters are asked?

There is no need to print their answer.

THE STORY IS NOT OVER

The third thing Chad Schlueter carried that night was a Christmas present for his girlfriend. A gold necklace. He had never bought such a gift before, certainly not for a woman. The family wondered, happily, if Chad were getting serious.

The necklace was found, alongside the highway, the morning of his death. Nicole kept it until just before the funeral. Then she put it around his girlfriend's neck, the way Chad had hoped to do. "You must have meant a lot to him," Nicole said.

They both cried.

There is enough irony in Chad Schlueter's story to fill a dozen Greek plays. There is Dennis offering to drive Chad home that night. There is Moskal who says "if someone sober had offered me a ride, I would have taken it." There is the family race team, Rampage Racing, that carried on Chad's tradition and won the SODA circuit this summer, his dream, after he was gone.

There is the fact that Chad, when he was killed, was within a mile of a gas station where he could have called home, where his family waited and where the Christmas tree was surrounded by gifts, including one box marked "To Chad, from Mom and Dad."

A car phone.

Instead today, the family has a most heartbreaking anniversary. They weep for the life they lost, and

Moskal—who says he hasn't had a drink since that night—weeps for his own. "I'm a good person. I feel such remorse. It hurts when people relate to me as a murderer. I am so sorry. I have no words."

The legal story is not over. A civil suit is still pending. But the important chapter can never be changed. Chad is gone. As part of the plea bargain, the Schlueters insisted that Moskal be constantly reminded of the horror he did, so he must write a check for $10, every month, to Mothers Against Drunk Driving—in Chad's memory. And he must speak to 20 groups about the crime. And he must sit and review materials chosen by the family—pictures, videos, letters—to show what kind of person their son really was, and what he will never be again.

"It's not enough," says his father.

How could it be? A drink. A drive. One less soul alive. All this from a stupid bottle, a stupid beverage, a stupid decision? Every year there are stories like this. And here we are, another holiday season, when more than half the highway deaths will be alcohol-related.

How much more can you warn? How much sadder can you get? Tonight is Christmas Eve, and in the small town of Howell a family waits, as they always will wait, for the roar of a distance truck kicking up gravel, the sweet sound of thunder, bringing their baby back home.

Writers' Workshop

Talking Points

1) Albom says he faced a challenge in this story: how to get the reader to care about Chad Schlueter, the young race driver killed by a drunken driver. He was looking for "a signature" that would bring the reader into his world. What detail did he settle on and how did he use it in the organization of his story?

2) The circle is a popular structural form for narrative writing. Notice how Albom employs it in this story. What details does he use to begin and end this story and how does their placement affect the reader?

3) Albom says he prefers to use dialogue rather than quotations uttered by a single source to give readers the freedom to interpret the reality of a scene that he's trying to communicate. "Dialogue can be interpreted in so many different ways," he says. Study the exchange between Chad's mother and the state trooper when the officer arrives to break the news of Chad's death. Discuss various interpretations that might be made of their conversation.

Assignment Desk

1) Write a story that uses the circle as its organizing principle. In your reporting, look for and begin your writing with a "signature" detail that you return to at the end to give the reader a sense of completion.

2) Examine the differences between quotations and dialogue. Paraphrase the dialogue between Chad's mother and the state trooper. Try a version where you quote only the mother or the trooper. How do such revisions alter the emotional impact and pace of the story?

3) Work hard to find opportunities to use dialogue in your stories. If you're reconstructing dialogue, remember Albom's observation that it can require close questioning of the participants and strict attention to accuracy.

Bone disease threatens basketball player's life

DECEMBER 28, 1995

She would not cry. She held back the tears as tightly as she once held her first basketball, cradling it all day, sleeping with it all night. Never mind this scary hospital, these sterile walls, these lousy blood tests; never mind what the doctor was telling her now, that she could die if she didn't have a bone-marrow transplant. *She could die? But she was only 18!* Never mind. Nekita Burnett, a college player the size of an eighth-grader, was used to laughing, clowning, cracking people up; she never was very good with the sad stuff. Besides, her mother was beside her, shocked by the doctor's words, and Nekita knew if she got misty then her mom would just lose it, start sobbing all over, and Nekita didn't want that. She just wanted out.

"Don't you cry," she told herself, fighting every impulse, *"Don't you cry...."*

This is the story of a kid they call "Small World," and if you met her, you would know why. She is compact and muscular and so full of talent, even her shadow has skills. She has survived the hardest stones the city has to throw: poverty, robbery, gangs, guns. One night she lay on the floor of a fast-food joint as a gunman threatened to shoot all the workers. The next night she was back, because this was her job, $4.40 an hour, and she couldn't quit, she needed the money. Besides, that was not her first holdup. A few months earlier, she had to hide behind the french fry machine as a gunman stole the cash through a drive-up window.

In her short life, Nekita Burnett has had every urban excuse for giving up: no father, no money, no status, no security. She has fought off those poisons with sports, art, good grades and college admission.

And now she could die—from a long-shot disease that's not supposed to strike young people, one that really makes you wonder how cruel fate can get.

Someone has to help this kid. It is just that simple. We cannot lose her.

Here is why.

* * *

"The building I have in mind is a homeless shelter," she says, sketching an invisible design on the desk in front of her. We are sitting in the student lounge of Wayne State, where Nekita takes freshman classes—in between her job at Rally's hamburgers, and watching her younger sisters, and practicing with the Tartars basketball team that she walked on to two months ago. Basketball is her passion—she has been playing since she was 9 years old, mostly with the boys, which explains her take-no-prisoners approach despite her 5-foot-1 frame—but her long-range goal is to be an architect.

A builder of cities.

She has wanted this since junior high, when she built a scale model of the Ambassador Bridge—out of toothpicks! A few years later, she met an architect on career day and she visited his office for a school report. There she saw a scale model of a proposed downtown Detroit. It looked so orderly, so breathtaking, so *possible.* "All the little buildings, the trees, the cars," she recalls, excitedly. This was what she wanted to do.

Build things.

"In this homeless shelter, I'm envisioning murals on the walls, and a library, and comfortable beds." She lowers her eyes and smiles. She has one of the 500-watt smiles, the kind that automatically make you smile back.

"And I was thinking...um, the building could be the shape of a 'N,' Like Nekita? You know, two towers, connected by a diagonal stairway?"

She waves her hand. Laughs again. "I have to work out the details."

Small world, big dreams.

OVERCOMING OBSTACLES

A few days later, we meet in the place where she lives. And you see why she dreams. Home is a decaying, upper-level flat off Washburn Street on the northwest side, with chipping paint, bars on the windows and a tilted porch that seems one strong breeze from collapsing. Music blares from the tenants on the lower level, too loud for this winter morning. Upstairs, Nekita sits with her mother, Carolyn, and younger sister

Toi in a tidy front room with a Christmas tree in the corner. On a table are some family photos, and behind a couch is Nekita's artwork—first-rate drawings of friends, teachers, even a self-portrait.

Still, of all the things that Nekita has done, her mother seems most proud of the fact that her eldest daughter is 18 and hasn't gotten pregnant.

"I keep reminding her of the three B's," Carolyn says. "Boys bring babies."

Boys bring babies. Carolyn learned that the hard way. She was pregnant with Nekita when she was 15. One day, walking home, some men started chasing her. She was wearing a leather coat. They wanted it. Carolyn ran. She ran down Charlevoix and onto Fairview, breathing hard, looking over her shoulder, they were still coming, so she darted across the street and *wham!* She was hit by a car, went flying and landed in a world of unconsciousness.

"I blacked out," she says. "I don't remember what happened next."

But it still haunts her. To this day, she suffers epileptic seizures that keep her from steady work. Because of this, she lives from week-to-week on welfare checks while fighting the paperwork for disability payments.

Carolyn was one of 11 children. Her three girls all have different fathers, and Nekita's father "doesn't bother with us." But Carolyn loves her daughters fiercely, so when Nekita began playing basketball with the local guys, her mother was skeptical.

"Are they looking at you funny?"

"What do you mean funny?" Nekita asked.

"You know, like they want something else?"

"What?"

"Sex."

"Naw, we're just playing basketball."

"Well just make sure that's all you do. Remember. Boys bring babies."

Boys bring babies. Nekita already knew that. Besides, she already had been taught another version of the three B's: "Books before basketball." This she was told by teachers in Noble Middle School and later at Mackenzie High, where she captained the team her senior year. She was a top point guard with a good long-range shot and a feel for the game born from countless afternoons on the asphalt court behind school, where in the winter Nekita would borrow a shovel to clear the snow, then keep on playing.

"With most high school girls, you just want to get the physical stuff down, let the mental part come in college," says Jan Chapman-Sanders, one of Nekita's coaches at Mackenzie. "But she knew the game already. She was a ball handler, a playmaker, and she could pass on a dime."

Unfortunately, as a senior, her team was mostly underclassmen. Nekita spent more time as a role model than as a star. She did not get recruited by major universities, and one potential scholarship, at Hampton Institute, fell apart when the coach there left.

So Nekita stayed home, went to Wayne State, prepared to focus on academics and get on with becoming the master builder she hoped to be. When she made the Wayne State team as a walk-on, it was just another plus. After all, unlike many black inner-city youths, she had passed her 18th birthday with no wounds, no children, a high school diploma and a possible ticket out. Things looked good.

And then the blood tests came back.

AN UNLIKELY VICTIM

She had known there was a problem a few years earlier. A routine physical revealed a troubling blood count. She was iron-deficient. For a while she took pills, and when these didn't help she was tested again. Her bone marrow wasn't right. The marrow, where the blood cells are formed, is the core of our human machinery—just as kids like Nekita are the core of our city's future.

When one is infected, so is the other.

In Nekita's case, the disease is called Myelodysplastic Syndrome, sometimes known as "pre-leukemia." It is very similar to the disease that killed radio star J.P. McCarthy this past summer. Only in McCarthy's case, the candidate fit the profile.

"This is a disease for 50- or 60-year-olds," says Dr. Steve Abella, who has seen Nekita at the Karmanos Cancer Institute at Children's and Harper Hospitals. "It's very rare to find it in someone Nekita's age...."

"Do we know what causes it? No. We wish we did. But most patients require a bone-marrow transplant between five and seven years of diagnosis. And Nekita, technically, was diagnosed two or three years ago. First she must find a donor."

And if she finds one?

"There is a 70 percent chance of long-term survival."

And if she doesn't?

"It is most likely fatal."

Small world. Big trouble.

THE SEARCH IS ON

Back in the student lounge, Nekita sits alone, with her baseball cap and her non-stop smile. To the outside observer, she is every inch the happy college student. She says she asked herself "Why me?" about a million times since that day in the doctor's office. She says she worries now that her basketball teammates might treat her differently when they know what she has.

"Maybe it's a test of my faith. Everything happens for a reason...at least right now it hasn't affected me. I can still play the same, still make the same moves, still do everything I always did."

When they told Nekita what a transplant would involve, she replied, in typical fashion, "I can't put my life on hold for that!" Sadly, she doesn't have a choice. Without new bone marrow, her system will be unable to ward off infections. Small colds might not go away. Bruises might not heal. In the end, if left unchecked, leukemia could move in and take over the body.

And so the search is on for a donor. Nekita's name is in a computer, which reaches potential donors all over the world. To succeed, their white cells must match. In Nekita's favor is her age, her good health and that 1,800,000 potential donors are in the system already.

Going against her: the acute shortage of minority donors, including African-Americans, like herself. The average wait for a bone-marrow transplant for blacks is between one and two years.

"It (her disease) is so rare," Abella says. "This is the first case I've seen all year in someone 18 or under."

And, meanwhile, the most precious currency of this city, a poor kid who survived without hate, without despair, with dreams of building a better life for people after her, must wait and take blood tests and hope a donor can be found to give her a future.

"How has this changed you?"

She pauses. She bites her lip. "Well, I've been thinking about how I can achieve my goals faster."

Faster?

She goes to college. She takes a bus to her fast-food night job. She works an hour and a half just to pay cab fare home, so she doesn't have to worry about getting shot at 2 a.m. And she dreams of building homeless shelters.

She is one of a thousand stories in this town that goes unnoticed in the finger-pointing over welfare and urban renewal, and whose responsibility is it anyway?

Nekita Burnett doesn't want to be anyone's responsibility. It's too late. She already is. When she learned her fate, she held back the tears. She didn't cry. She went home, made sure her mother was OK, then slipped into her room, shut the door, sat on the bed and, finally, wept.

We have too many kids weeping in this city already. Too many we can't help. Small world. Big problem.

Can't we do something?

Writers' Workshop

Talking Points

1) Albom says he "puts details between commas." "Nekita Burnett, a college player the size of an eighth grader, was used to laughing...." Look for other examples of this technique and discuss the effect.

2) After this story was published, several readers volunteered to donate bone marrow. Discuss the ethical implications of such a story. Is it fair to single out one person when thousands of others may suffer a similar fate? Is it proper for the journalist to play the role of social worker or charity fund-raiser?

3) Notice how frequently Albom, and many other newspaper writers, use the phrase, "This is the story of...." This can be viewed as literary scaffolding, writing that helps the writer build the story, much like scaffolding on a building makes construction work possible. But construction scaffolding is dismantled once the building is finished. Story scaffolding may be necessary to discover the focus or organization of a story. Could it be removed without harming the story?

Assignment Desk

1) Adopt Albom's technique of weaving details between the commas in your stories.

2) A musician and songwriter, Albom often uses words like a lyricist. "A drunk. A drive. One less soul alive." "Small world. Big trouble." Look for other examples. Weave such phrases into your own stories.

3) Many writers use "This is a story about..." as scaffolding. Look for examples in your work and your reading. Remove the scaffolding and study how it affects the story. Consider using scaffolding as builders do, as a temporary device that enables you to build your story but which can be removed before the reader occupies the space.

A conversation with
Mitch Albom

CHRISTOPHER SCANLAN: What's your job at the *Detroit Free Press?*

MITCH ALBOM: My job title is lead sports columnist. My job is to go to all major sporting events and offer my insights, or analysis, or opinion. What my actual job turns out to be is a lot of that, and a lot of seeking stories—and I emphasize the word "stories" —that all people can relate to because they express basic human emotions, such as fear, courage, desire, dedication, humor.

A lot of what I end up writing is not the seventh game of the World Series. It's a story about a kid in a Detroit school who plays football with a bullet in his eye. Or the story of an Iditarod sled dog racer in Alaska who sold all his possessions and traded in his life for one run at the 1,100-mile sled dog race.

It's the story that matters. You can weave lessons and commentary out of almost anything in life. The trick is to make sure you are playing the human chords because the music attracts the audience.

What does "story" mean to you?

An episode in a person's life when something took place, usually when something changed for them, or they were changed by it. The reader is attracted simply because they want to see what happens next.

If you can hook them with the story that way, you really don't need to pound them over the head with a hammer, and say, "This is the message of the column."

You can almost wait until the very last paragraph and deliver the whole wallop of the column in a single line. And I feel if I've done that, then I've done my job, not only as a columnist, but as a reporter.

How important is being on the scene?

I've never seen a story break in an office. Because of portable computers you can use anywhere, I frequently like to set up shop right where the story took place and just start writing there. It's fresher. It's in your mind. The smells and the sights and the sounds are all there, and it's a lot easier to capture them by just looking up from your computer and looking around than it is to run back to the office, grab a sandwich, and all of a sudden try to remember it. Sometimes, just the color of a building, or the texture of a building's material, or the type of tree, or things like that really help your writing to be explicit and colorful.

You have to get out of the office. I think a lot of columnists feel that when they get a column job, that means they're being rewarded for the hard work they've done in the business up to that point, and now they're allowed to sit by their computer and think great thoughts. I see it as you're almost more obligated to get out and see more things now. You don't have a beat any more. Your beat is the human race, or the sports world—you have to go all over it, but the luxury is that you are now allowed to report not only what you see, but then put your spin on it.

I almost never go to the office, maybe once a month to pick up mail and say hello to everybody. The office is, in addition to being a tough place to work because a lot of people want to talk, the phone's always ringing, and there's no news ever breaking out of the office. But it's also a breeding ground for cynicism.

We all seem to want to impress one another with our cynicism. That's almost a language of journalists, especially in the office. And that's not the language of the average person. I don't think that our writing should be infused with cynicism. And it's not going to make me better to the readers. Until somebody tells me otherwise, I still think I'm writing for the people who pay for the newspaper, not the people who get to read it for free at the office. I can be a little purer towards things if I write at home, looking out the window, than if I'm down at the office.

What was the genesis of the story about the press conference for the high school basketball player?

I knew that there was a press conference in an inner city Detroit high school, which to me, in and of itself, was a story. All the press, with their TV trucks, driving down to a school that they would otherwise never go to for a press conference held by a student—not by a teacher or the school board principal—a student, and a marginal student at that, but a basketball player. I knew the scene was just going to spell out the lunacy of that situation.

I went there simply to report on the scene. I was watching this parade of people behind Robert Traylor, all the excited coaches, all these sports reporters, and cameras, and little doughnuts that they served, and kids peering into the room.

Bells were ringing out in the hallway, and kids were standing on their tiptoes. And it struck me that there was all this school stuff going on around this basketball player's press conference.

Did you stay for the entire press conference?

I'd heard all the clichés of press conferences before. I listened for a few minutes, and then I got the idea to just wander around the halls and see if I could find anything that would point out a contrast of what the school should be versus what school had become on this day.

I wandered into the computer library. There was a young man there. I asked one of the teachers about him, and he said, "Well, he's going to Michigan on a computer scholarship." And I said, "Well, there we have it."

I asked the young man if I could talk to him, and of course we had to go to the principal and make sure it was OK. It was all right to bring in press trucks from all over to talk to a basketball player, but in order to talk to a kid about his computer scholarship, I had to go through three levels of bureaucracy.

But they finally let me, and I found that he was from a very similar background. Tough home. Single parent. His mom worked as a janitor, all the tough stories, and yet he was going to stay four years at Michigan, not two or three as a lot of basketball players do.

My job in those kinds of situations is to get out of the way, set it up, and just come in at the end, almost like the chorus in a Greek play, and sum up what it's about. I think that was a good marriage of reporting and commenting without my having to tell you, every two paragraphs, "This is what I think."

How much longer did you stay on the scene?

I really just thought I was going to write about the press conference. I didn't know when I got there that I was going to find Kevin Jones.

First and foremost you have to go with an open mind. Don't go and say, "Well, this is it. This is what I've got to do. I'm not moving." You sort of follow your nose a bit. That's one of the luxuries you have as a columnist. You're not there to report every single word.

I watched the first 15 minutes of the press conference. By the time I found Kevin, school was close to out. By the time they allowed me to talk to him, school was out. We talked for probably 45 minutes, I went back to the press conference and just verified the scene in my mind.

What's your deadline for a column?

The *Free Press* has the worst deadlines in America, and always has, for a major paper. My first edition has to be in by 7:30, and my second edition has to be in by 10:30. As you can imagine, there aren't a whole lot of games that are over by 10:30 or 10:45, or they just got over, and I have to write an analysis, complete with quotes and everything in 10 or 15 minutes. There have been times when I've had to file before the game is over, which is pretty interesting when you're trying to make a commentary on the game and you don't know who won it.

I've written many columns that have never seen the light of day because, on big games, I would have a "Pistons Win" column, "Pistons Lose" column, and "Pistons Are in Overtime" column. I've had pretty good training through the *Free Press* at writing quickly.

When you sit down to write, have you already formulated the column in your mind? How do you decide on your focus for a story?

I try to tell the story out loud and see if I can come up with a single sentence, a summation, or a question that speaks for it, and then keep my eye on that, no matter where I go. And not try to lose it, because those kind of stories can ramble on you.

You get lost and you throw in everything just because you don't want to leave anything out. That's the old Dizzy Gillespie rule that I live by. I learned that when I was a musician.

Dizzy Gillespie said, "It took me my whole life to learn what *not* to play." I write by that philosophy. I'm assuming by the time I'm ready to kick off, I'll finally have this writing business down, and I'll be able to say everything that I'm taking 50 inches to say now in 10 inches, because I'll know what *not* to play.

What am I saying here? When people are done reading it, they walk away, and they tell somebody, "Here's what that column was about." Can they do it in one sentence? Or do they just ramble?

Do you write an outline?

No outlines. No formal ones, anyhow. Don't have enough time. Mental outlines. Generally, I know the length. That is almost automatic.

The most important thing has got nothing to do with that. It's where do I line up? Like lining up a shot or a pitch. The key is in where you stand. If you line up wrong, the column is always going to be awkward, and you're going to be stretching to make your point. If you line up right, if you are any kind of storyteller, you really do just have to get out of the way.

How does "lining up" work?

Lining up the angle. Where do I begin? Do I begin with Kevin Jones? Do I begin with some big sweeping statement? Do I begin with my trip down to the school?

All this thinking takes place in a couple of minutes. The key is to just keep your eyes open. And the thing I saw was those little doughnuts on a tray by a coffee urn. And that was just so non-high schoolish, and so much like a movie, where a camera focuses in on a close-up and then pulls out to establish a scene. That's where I lined up. "I'm going to start with the grandiosity of the press conference." Never having to state that this is crazy, because it will be very apparent by what I choose to relate that this is not like high school.

I have the doughnuts, and the press, and the cameras, and in comes the man of the hour. He's got an entourage of people behind him. He introduces them. They all sit down. He steps to the microphone.

I knew once I did that I would have my angle, my second angle, established for Kevin Jones, which was to be a much quieter, small room working on a computer. All I would have to do is describe him, some of the things that he said, his life, contrast it to make the point, and that's the column.

You have to be able to break it down like that, because when you have two hours, you can't start pouring through tapes and making outlines. Life just doesn't work that way. The scene has to hit you, and you have to know what you want to say. I knew in the car ride home what I was going to do with it.

Are you peppering yourself with mental questions?

Sometimes if you ask yourself so many questions you get confused, I say, "OK. Don't think about it for a couple of minutes. Turn on the radio. Just think about something else. Let it come back to you."

And I don't think about it for a while—"a while" being five minutes—and then I wait for something to pop into my head, the impression that stayed with me. It might have been the doughnuts or that silver coffee urn. It just looked so out of place in a room with a blackboard.

You look for symbols that will help you tell your story. Understand, there are probably a thousand ways to write a column. The trick, if you want to get good at this job, is to choose one and make it work the best you can. Don't worry about what's *not* being written. Don't worry about what's *not* being included.

The trick is what you are putting on the page. No one is going to read your column and say, "You know he should have put this other thing in there—I think the first paragraph he was considering was better." They only know what you give them.

So make sure what you give them is good, and don't worry about the permutations of a column, because you'll drive yourself crazy.

If you keep thinking great thoughts right up until the time that you file, no one's going to appreciate all the wonderful thinking that you did. They're just going to know there's a big empty white space under your face in the newspaper.

How important is the lead?

I look at leads as my one frail opportunity to grab the reader. If I don't grab them at the start, I can't count on grabbing them in the middle, because they'll never get to the middle. Maybe 30 years ago, I would give it a slow boil. Now, it's got to be microwaved.

I don't look at my leads as a chance to show off my flowery writing. My leads are there to get you in and to keep you hooked to the story so that you can't go away. I'll make my points later if I want to flex a writing muscle.

How do you revise?

A lot of times at the *Free Press,* I only have time to write one shot. The ultimate one was the second time the Pistons won a championship against Portland, on the West Coast, and I had to file a story five minutes before they won, and they won the championship on a shot with .007 left on the clock. Not only was that literally patched together over the phone, but they turned it into a commemorative poster because it was the front page.

So now, the worst thing I ever wrote is on kids' bedrooms all over Detroit. I always have this vision of these 11-year-old kids waking up in the morning and reading it and they're all thinking, "God, this guy's terrible. Why did they ever give him that job?"

Usually, I file for the first deadline. And I make sure it fits. Then I go downstairs, get a cup of coffee or something to eat, come back up, and start working on it again.

I file again for the 10:30 deadline, either a whole new column, or I modify it over the phone: "Take this line out. Put this line in."

Sometimes I'll modify a few more lines for the 12:30 deadline. And once in a while, one or two more for the chaser edition. A lot of times I go out to dinner and the column is still in my head. I'll be eating with my wife or friends, and all of a sudden, my eyes will get glassy and I'll say, "Excuse me a minute," and I go running to a pay phone. I'm fortunate enough to work with really good people who know my quirks.

And they say, "Ah, Mitch is on the phone again. Somebody take him. He wants to make a change in his column." And I won't even have the column in front of me. I'll know it in my head. "You know that paragraph that begins with such and such? Can you put in a sentence and take out a sentence?" "Yeah, yeah. Sure, Mitch."

And I'll do that up until 1 o'clock in the morning because it just never leaves me.

That's a long work day.

I have accepted the fact that I don't get any mental time off unless I'm literally not working. If it's a column day, my column writing responsibility ends when there are no more papers to go out. I've always looked at it that way. If I can make it better for one more edition, there's a hundred people that are going to get a paper that's got a little bit better take on it.

It ruins some dinners and some movies. Sometimes, I take a printout of a column with me. My wife and I go see a movie, and I stick it in my pocket, and she'll see it. "Now you're going to walk out in the middle of the movie." I say, "Oh, no. I'm taking it just in case."

And then, sure enough, an idea will come to me and I'll say, "You want some popcorn or something?" I'll miss the whole movie. I'll come back with the popcorn when the movie's over, and she'll say, "You called the office, didn't you."

When you become a columnist, you've got your name up top with a picture of you, you don't want people to associate your name and your picture with bad work. If I can keep sculpting it, or working on it, I'll continue to do it.

This impetus sounds like it's from within.

That's where your writing should come from.

What's your sense of the reader reaction when you zag when everybody else is zigging?

Very positive. Do people take to the odd or the off-beat? I think they're starved for it. I think they're really tired of hearing the same Michael Jordan column over and over again.

Are there lessons that the news side could learn from the sports side—I hear people saying, "I don't read the paper," but I don't hear people saying, "I've stopped reading the sports pages."

In this age of CNN and ESPN, the only thing we really are going to be able to offer our readers that they can't get someplace else is the analysis, the unusual take, the long feature story. If we're not already there.

Let's face it. You can log on your computer now any time, day or night, and get all the scores. And that's a lot easier to do than to walk down your driveway in 7 degree below weather and get your newspaper, which had to be printed at 10:30 at night and doesn't even have the box score. This frequently happens with us and we have to write "incomplete" after the game. "Detroit at San Francisco—incomplete."

That's terrible. I hate seeing that in a newspaper. It goes against my whole notion of what a newspaper is. All the news that's fit to—incomplete.

So the days of us being the first people to bring you the box scores are gone. They have been gone for some time. And I really do think it's the personalities, columnists, feature writers, long investigative takes on things, that are the only plasma left for the blood supply of newspapers.

There's nothing else. Anyone who thinks, "We're still going to beat the electronic age," are kidding themselves. That's like throwing pebbles against a machine gun.

The Kevin Jones/Robert Traylor piece was a short column. Are you talking about just long features?

It doesn't have anything to do with length. The Traylor/Jones column is a perfect example of something that a newspaper can do. The day after that came out, two television stations called me at home and asked me how they could get in touch with this kid to do a feature on him.

TV still takes its cues from what they read in a newspaper. It's amazing. We're afraid of Goliath, and Goliath is reading us.

The newspaper's resources are its people, and the people's eyes. And newspapers still employ far more people than any local TV news station. How many reporters does the local TV news station have? Five? And sports reporters, they have one? They can bring you results, but they can't bring you upbeat stories, or angles, or whatever. They don't have enough time. They have 22 minutes per broadcast.

Our strength is we've got 80 pages a day to offer people, and we can fill those pages in a lot of ways, but trying to fill them with box scores is not where we're going to be able to differentiate ourselves.

What kind of reading do you do on a daily basis?

I read voraciously, and I don't read sports things. I wasn't a sports geek when I grew up. I wasn't even a sports page reader. I was a musician. And I trained to be a musician. I traveled as a musician.

I didn't go to college for writing, I never wrote a word. I never wrote for my high school newspaper. I never read my high school newspaper. I never wrote for my college newspaper or read my college newspaper.

I was playing music and going to school overseas for a while, and I lived in New York as a starving artist. I only fell into journalism as something to do, and I think, in a weird way, that's really served me well.

Early on, I interviewed a photographer of famous people. He told me a story that I have never forgotten. When he was beginning as a photographer, he took all the work he had done, and he sent it to the guy who at the time was the biggest photographer in the business, with a note saying, "Please look at my work and analyze it and tell me what I should do, and how I can improve."

And he didn't know if he'd ever get anything back, but sure enough, a week later, he got his stuff back with a short note: "Based on your work, based on what you sent me, obviously you've mastered the basics of photography. Here's what I suggest. Surround yourself with the finest music, the finest art, the finest theater, the finest drama, and everything else will take care of itself." Signed such and such.

The point was that sometimes the way you get better in your own field is by making sure you surround yourself with excellence in other fields. And I've never forgotten that, and I've always tried to do that with writing.

Watching good movies, reading great novels, seeing great plays all help you become a better sports writer. You just have to be open to absorb it. Observe how they do things in drama, and how they do things in good novel writing—I dog-ear all the pages of books that I read. I underline phrases that catch me.

When I pull a book off a shelf, I can just open to a page and read a couple of really inspirational sentences—absorb them like a sponge, and ultimately, your own writing becomes better.

I don't think reading *The Joe Namath Story* or Joe Montana's book is going to necessarily make me a better sports writer. But I do think that reading Tom Wolfe or John Updike will. And so that's what I try to do with my spare time.

Are there writers who have been particularly influential?

Hemingway. There are some great lessons in his work about how to say a lot with a little. Which is a great lesson for a newspaper writer.

Mike Royko's early work as a columnist is a great lesson to people in terms of how you can say a lot and really be a good columnist without ever using a fancy word. You won't ever find a three-syllable or four-syllable word that you have to run to a dictionary to look up in a Mike Royko column. And yet, he says it perfectly. He also is real big on saving the punch line till the end. If you were to trim the final half-inch of every Mike Royko column, you wouldn't get any of them. That's where the message is.

If I really like a writer, I'll even analyze how they did what they did with little things. I read humor writers because I like to laugh, but also because I think that's something people don't do very well, and try to analyze how you make something funny, and what are the mistakes people make when it's not funny.

This is my craft. I can't learn enough about it. There are always media guides to learn who led the league in triples in 1961.

Who are you writing for?

The crowd that might otherwise walk past the sports page, because it's too many numbers. I have a cardinal rule that I don't use numbers in my writing.

If I have to use them to illustrate a point I'll drop in a batting average here and there. Generally, if I can say, "Three out of four times he comes to the plate something good happens," I'll say that rather than say, "He hits .750."

I'm not an accountant. I don't want to have to figure it out. Use your creativity, you know. Explain what the numbers mean. I always try to figure, what if somebody's visiting from another country and they speak English, and they read English, but they really don't know the game of baseball. They pick up your column and they say, "I'm going to read one thing about the game of baseball. And if it holds my attention, maybe I'll read a second thing. If not, I'll never read anything again."

Are you going to serve that person by saying, "Barry Bonds, coming off a .333 season, heads into June with a 15 for 27 streak from the left side of the plate, with a .46 slugging percentage"?

What was the genesis of your "Dream Deferred" series?

I've done it a couple of years now. There are so many stories that I come upon that are never going to make headlines.

Working with some of these famous people, it always stands in contrast to me. I'm always aware of and looking for people who don't get a crack at being famous, who might have had a chance.

And I tried to do it around Christmastime. It often provides an interesting backdrop. Everybody's out celebrating, and frequently a lot of the people I write about can't. Or it's a time of sadness for them, like in the case of Chad Schlueter who was killed on Christmas Eve.

Often those columns help the people who are involved, too. Which I don't think violates journalism, at least in Detroit. We feel that we're part of the same community here, it's a big small town.

I remember writing a column once about a kid who was shot on a pick up playground, playing basketball out in the suburbs. He was from Detroit, and had never gotten into any trouble in inner city Detroit. He and his friends one day said, "Let's go out to the suburbs and see what kind of basketball they play there." And they went out and he got shot on a suburban court by a guy who was aiming for somebody else and just hit him.

He was paralyzed, and he lives in a one-room place with his mom and he can barely get out of bed. And this is going to be his life. I asked him, during the course of the interview, what he wanted for Christmas, and he hoped his mom was going to get him a little television set, because the TV was in the other room and it was really hard for him to get from his bedroom to the other room.

It was probably a 40-inch story, and that probably appeared at inch number 28. Hardly prominent. But the next day, three different people drove to that kid's house and delivered television sets. And two others sent money to the paper.

It gives me goose bumps. It's astounding that a newspaper can engender such kindness from people. In the case of Nekita Burnett, they had a lot of people call up to donate their bone marrow to see if it matched hers. In that case, you may be saving somebody's life.

You made that pitch, in a sense, with the story.

The key is the story. Everybody's getting pitched. You turn on your television in the morning and you're getting pitched from the time you hit the on button until the time you go to sleep. You open your mail, and you're getting pitched for charities, and you go on the street and there's people begging and asking—everybody wants something.

I think it's led people to turn away the minute they hear a request. The best bait for your readers is a story. Always a story. And if you can get them into the story, they'll care about the people in the story. And once they care about the people in the story, then maybe they'll do something about it.

What in your past influences you as a writer?

Music has helped—being a musician and a songwriter before I was a journalist has really helped my writing, particularly the pace of the writing. You'll notice how sometimes you read one person's 15 inches, and it just flows like melted butter. You're at the bottom before you even know what happened to you. Then others, you read the same length story, and you have to blink a couple of times and stop and go back and read, and why? It's the same amount of words.

A lot of that has to do with pace and rhythm, and I think I learned that from music. When to use a short sentence, when a long sentence, when a one-word sentence, when to break a paragraph. Songwriting is a verse, a chorus, a verse, a chorus. I'll use the chorus technique in the single line.

"A drink, a drive, one less soul alive."

I'll repeat a line two or three times during the course of a column. That's like the shoelace that goes through it, and then you just tug on the shoelace to tighten up the story. Sometimes it's just—"I Love You, Yeah, Yeah, Yeah."

God! Did you write that?

Yeah. That was one of my early ones. I wrote "I Love You, Yeah, Yeah, Yeah," and it was never quite a hit, and then a few years later, wouldn't you know it? The Beatles come out with "She Loves You, Yeah, Yeah, Yeah." I gotta sue those guys sooner or later.

How did you become a writer?

The storytelling actually comes from my family. I had a pretty big extended family, and we would have a lot of family get-togethers where, like at Thanksgiving and Easter and times like that, we were really big at staying at the dinner table for two or three hours. Nobody watched TV. Everybody stayed at the dinner table, and everybody told stories.

In order to keep the floor, you had to be really good at telling a story. And I had a few uncles who really were good at it, and everyone wanted them to tell stories, and then someone else would jump in, and they weren't very good, and you could see the pained expressions—"Oh, God. Get this one over with."

Sometimes my uncles would turn to my aunts and say, "Will you hurry up? Get to the point." I kind of learned as a kid that you don't get too long before they yank the carpet from under you. I had a pretty critical audience there at that dinner table. You really had to learn to keep their attention, and you had to get to the point fast, and paint a good picture, and throw in a good couple of humorous lines to keep them interested.

You use dialogue: "Ma'am, I need to talk to your husband." "Is Chad all right?" she gasped. "Is anyone else hurt?" "I need to talk to your husband." "Anything you can tell him, you can tell me. Tell me!" Are you deliberate about looking for dialogue?

Absolutely. That's something people really should do more of. It's hard, because you're recreating dialogue, and so it requires a lot of questioning that I think sometimes reporters don't like to do with people.

When I asked Mrs. Schlueter the question about that, and I said, "Well, what did he say?" You know, they described the cop coming to the house. And first people always recount it, they say something like, "Well, a policeman came to the house, you know, and he—you know, wanted to—he wouldn't tell me what was going on, and he wanted to see my husband." And I could see she was bothered by that.

"Well, what did he say?"

"Well, he said, you know—you know, 'I have bad news.'"

And I said, "Yeah. And what did you say?"

"Well, tell me, and my husband."

You have to take two, three, four questions to try to recreate that, and a lot of people don't want to do that. But I find it gets your subject more into the story, too, because they start remembering what they said.

Of course, you want to be as accurate as you can, so you need to really double-check and ask over and over. But it's worth it to me, because I think most of the world exists in dialogue, not in people's thoughts. That's how people relate to people. Dialogue reads quicker, and people can relate to it more.

With dialogue, somebody might get something else out of it that I didn't. Somebody might read that dialogue. "Oh, isn't that sad? The way she had to find out was someone said, 'I have bad news for you.'" Another person might look at it and think, "Why is that cop so sexist?" Another person might think, "Well, when does the father come in?"

Do you use a tape recorder?

Sure. I was there for four hours. Can you imagine my handwriting at the end of four hours?

Do you have a transcriptionist?

You're talking to him. Without a tape recorder, you really can't capture the full emotional breadth of what people are saying to you. When you're talking to a family, a grieving family, the way they say things, sometimes even a small little sentence, or the way their voice trails off, is very important to recreate the mood and the spirit. I don't trust my penmanship to try to get it down.

I find sometimes it's a little disrespectful. The physical act of jotting down what they're saying as they're crying is a bit cruel. I should add that I work with a notepad even with the tape recorder, because I don't trust technology.

Are there techniques you've found helpful in getting people to reveal themselves to you?

In general, I go in, I introduce myself, and sometimes that helps, because they might know me. That's just the reality of having been in the town for 10 years. But other times they don't.

In the case of Chad Schlueter, I called his father and introduced myself and said, "Here's why I'm calling." I always try to get right to the point. I don't make silly talk, because I think people distrust that. I think the minute you say you're from a newspaper, everybody's antennae go up.

So get to your point. Don't say, "So, how you doing? How's things going?" "Hey, you're working at Ford. Ford's got a nice new Taurus out, don't they?"

I wouldn't want to be insulted like that. Never assume that you can pull the wool over anybody's eyes, just because you're a reporter and they're an average citizen, you know. You wouldn't try that with a savvy politician or athlete. Don't try it with the average person.

I always say, "Here's why I'm calling. I know about your son's story. I know it's probably a very painful thing for you to talk about, and I certainly understand if you can't." And I always offer them that option, right from the start. In any situation that is uncomfortable, they need to know they don't have to do it, and they need to hear you say they don't have to do it.

Remember, I am not investigating a criminal offense by a prominent politician, in which case he shouldn't have an option not to do it. He owes his public an explanation. These are people who have suffered private tragedies, and owe nobody anything. They don't owe me a story, and they don't owe the newspaper a story, and they don't owe the public anything.

Right off the bat, you can't make them feel that they have to give you a story. And so I try to state to them, "Listen. You know. I'm going to ask you something here that may be too tough for you, and I understand perfectly, and so please don't think I'm pressuring you.

"Here is why I'm interested in your story. Here's what good I think can come out of it. I'm not here to try to exploit your weaknesses, or exploit your son, or exploit his memory, or exploit your tragedy. I think what happened to your son has happened to a lot of people. It's going to come up on the one-year anniversary of it. He was an athlete and I write for the sports section, and I think maybe, after telling your story, other people will not only appreciate him and the story, but maybe learn something about drunken driving. I can't promise it, but maybe there's something there. Would you be willing to help me in a project like this, and talk to me?"

I don't walk up to people with a notepad. That's so frightening to the average citizen. I keep my notepads and my tape recorders in my pocket if I go up to somebody, and I ask them if it's something they want to do. And if it is, then I say to them, "OK. Let me explain how this works, if you've never been interviewed before. I'm going to use a notepad and a tape recorder, and I can't often read my notes and so I have a tape recorder"—try to put them at ease with it, and they usually laugh.

I say, "So is that OK with you?" And they say, "Yes." So I reach in my bag and I take it out. Then already they don't look at it as a weapon.

Somebody once wrote that there's no more seductive sentence in the English language than, "I want to hear your story," and maybe they're right. Because often you don't have to do any more than just say that.

As a columnist, you are allowed to have what reporters generally are not allowed to have in their stories: an opinion.

But an opinion doesn't make you God. There are many kinds of opinions, and some of them are wrong. Just because you have an opinion doesn't mean you have the right to assume that it is the correct one. You have the right to tell people that this is your opinion.

But you are still a reporter, too, in a column. You don't get to say, "Oh, I'm trading in my reporter's credentials, and I'm going to be a columnist." It's like another stripe in the military. You don't throw out the other ones that you got on your patch. You just get a new one on top of it, and you're still obligated to report, and you're still obligated to give people enough of the story that if they choose to disagree with you, there's the detail and the evidence in your column to allow them to disagree with you.

That is much more of a challenge than to just be dogmatic or ignore any evidence that might suggest the contrary. And I always give myself that acid test when I write a column. I say, "Well, can I work in the other side here, and still make a case for the point that I'm trying to make?"

And if I feel that I do, then I feel justified in making my opinion. But if the only way I can get you to believe that this guy's a bad guy is to leave out all the good things he's done, not mention them, ignore them, and completely pretend they don't exist, then that's not really a fair opinion, and I don't really have the right to make it.

The Boston Globe

Dan Shaughnessy

Finalist, Sports Writing

Dan Shaughnessy is a sports columnist for *The Boston Globe.* He was born in Groton, Mass., graduated from Holy Cross in 1975, and worked at the Baltimore *Evening Sun* and the *Washington Star* from 1977–1981. He joined the *Globe* in 1981 and covered the Celtics from 1982–1986 and the Red Sox from 1986–1989. In 1989, he became a sports columnist. He has been named Massachusetts Sportswriter of the Year in each of the last six years, and four times has been voted one of America's top 10 sports columnists by Associated Press Sports Editors. He was an ASNE finalist in sports writing in 1995. Shaughnessy has written five books: *The Curse of the Bambino, At Fenway, Seeing Red: The Red Auerbach Story, Ever Green,* and *One Strike Away.* He makes regular appearances on television and radio sports shows.

In his graphic portrait of the mood and the maimed on the bus carrying Boston Marathon runners whose bodies gave out, Shaugnessy demonstrates a variety of effective reporting and writing techniques: the power of the detailed list, the telling observation, and the value of zigging when all the other reporters are zagging.

On this bus, they've paid a heavy fare

APRIL 18, 1995

It's 10 minutes to five and we're on bus No. 10, stuck in traffic on Huntington Avenue.

Aboard are one licensed driver, one registered nurse, one medic, one ham radio operator, one reporter, a case of Vermont Pure Natural Spring Water, barf bags, swab sticks, mycitracia packets, Band-aids, mylar wraps, tape and 21 aching marathoners.

Ours is the tragic bus, not the magic bus. It's the big yellow taxi, the finishing kick for the runners who just couldn't finish. Ours is a bus of cramped quads and dashed dreams. Appropriately enough, our first pickup was at the bottom of Heartbreak Hill, a good 20 miles into the course.

In the back of our bus, there's a guy with hypothermia. We've been told that he exits the bus first. At least one wheelchair is on order at the medical tent at the corner of Dartmouth and St. James streets.

All things considered, there's a decided lack of groaning on our bus. No complainers here. We've got a guy wearing a Marine T-shirt, stained with what appears to be vomit. We've got a young woman crumpled across a seat who makes no noise at all. Jane Catavella, R.N., checks to make sure she's OK.

As we plow our way through the traffic toward the finish line, 53-year-old Joe McCusker, a veteran of 17 Boston Marathons, considers the plight of the folks on our bus.

"It's like the old man and the sea," says McCusker. "He thinks he's got the big marlin, but he doesn't have the marlin, because they keep taking bites out of it. That's what we've got here today. That's what the marathon does to you. Little bites all over."

McCusker is a high school science teacher in Boston and this is the second time he has failed to finish his city's marathon. "I cramped up," he says. "The batteries are getting old."

In the front of the bus, Wendy Holdsworth, a 27-year-old office manager from Marlborough, stands up, turns around and holds up a camera that's attached to a string around her neck.

"Everybody smile," she says, snapping the picture.

No one smiles.

There aren't many smiles on this bus. This is the bus for the tired, the deflated, for the huddled-in-a-puddle-of-sweat masses. This is a bus full of runners who fizzled early in the the 99th Boston Marathon. This is a quiet bus. No one on it expected to be rolling across the finish line in a yellow school bus.

There are as many reasons as running styles. Some of them hadn't trained hard enough. Some hadn't loaded enough carbos. Some couldn't help downloading carbs right on the course. Some were plain unlucky, getting cramps, a sprained ankle or hypothermia. Some just got cold before their time.

Monica Stobbs, a 33-year-old nursing consultant for the state Department of Public Health, sighs and says, "Next year I'll train better. I finished last year in 4:33. I was actually on a better pace today. But then I saw the bus at 20 miles and it was too tempting. I like biking, swimming and all the outdoor activities. I suppose I could have finished, but I didn't want to get laid up for any period of time."

Dave King ran 18 miles to pace his friend, Liz Skiba. She went on to finish and Dave headed for the bus. He had not a single urge to go those last 8 miles.

More than 9,400 (official) runners lined up in Hopkinton for the start. Today's front pages and TV broadcasts will highlight Cosmas Ndeti, Uta Pippig and other emaciated mutants who can run this race and finish looking like they just walked off the 18th green at Augusta. But that's not what the race is about. The race is about real people, and the real people were on our bus.

The real people are winners, even if they looked and felt like losers yesterday. The bus has that effect on people.

When you watch the marathon at Mile 20, you see the Inverted Rule of Finish. The longer you watch, the worse shape the runners are in. Four hours into the race, you see more pain, more goofy T-shirts, more body fat, more bald heads, more hats, bigger bones, older shoes, more walkers, more runners without numbers, more runners with partners and fewer fans. There are also more drunk fans cheering them on.

As the shadows grew longer, the runners grew more outrageous. Late in the race we saw the Blues Brothers, down to the shades and shiny shoes, two young women, wearing "Dumb" and Dumber" T-shirts, and a man who ran with a beer can dangling in front of his face for 26 miles. It was just the carrot he needed.

But there was also more pain. And so some opted for the bus.

"Everybody did very well," says Dave Kugler, the medic on our bus. "Most of the people on this bus seemed like they could have continued. They all finished —one way or another."

In the end, the boys and girls on the bus made it to Copley Square the same way as thousands of other runners. They chugged into town. They had their pride. They tried. Sometimes you think better off your feet.

Lessons Learned

Writing a column on the Boston Marathon for *The Boston Globe* is a daunting assignment. Our paper covers every possible angle of the race. We feature stories on the men's winner, women's winner, wheelchair winner, over-40 winner, sick tent, crowd color, etc. It's difficult to come up with anything original. Compounding these woes, the event is a logistical minefield with hundreds of thousands of spectators along the route. It's almost impossible to see the race from more than one vantage point.

I was lucky in April 1995 because Bill Griffith, one of our assistant sports editors, furnished me with a fresh idea. He told me about a bus that drove the course route picking up runners who were unable to finish. He called it the "Dead Bus."

It turned out that there were more than a dozen of these buses. I got permission to ride one of the buses and introduced myself to the driver, radio operator, nurse, and medic. We stationed ourselves about three miles from the finish, bought doughnuts, and stood around waiting for the runners to pass.

This was a long day. Our bus was in place well before the noon starting time and runners didn't start to pass until 2 o'clock. Naturally, the first runners were the strongest and we didn't see many stragglers until about four hours into the race.

Just after 4 p.m., our bus pulled out and chugged down the final miles of the route, picking up runners who were too injured or tired to finish. It was difficult to interview these folks. I had to pick my spots carefully. Many of the runners were too ill to speak, while others were too discouraged to cooperate. But it was a big bus with a lot of runners and by the time we got to the finish line, I had enough quotes to make the story work.

I wrote the column in the press center near the finish line. I opted to write in the present tense because I wanted to put the reader on the bus with the rest of us.

I had to explain what the bus was all about without cluttering the story with too many details. I find this to be a common dilemma for a columnist. The story needs to be entertaining, but details are necessary to avoid confusion. Readers will give up and move on if you don't tell them what your story is about. The third paragraph of this piece solved the problem. Then I was able to go back to the description of people on our bus.

Quotes helped make the column. And the kicker works. It was important to exit with a good feeling. I didn't want the runners or the readers to be left with a negative impression. This was not designed to be a story about failure.

It would be dishonest to claim I did this column without considerable editorial help. The older I get, the more I try to bounce thoughts and ideas off other writers and editors. There are too many complacent columns. It's an occupational plague. It was no later than 6:30 when I finished the first draft. Many times—all late-night sporting events—the first draft goes in the paper without any rewrite. But sometimes you get to sculpt a little.

I shared the first draft with Lynda Gorov, a writer/editor at my paper. She read it and ran it back at me, punching up some of the one-liners. I have found this kind of writer-editor exchange to be very helpful. The writer, of course, gets too much credit, and the editor none. It's like a running back making the big money and grabbing the headlines thanks to the hard work of the nameless blockers in the offensive line. Having written five books, I am a big fan of creative editors. Too many columnists are threatened by the editorial pencil or blinded by their lofty perch at the paper.

Looking at the column now, there are several things I would change. I think it got a little busy with detail near the end. There was more description than necessary. Sometimes it's better just to wrap it up and get out. So that's what I'm doing now.

The Dallas Morning News

Kevin Sherrington

Finalist, Sports Writing

Kevin Sherrington is a sports feature writer for *The Dallas Morning News.* He was born in Dallas, grew up in Houston, and graduated from the University of Houston in 1979. He worked for three newspapers in the Houston area before going to work for *The Houston Post* in 1981 where he covered the University of Houston's basketball team. He went to the *Morning News* in 1985, where he covered Southwest Conference basketball and football until 1988. He covered baseball for a year and a half before becoming a full-time feature writer. He has won state and regional awards for game stories, features, and columns. One of his features appeared in *The Best American Sports Writing 1991.*

In his profile of Dennis Rodman, the basketball star of many tattoos, hair colors, and on-court outbursts, Sherrington's fly-on-the-wall reporting and staccato style give readers a series of intimate and revealing glimpses of a provocative public figure. In our television age, his entertaining story demonstrates why newspapers still retain a franchise.

It's a colorful life

MARCH 5, 1995

SAN ANTONIO—The white Jeep is roaring away from the loading dock of the Alamodome, hurtling toward the parking lot and 200 or so fans. They have been waiting more than an hour for the last of the San Antonio Spurs. But Dennis Rodman is not stopping, and the faces of the fans fly past in one long streak of disappointment.

"Can't stop...can't stop," Rodman says under his breath, veering toward the exit.

He stopped last week and nearly didn't get away. Must have been 2,000 of them, he says, shaking his head.

He will not allow himself to be trapped again. The man former NBA coach Chuck Daly calls the best rebounder in history will admit to only a couple of fears, and this is one: feeling trapped, whether by fans, friends, family, management or the constraints of a league and society he deems too conventional for his often-outlandish tastes. He acknowledges that he is known as "the bad boy of the NBA." Over the course of the evening, his favorite word to describe himself will be "free." Free to wear a dozen tattoos, free to pierce his ears, nose and navel, free to choose his hair color as if by flavor. *Leapin' Lime Lizard, please.*

He will sum up his attitude with the letters "WFO," inscribed in hot pink on the tailgate of another Rodman vehicle.

WFO?

"Wide (expletive) open," Rodman says, smiling.

The Jeep seems wide open now, hell-bent for the access road fronting the Alamodome. At the stop sign, more fans stand watch. It doesn't seem to matter that, just three months ago, Rodman was on a 3½-week paid leave of absence after a series of insubordinate acts. To these people waiting in the yellow sodium light, Rodman is a technicolor hero, every bit as popular as his teammate and alter ego, the exceedingly tall and proper David Robinson.

As the Jeep bears down on the stop sign, a few of the bolder fans move across the exit in a foolish attempt to block it.

"Do not stand in front of me," Rodman says, still talking to himself. Something threatening lurks in the soft tone, as if the fans are inviting disaster beyond Rodman's control. His two passengers brace themselves; one emits a long low groan as Rodman repeats his warning.

"Do not stand in front of me."

The fans seem to sense their predicament at the last moment, jumping back as the Jeep barges through.

No longer boxed in, Rodman will feel free to discuss his other great fear: He doesn't like to trust anyone. He will talk about how mistrust is such a powerful force in his life that he will negotiate with Spurs management only through an intercessor, teammate Jack Haley. Rodman has hardly spoken to the rest of the Spurs since they acquired him from Detroit last season. This is the way he wants it. He says he is close to only three people: his girlfriend, his daughter and a friend he made during college.

Despite his claims, he embraces all manner of people outside basketball, from Madonna to mailmen to mechanics. He gives them his unlisted number, tells them to write, even puts them up in his home. His mother, Shirley, says he "hasn't learned yet that he can't save the world." At dinner, his guests include a middle-aged couple from Michigan and their two teenage children; the brother of a man who once worked on his truck in Michigan, and four young women from Incarnate Word College, where the Spurs practice.

The members of this eclectic entourage will see a side of Rodman withheld from the NBA and anyone else he thinks could hurt him.

"When Dennis gives you his affection, it's all the way," his mother says. "And when you hurt him, it's all the way gone."

Half the entourage will accompany Rodman on the evening's last stop, a bar near downtown. Outside, Rodman turns to one and asks, "Ever been in a gay bar before?"

Not that we know of...

"Well," he says, "you're about to go in your first."

Entry is both a statement by Rodman—"He likes to shock you," Haley says—and a rite of passage into his world. He says there never will be another NBA player like Dennis Rodman, simply because no one else will frequent a gay bar, or at least be interviewed in one.

"I love gay people," he says, looking about the dimly lit room, where people are playing pool and darts and drinking at the bar. "They're free and wide open. They're saying, 'Hey, we're people, too.'"

UNLIKELY FRIENDSHIPS

Haley learned about Rodman's haunts on their first outing, when he took Haley and his wife to a gay bar. Haley—an awkward 6-10, preppy, unmarked by tattoos, as white as an episode of *Leave it to Beaver*—was determined to show his worldliness.

"Guys danced up to us," he says, "and I stuck a buck in their G-strings."

Haley and Rodman seem an unlikely pair. Even Rodman calls their friendship "a fluke," though he long has attached himself to people who would seem to have little in common with him. Reared in the projects of South Oak Cliff, Rodman lived with a rural mail carrier's family while a student at Southeastern Oklahoma State, and he became best friends with their 13-year-old son. Bryne Rich, now 25, remains his closest friend. An acquaintance described Rich, who accompanied Rodman on several road trips this season, as "Dennis' personal attache."

In some ways, Haley has filled the same role. The Spurs assigned Rodman a locker next to Haley's last season. Haley walked up, introduced himself, stuck out his hand and got nothing but air.

"He didn't even open his eyes," Haley says.

Rodman didn't open his mouth for nearly three months. Gradually, working against each other in practice, they built a relationship. Haley says he is "Dennis' liaison with management, the team and the outside world."

Asked why, Haley looks up from his locker room seat to see Rodman make a brief appearance.

"Why am I your liaison, Dennis?" he asks.

"I don't trust anybody else," Rodman says, before retreating quickly to the training room.

The mutual trust allows Haley the liberty to question Rodman on subjects that would be impossible for other teammates. At a dinner earlier this season with Rodman and Daly, Rodman's first coach with the Pistons, Haley told Rodman he still was stuck in Detroit. He talked about it every day. Rodman contends that players were tougher when he came into the league nine seasons ago, or at least they were allowed to be tougher. The game is softer now, he says, peopled by overpaid, overrated athletes.

But his feelings for Detroit run much deeper than an affection for style of play, Daly says. "It was like a real family to him," he says. "To some degree, he lives in the past."

Rodman admits he has had difficulty dealing with the split from Daly, who left the Pistons after the 1991-92 season. The only person Rodman says he respects as much is James Rich, the Oklahoma mailman whose family all but adopted him. Rodman's respect is so great that, when Rich suggested he back a business venture by one of Rich's sons and another man, Rodman did. He provided a line of credit against the advice of his agent and Pistons officials. "Everyone told him not to do it," says Rod Vilhauer, president of Rodman Excavation, Inc., in Frisco. Since 1990, the company has gone from a two-man operation to 120 employees, Vilhauer says.

Men like Daly and Rich "gave me the opportunity to express myself and be who I am," Rodman says. "They let me be free, let me learn from my mistakes."

Daly saw no choice. Rodman was the NBA Defensive Player of the Year in 1990 and 1991 and was runner-up two other seasons. The past three seasons, he has led the league in rebounding. At 6-8 and 210 pounds, he is the only forward to win a rebounding title in back-to-back seasons. The only players to lead the league in rebounding more times than Rodman were Wilt Chamberlain, Moses Malone and Bill Russell, all centers, all taller and heavier.

The reason Rodman is the best rebounder ever, Daly says, is his relentless drive. The balls he can't grab he tips out of the reach of others until he can chase them down, at times going into the seats for a loose ball.

"The two most bionic athletes I've ever seen," Daly says, "are Michael Jordan and him."

THE IMAGE

Despite his talent, Rodman was traded because his relationship with the Pistons deteriorated after Daly's exit. His mother says he "wanted to be someone else," and it began to show in his appearance. His hair color eventually ran through the spectrum and now has come back to blonde. Before that, the "flavor of the month," as former Pistons teammate Joe Dumars put it, was raspberry, with a dollop of blue.

Rodman says the colors don't mean anything. He leaves the dye up to his hairdresser, David Chapa of San Antonio's K. Charles salon. Chapa promises something "really vivid" for Rodman's Monday night appearance on *The Late Show With David Letterman,* maybe something "short and straight with Mamie Eisenhower-type bangs" or a red ribbon, the symbol for the support of AIDS victims.

He does not worry that the dye might cost him his hair.

"If it falls out," he says, eyes half closed, "I'll just tattoo it."

Pop psychology holds that people with multiple tattoos do not like themselves, or at least that's what a January *GQ* story on Rodman contends. The story was memorable for a couple of reasons, notably a picture of a nude Rodman, posed fortuitously in a running stance in a field outside Frisco, and Rodman's brief but colorful description of sex with Madonna.

A third of Rodman's tattoos have been drawn by Erik Inclan, a 22-year-old artist at Trilogy in Dallas. His are the largest works on Rodman's muscular body: a black tribal design on his back and neck; a tribal symbol on his left biceps around Rodman's zodiac sign, Taurus; a "naked devil girl" on the back of his right biceps; and a black sun encircling a shark on his left arm.

When he wants a tattoo, Rodman sets up the appointment through his girlfriend, Stacy Yarbrough of Dallas. She calls Inclan, who does the work after the shop closes at midnight. He says he gives Rodman a price break, charging between $100 and $150. Afterward, the artist and his canvas usually go to the International House of Pancakes or Denny's.

"He's a real cool guy," Inclan says. "I've never treated him any different from anyone else. No one here cares who he is. We're not gonna ask him for any autographs."

His play would seem to warrant it. Against Golden State last week in a 129-99 victory. Rodman had 22 rebounds in 26 minutes, including a club-record 15 in the third quarter. He missed the shootaround the morning of the game, claiming a head cold. But he didn't look any weaker for it during the game. He runs the court as if he were on a lark, his heels kicking high behind him. Almost no factor on offense, he is content to set picks and screens, raising his hand and conducting the movement of his teammates in the half-court offense like a headwaiter waving in patrons from the door.

The amusing images are misleading at times. He calls his style of play "getting psycho." He drew a technical against the Pistons two weeks ago and had to be restrained by two teammates. Appearing on the verge of being ejected at one point, he looked at Spurs coach Bob Hill and mouthed the words, "I'm all right, I'm all right."

His self-control wasn't as good much of his first year in San Antonio. He was suspended twice last season and fined twice in training camp. After being ejected from an exhibition game, he was suspended three games and then took his 3½-week leave of absence, during which he missed two scheduled meetings with Spurs officials.

He returned to the team on Dec. 10. Spurs team members and officials say they see a change in him. Robinson says he senses from Rodman more respect toward his teammates. Hill says that, underneath the tattoos and hair, Rodman is "a good person."

Spurs officials do not like to comment on Rodman, though. Told that they do not want to upset him, Rodman smiles.

"They don't want to mess up the chemistry," he says. "They're afraid I might go off."

He says he is no different now. He told his girlfriend during his suspension that he was going to
"kick ass when I come back, and nobody's gonna say
nothin' if we're winning."

He has played so well that he says he will ask the
Spurs after the season to renegotiate the remaining year
of his contract. He wants $15 million. He says the Spurs
would be "sick in the head" not to pay it, considering
what he has done for the team. Despite his occasional
problems making practice, he is a workaholic, riding an
exercise bike for up to 45 minutes after games.

Since Rodman's return to do what he calls "the
dirty work," the Spurs have gone 31-7.

"If we were 16-36," he says, throwing a thumb
over his shoulder, "I'd be gone."

He'd be missing a good time. Against the Pistons,
he briefly demonstrated for Haley the proper free
throw form. In the Golden State game, he motioned to
the crowd whether he should try a three-point shot,
then passed off for a give-and-go layup. He does these
things, he says, because he should entertain the fans,
an obligation he does not feel toward his teammates.

"I guess Dennis Rodman wants to keep his personal
life away from everything else," Rodman says. His tone
is soft, almost apologetic. "I don't hate these guys.
They're great guys. I just believe I should keep my distance. I have been hurt many times in this business.

"This business is rotten."

So he finds his friends elsewhere.

FAMOUS FLING

He met the most famous one during a photo shoot
last year, leading to a brief but notorious romance with
Madonna. Haley says he was shocked to find Madonna somewhat demure, polite and overwhelmed by
Rodman.

"No question," Haley says. "She wanted to get
married and have Dennis' babies. She said it several
times. She thought Dennis Rodman was the perfect
physical specimen."

Madonna still calls occasionally, and the two
friends trade faxes. She calls him Daddy Long Legs.
But they no longer are an item, says Rodman, who
seems uncomfortable discussing it.

Asked whether Madonna really wanted to have his baby, Rodman looks away and thinks a long time.

"She did," he says.

Did you think about it?

Another long pause. "A little bit."

Shirley Rodman says she never worried that Madonna would end up her daughter-in-law. Asked if she ever met Madonna, she says, "Thankfully, I did not."

Her only conversation with her son about Madonna was short.

"Dennis, why would you go out with this woman?"

"She has $250 million, Mama."

SEPARATED

Shirley Rodman does not claim to understand her only son. He grew up sheltered by his younger sisters, Debra and Kim, both basketball stars. Clumsy and shy, he was 5-11 when he was graduated from South Oak Cliff High School and did not play basketball. His sisters were "very protective of him," Shirley says. The trait persists in the family in some ways. Shirley Rodman lives in a North Dallas apartment; her daughters live on either side of her. Dennis may be nearby after his playing days. He wants to open a bar in Dallas.

They do not see much of Dennis unless it is by their initiative. On some of his trips to Dallas, Shirley says, he doesn't call. She has a key to his San Antonio house and occasionally visits. Often, she will not see him there, either.

"We respect his privacy," she says. "He has his own life. Dennis knows I have no desire to be in the limelight. Everybody's surprised that I don't own a great big house, but this is the way I like it. I like to maintain my own identity."

On the few occasions that national media have contacted her, she says, the results are the same. Little of her story finds its way in. Mostly, all anyone reports is that she kicked Dennis out of the house when he was 20.

He had a part-time job at Dallas/Fort Worth International Airport and was running with the wrong people. One day, the police came to arrest her son. They said he had stolen some watches, which she didn't believe until Dennis produced the watches. She still isn't sure if Dennis took them or was protecting someone else.

They took him away in handcuffs. No charges were filed. But, exasperated with her son's aimlessness, bewildered that he seemed to be growing by the day, Shirley gave him three choices: Go to college, enlist in the military or find a job.

He chose to do nothing. Shirley packed some of his belongings and put them and Dennis out on the porch. She told him that, if he wanted to run with people who were no good for him, he could go live with them.

"Dennis thought I abandoned him," Shirley says. She kept up with him, though. Three months later, a coach called and asked if her son might be interested in playing basketball. He took the opportunity. But damage was done to the mother-son relationship. She believes Dennis already resented her for divorcing her husband, Philander, when Dennis was 8. Kicking Dennis out of the house "saved his life," she says, but he never has forgiven her. "I think he reflects on that," she says.

"I'll just say this," Dennis says. "It left a hole in my life I can't fill up."

He dismisses the loss of his father, who lives in the Philippines with his new family and has not seen his son in 25 years. "I pretty much wiped my father out of my mind," he says.

His own marriage fared no better. He was married for 80 days. His ex-wife, Annie, lives in Sacramento, Calif., with Rodman's 6-year-old daughter, Alexis. He says he rarely sees Alexis, unless he looks inside his left forearm. He celebrated her third birthday by having her chubby likeness inked just underneath the crook of his arm. Of his dozen tattoos, it is his favorite.

Perhaps because of difficulties inside his own families, he has been adopting people for years. The first were the Riches of Bokchito, Okla., 14 miles east of Durant, a two-hour drive from Dallas.

"He comes up here every once in a while," James Rich says. "It used to be his hangout, but it's a little slow for him now."

When the Riches first knew Rodman, the only thing different about him was his race. That admittedly was a problem for them at first. His hair and tattoos have been a minor adjustment.

"I just kindly think Dennis is over 30," Rich says, "and if a man wants to put a color on his hair, he can do anything he wants."

FINDING HIMSELF

Dennis Rodman the player expects respect from his peers. He thinks it should come in the form of another Defensive Player of the Year Award, maybe even an MVP if the Spurs win it all.

Or at least that is what he is saying at the moment. One minute he says he should be rewarded with a fat new contract and trophies; the next, he says he can't believe he is anything other than that 20-year-old guy from the projects. He never expected much from his life growing up, he says. Perhaps it is why, when he was being presented his first Defensive Player of the Year Award, he broke down, sobbing, unable to comment.

"I'm something I shouldn't have been," he says. "I should be an average Joe Blow, 9 to 5."

He still can retreat to the life he wants. At 2015 Place, no one cares about his tattoos or piercings or hair color. They aren't too concerned that he's a basketball star, either. Here, Rodman raises his glass to silly toasts with a middle-age gay couple, the Incarnate Word students and the brother of the Michigan mechanic. One of the women says she never met a gay person until Rodman showed them 2015. "Dennis is so unlike everything I read or heard about," she says, watching Rodman dance in place next to the table, his head rocking slowly side to side.

He is wearing a white T-shirt, jeans cut off at the knees and black canvas sneakers. A pair of black Harley Davidson socks reach halfway up his skinny calves. His famous hair of many colors is hidden underneath a black cap, worn backward.

He colors his hair, he says, "because it makes me feel free. It's another side of Dennis Rodman, free, open. I'm finding out I'm going in the right direction. And I'm not hurting anybody."

Nobody but himself.

"I hurt myself all the time," he says. "I have a tough-man contest inside myself. Me and me go at it all the time. Ain't nobody on the outside that give me any trouble after that."

Nobody in 2015 gives him any trouble. Here he practices none of his vaunted defense. He laughs, teases, hugs. He patiently endures a drunk who congratulates his play in the game that night. His only complaint comes when the music turns country-Western. He barks for the bartender to change the song, and he does. "I like country-Western music," Rodman says, "but on Tuesday or Wednesday. Not tonight."

He is drumming his hands on the table top, his head back. "I feel great," he says. "I can't love life any more. I'm a free, wild, exotic animal loving life, such as it is in the confines of the rules and laws of the universe."

The only rule here is that the bar closes at 2 a.m., and he has to take his party elsewhere. He walks outside into the warm winter night and gives a stranger directions to the interstate, cautioning him to be careful on the way home. As the stranger pulls away from the curb, he chances a look at Rodman. The bad boy of the NBA is standing with his hand raised over his head, the expression on his face tentative, as if he were afraid his good-bye might not be returned.

Lessons Learned

BY KEVIN SHERRINGTON

Dennis Rodman had been the subject of a good story done by a reporter at *The Dallas Morning News* years ago. When he was with the Pistons, before the tattoos and the dye jobs and Madonna, Rodman was just a tough defender and a good rebounder. He received his first real notoriety when he alluded that the Celtics' Larry Bird received so much acclaim only because he was white. The *News*'s Jan Hubbard, now with the NBA, wrote a story that showed the irony of that statement. Rodman was all but adopted by a white family while he was in college in Oklahoma.

We had three interests in Rodman: the Oklahoma background, he is from Dallas, and he had evolved into this Buck Rogers character. But he also had a reputation as a very difficult interview. So David Moore, who covers the NBA for the *News* and also works for ESPN, went with me to a home game of the San Antonio Spurs. Moore has a good relationship with Rodman, and he planned to ease the transition for me.

After the game, Rodman worked out for almost an hour, as is his custom. A few reporters waited him out. Moore introduced me; Rodman, showing no emotion, barely even talking, agreed to meet the next day after practice.

Moore and I showed up at practice. Rodman left the floor, went to the locker room...and was gone. Either he forgot, or he didn't want to do it.

I had three options: I could forget the story, do it without him, or wait him out. I was doing the story. I'd already talked to his mother, who had been brutally frank about their relationship. I could have done the story without him. I've done it before with other subjects, several times.

But I was still bugged by what I considered my most disappointing experience in journalism. Only the year before, I decided I was going to do a story on Mickey Mantle's stay in a rehab center. I thought it would be the story of my career. I thought he would give us access because he had lived in Dallas for the previous 40 years, and the *News* had nearly ignored him for most of it. I figured he owed us one.

But I didn't get Mantle. He talked only to NBC and *Sports Illustrated,* and he was so good in both venues that I had to use his quotes and credit those sources in my story.

Maybe I didn't try hard enough to get Mantle. I was determined not to let it happen again with Rodman. I stayed two more days in San Antonio. After the next game, I waited in the locker room. The club's public relations director, who had been no help previously, went in and said something to Rodman, who sent a message back: Wait out back, and we'll go to dinner.

We ended up at dinner with a family Rodman knew from Detroit. He could not have been more accommodating to them, or me. He apparently liked the fact that I was so persistent, because he wasn't ready to end the interview. During dinner, he told me to hang with him, that we would go to a club and talk some more.

And so it was that I ended up with the first interview ever done with a professional athlete in a gay bar, as far as I know.

Rodman likes to shock people. He does it to gauge their reaction. If they act indignant, he crosses them off. He wants to see if you're willing to look past his act, to see what he really is: an immature but sensitive, hurt, caring person. He also is amazingly tolerant once he lets someone behind that façade.

It is easy to make Dennis Rodman a scapegoat for whatever it is that people don't like about the NBA or professional athletes. I don't agree with some of the things he does. But, too many times, reporters draw characterizations of athletes by what they read in other papers or see on television. Or they react to how they're treated by the athletes. That is a mistake. The Cleveland Indians's Eddie Murray hates the media, but his teammates love him. How bad could he be? On the other hand, former Los Angeles Dodger Steve Garvey was one of the media's favorites. But he was held in considerably less esteem by his teammates, who thought he was a politician.

Dennis Rodman was worth the wait. He made two good stories for the *News,* which is more than most reporters can ask.

A writing improvement quiz

BY CHRISTOPHER SCANLAN

Writing isn't like the Army. You can't command it. Good writing grows up from the staff. It thrives in an environment where the people who are interested in writing can take a leading role in improving it.

In too many newsrooms, writing programs are remedial. But at a growing number of newspapers, the best writers and editors are talking to their colleagues about what they do well.

What's the situation in your newsroom? Is it writing-friendly? Are people talking about writing?

If not, how can you encourage the kind of sharing of success that breeds new successes?

Find out by taking the writing improvement quiz below. The commentary following each question introduces some of the most useful and popular programs adopted in newsrooms across the country.

1) Do you have a regular writing contest, judged not by editors but by reporters? **Yes. No.**

Editors have the responsibility to judge the paper's writing every day. A writing contest judged by reporters gives them responsibility for critical evaluation to writers, and involves writers in an important way by making them responsible for creating and judging work that merits their colleagues' praise. An editor can be part of the contest, of course, by writing a story.

2) Do the winners of your writing contest have to write a "How I Wrote the Story" essay that is shared with the staff? Do you also ask editors of winning pieces to contribute "How I Edited the Story"? **Yes. No.**

There may be no better vehicle to share the lessons of good reporting and writing. Among the papers that have collected "How I Wrote the Story" essays: *The Providence Journal, Los Angeles Times, St. Petersburg Times*. At their worst, these essays read like bad Academy Award acceptance speeches ("I want to thank my editor, my dog, my spouse, my _____ ."). At their best, they are valuable teaching models.

3) Does your newsroom have a writing bookshelf stocked with books about writing, editing, interviewing, and anthologies of great writing? **Yes. No.**
Newsrooms stock city directories, dictionaries, and style books to ensure accuracy. Why not a collection of *The Paris Review Interviews* or *Best Newspaper Writing* to inspire editors and writers to reach new heights?

4) Does your newsroom have a "Write Stuff" bulletin board where examples of good writing are posted? **Yes. No.**
Take advantage of your electronic network to create an ongoing dialogue about effective writing and editing, and encourage writers to praise and learn from one another and to share examples of good writing and writing about writing from within the paper and outside. Scientists learn from failure. Writers learn best from what works.

5) Have you organized an in-house training program that features courses taught by your own staffers? **Yes. No.**
"Slug U" at *The Philadelphia Inquirer,* "Newsroom University" at *The Orlando Sentinel,* "USAT University" at *USA Today,* and "Deadline U" at *The New York Times* offer sessions on reporting and writing, computer-assisted reporting, law, grammar, and other subjects. They represent efforts "to harness the enormous wealth of talent" in the newsroom, in the words of Joan Motyka, director of staff development at *The New York Times.* "We want to encourage excellence. And most important, we want to nurture an environment infused with creativity, energy, and support. Some people call this professional development or enrichment. I like to think of it as gifts we give each other."

6) Do you invite outsiders to share writing and editing tips with the staff? **Yes. No.**

Invite a top homicide detective to talk about interviewing techniques, a poet to discuss writing with economy, a historian to present the background of zoning development in your city.

7) Do you hold regular brown-bag lunches where writers, editors, and other newsroom staff can share ideas about reporting, writing, and editing? **Yes. No.**

Assign a staffer to present the works of a favorite writer. Invite the winner of the writing contest to talk about reporting details. Ask photographers to discuss how they get people to open up.

8) Do you have a staffer with a strong interest in writing assigned to run the writing improvement program? **Yes. No.**

Like plants, a writing program can die without regular and devoted care. Form an editor/writer team or a writing committee to brainstorm ideas and keep track of progress.

9) Do you publish a regular newsletter that features articles about writing craft and celebrates successes? **Yes. No.**

"Second Takes," edited by Jack Hart of *The Oregonian* is a regular provider of good advice. "Wordsmith" is a rich new offering from Kevin McGrath, an editor at the Munster, Ind., *Times*.

10) Do you celebrate "Great Saves by the Copy Desk?" **Yes. No.**

Don't ignore the newsroom's first readers and last line of defense against inaccuracy and foggy writing. Editors make better collaborators than enemies.

11) Do you have computer links to writing resources on the Internet? **Yes. No.**

Writer_L is an electronic roundtable created by two-time Pulitzer Prize winner Jon Franklin and

visited by some of the country's leading writers and writing teachers. The World Wide Web is loaded with writing resources. The Poynter Institute offers links on its home page:
http://www.poynter.org/poynter

12) Are top editors actively involved: attending workshops, writing occasionally? **Yes. No.**
Before writing coach Don Murray would agree to serve as *The Providence Journal*'s coach, he insisted that top editors take part in all seminars. High-ranking involvement sends a clear message: We really care about good writing.

YOUR SCORE

8–12 Yes answers – Congratulations. You're working in a writing-friendly newsroom.

4–7 – You care about writing, but could even be doing more.

3–5 – You're spinning your wheels. Get in gear.

0–2 – Don't complain about the writing in your paper. Do something about it.

BONUS ROUND

For extra points, itemize any additional programs, methods, or techniques you use to improve writing in your newsroom. Add a point for every item.

Does your newsroom offer an innovative program to encourage good writing? The Poynter Institute wants to know about it. Write to the Director of Writing Programs, The Poynter Institute, 801 Third Street South, St. Petersburg, FL 33701 or send an e-mail message to chipscan@poynter.org.

Annual bibliography

BY DAVID SHEDDEN

WRITING AND REPORTING BOOKS 1995

Charity, Arthur. *Doing Public Journalism.* New York: Guilford Publications, 1995.

Evensen, Bruce J., ed. *The Responsible Reporter.* Northport, AL: Vision Press, 1995.

Garrison, Bruce. *Computer-Assisted Reporting.* Hillsdale, NJ: Lawrence Erlbaum Associates, 1995.

Hohenberg, John. *Foreign Correspondence: The Great Reporters and Their Times.* 2nd ed. Syracuse, NY: Syracuse University Press, 1995.

Houston, Brant. *Computer Assisted Reporting: A Practical Guide.* New York: St. Martin's Press, 1995.

Keyes, Ralph. *The Courage to Write.* New York: Henry Holt and Company, 1995.

Laakaniemi, Ray. *Newswriting in Transition.* Chicago: Nelson-Hall, 1995.

Lauterer, Jock. *Community Journalism.* Ames, Iowa: Iowa State University Press, 1995.

Lorenz, Alfred Lawrence, and John Vivian. *News: Reporting and Writing.* Boston: Allyn and Bacon, 1995.

Merritt, Davis. *Public Journalism and the Public Life: Why Telling the News is Not Enough.* Hillsdale, NJ: Lawrence Erlbaum Associates, 1995.

Mitchell, Catherine C., and Mark D. West. *The News Formula: A Concise Guide to News Writing and Reporting.* New York: St. Martin's Press, 1995.

Murray, Donald M. *Writer in the Newsroom. Poynter Paper: No. 7.* St. Petersburg, FL: The Poynter Institute, 1995.

Pew Center for Civic Journalism. *Civic Journalism: Six Case Studies.* (Published jointly with The Poynter Institute.) Washington, DC: Pew Center, 1995.

Rhodes, Richard. *How to Write: Advice and Reflections.* New York: William Morrow and Company, 1995.

Rivers, William L., and Alison Work Rodriguez. *A Journalist's Guide to Grammar and Style.* Boston: Allyn and Bacon, 1995.

Scanlan, Christopher, ed. *Best Newspaper Writing 1995.* St. Petersburg, FL: The Poynter Institute, 1995.

Ullmann, John. *Investigative Reporting.* New York: St. Martin's Press, 1995.

Vivion, Michael J., and Sarah Morgan. *Circles of Influence: A Writer's Rhetoric.* Boston: Allyn and Bacon, 1995.

Weinberg, Steve. *The Reporter's Handbook: An Investigator's Guide to Documents and Techniques.* 3rd edition. New York: St. Martin's Press, 1995.

Wilber, Richard A. *Magazine Feature Writing.* New York: St. Martin's Press, 1995.

CLASSICS

Atchity, Kenneth. *A Writer's Time: A Guide to the Creative Process, from Vision Through Revision.* New York: Norton, 1986.

Berg, A. Scott. *Max Perkins: Editor of Genius.* New York: Dutton, 1978.

Bernstein, Theodore M. *The Careful Writer: A Modern Guide to English Usage.* New York: Atheneum Press, 1965.

Biagi, Shirley. *Interviews That Work: A Practical Guide for Journalists.* 2nd ed. Belmont, CA: Wadsworth, 1992.

Blundell, William E. *The Art and Craft of Feature Writing: Based on The Wall Street Journal.* New York: New American Library, 1988.

Brady, John. *The Craft of Interviewing.* New York: Vintage Books, 1977.

Brande, Dorothea. *Becoming a Writer.* Los Angeles: J.P. Tarcher; Boston: distributed by Harcourt Brace, reprint of 1934 edition, 1981.

Brown, Karen, Roy Peter Clark, Don Fry, and Christopher Scanlan, eds. *Best Newspaper Writing.* St. Petersburg, FL: The Poynter Institute. Published annually since 1979.

Cappon, Rene J. *The Word: An Associated Press Guide to Good News Writing.* New York: The Associated Press, 1982.

Clark, Roy Peter. *Free to Write: A Journalist Teaches Young Writers.* Portsmouth, NH: Heinemann Educational Books, 1986.

Clark, Roy Peter, and Don Fry. *Coaching Writers: The Essential Guide for Editors and Reporters.* New York: St. Martin's Press, 1992.

Dillard, Annie. *The Writing Life.* New York: Harper and Row, 1989.

Downie, Leonard, Jr. *The New Muckrakers.* New York: NAL-Dutton, 1978.

Elbow, Peter. *Writing With Power: Techniques for Mastering the Writing Process.* New York: Oxford University Press, 1981.

Follett, Wilson. *Modern American Usage: A Guide.* London: Longmans, 1986.

Franklin, Jon. *Writing for Story: Craft Secrets of Dramatic Nonfiction.* New York: Atheneum, 1986.

Goldstein, Norm, ed. *The Associated Press Stylebook and Libel Manual.* 27th ed. Reading, MA: Addison-Wesley, 1992.

Gross, Gerald, ed. *Editors on Editing: An Inside View of What Editors Really Do.* New York: Harper & Row, 1985.

Howarth, William L., ed. *The John McPhee Reader.* New York: Farrar, Straus, and Giroux, 1990.

Hugo, Richard. *The Triggering Town: Lectures & Essays on Poetry & Writing.* New York: Norton, 1992.

Mencher, Melvin. *News Reporting and Writing.* 5th ed. Dubuque, Iowa: William C. Brown, 1991.

Metzler, Ken. *Creative Interviewing: The Writer's Guide to Gathering Information by Asking Questions.* 2nd ed. Englewood Cliffs, NJ: Prentice Hall, 1989.

Mitford, Jessica. *Poison Penmanship: The Gentle Art of Muckraking.* New York: Knopf, 1979.

Murray, Donald. *Shoptalk: Learning to Write With Writers.* Portsmouth, NH: Boynton/Cook, 1990.

—. *Writing for Your Readers.* Old Saybrook, CT: Globe Pequot Press, 1992.

Plimpton, George. *Writers at Work: The Paris Review Interviews.* Series. New York: Viking, 1992.

Ross, Lillian. *Reporting.* New York: Dodd, 1981.

Scanlan, Christopher, ed. *How I Wrote the Story.* Providence Journal Company, 1986.

Sims, Norman, ed. *Literary Journalism in the Twentieth Century*. New York: Oxford University Press, 1990.

Snyder, Louis L., and Richard B. Morris, eds. *A Treasury of Great Reporting*. New York: Simon & Schuster, 1962.

Stafford, William, and Donald Hall, eds. *Writing the Australian Crawl: View on the Writer's Vocation*. Ann Arbor, MI: University of Michigan Press, 1978.

Strunk, William, Jr., and E.B. White. *The Elements of Style*. 3rd ed. New York: Macmillan, 1979.

Talese, Gay. *Fame & Obscurity*. New York: Ivy Books, 1971.

Wardlow, Elwood M., ed. *Effective Writing and Editing: A Guidebook for Newspapers*. Reston, VA: American Press Institute, 1985.

White, E.B. *Essays of E.B. White*. New York: Harper & Row, 1977.

Witt, Leonard. *The Complete Book of Feature Writing*. Cincinnati, OH: Writer's Digest Books, 1991.

Wolfe, Tom. *The New Journalism*. New York: Harper & Row, 1973.

Zinsser, William. *On Writing Well*. 4th ed. New York: Harper & Row, 1990.

—. *Writing to Learn*. New York: Harper & Row, 1988.

ARTICLES 1995

Adock, Beryl. "Attention, Please, for Some Words from the Copy Desk." *The American Editor,* October 1995, pp. 34–35.

Auman, Ann. "A Lesson for Instructors: Top 10 Copy-Editing Skills." *Journalism and Mass Communication Educator,* Autumn 1995, pp. 12–22.

Banaszynski, Jacqui. "My 10 Requisites for Writing Excellence." *Workbench: The Bulletin of the National Writers' Workshop,* Vol. 2, 1995, p. 9.

Clark, Roy Peter. "Music and Writing. Growing as a Writer: A Workshop." *Workbench: The Bulletin of the National Writers' Workshop,* Vol. 2, 1995, p. 10.

Fry, Don. "Deal with the Demons in Your Writers' Heads." *The American Editor,* July/August 1995, p. 23.

— . "We Can Talk About Change All We Want, But Doing It Is Tough." *The American Editor,* November 1995, p. 19.

Germer, Fawn. "Are Quotes Sacred?" *American Journalism Review,* September 1995, pp. 34–37.

Hart, Jack. "The Power of the Paragraph." *Editor and Publisher,* March 11, 1995, p. 43.

Harvey, Chris. "The High-Stress Police Beat." *American Journalism Review,* July/August 1995, pp. 28–33.

Kirtz, Bill. "Writers Offer Advice To Writers." *Editor and Publisher,* July 1, 1995, pp. 14–15.

Land, F. Mitchell. "Awakening the Right Brain in Feature Writing." *Journalism and Mass Communication Educator,* Autumn 1995, pp. 52–60.

LaRocque, Paula. "Familiarity Need Not Breed Stilted, Boring or Lifeless Writing." *Quill,* September 1995, p. 40.

— . "Here's a Tough Little Quiz to Check Your Language Skills." *Quill,* April 1995, pp. 46–47.

Lieberman, Trudy. "Plagiarize...Only Be Sure to Always Call It Research." *Columbia Journalism Review,* July/August 1995, pp. 21–25.

Mann, Raleigh. "Restructuring Adds to Stress on Desks — But Help is at Hand." *The American Editor,* November 1995, pp. 5–7.

Murray, Donald M. "What Writers Can Do for Newspapers." *Workbench: The Bulletin of the National Writers' Workshop,* Vol. 2, 1995, p. 2.

Olson, Lyle D., and Thomas Dickson. "English Composition Courses as Preparation for News Writing." *Journalism and Mass Communication Educator,* Summer 1995, pp. 47–54.

Panici, Daniel A., and Kathy B. McKee. "Writing-Across-the-Curriculum in Mass Communication Courses." *Journalism and Mass Communication Educator,* Summer 1995, pp. 55–61.

Rife, Judy. "So You've Been Assigned to Cover City Hall..." *ASNE Bulletin,* April 1995.

Rosensteil, Tom. "Yakety-Yak: The Lost Art of Interviewing." *Columbia Journalism Review,* January/February 1995, pp. 23–27.

Scanlan, Christopher. "Eye to I: Writing the Personal Essay." *Workbench: The Bulletin of the National Writers' Workshop,* Vol. 2, 1995, p. 4.

— . "Storytelling on Deadline." *Quill,* May 1995, pp. 42–44.

Smith, Patricia. "Patricia Smith: Poet in the Newsroom." *Workbench: The Bulletin of the National Writers' Workshop,* Vol. 2, 1995, pp. 11–12.

Steinke, Jocelyn. "Absentee Coaching Puts the Focus on Feedback." *Journalism and Mass Communication Educator,* Autumn 1995, pp. 71–76.

Stimson, William. "Two Schools on Quoting Confuse the Readers." *Journalism Educator,* Winter 1995, pp. 69–73.